Grant's Getaways II

More Outdoor Adventures with Oregon's Grant McOmie

Text by Grant McOmie

~

Photography by Steve Terrill

WestWinds Press®

For my mom, dad, brother, and sister
and childhood memories of travel that keep me young at heart.

Text © 2003 by Grant McOmie
Photographs © 2003 by Steve Terrill
Book compilation © 2003 by WestWinds Press®
An imprint of Graphic Arts Center Publishing Company
P.O. Box 10306, Portland, Oregon 97296-0306
503/226-2402 • www.gacpc.com

All rights reserved. No part of this book may be reproduced or transmitted in any form or by any means, electronic or mechanical, including photocopying, recording, or by any information storage and retrieval system, without written permission of the publisher.

McOmie, Grant.
Grant's getaways II : more outdoor adventures with Oregon's Grant McOmie / text by Grant McOmie ; photography by Steve Terrill.
p. cm.
Includes bibliographical references and index.
ISBN 1-55868-697-5 (softbound)
1. Oregon—Guidebooks. 2. Washington (State)—Guidebooks. 3. Outdoor recreation—Oregon—Guidebooks. 4. Outdoor recreation—Washington (State)—Guidebooks. I. Title: Grant's getaways 2. II. Terrill, Steve. III. Title.
F874.3.M395 2003
917.9504'44—dc21
2003002520

President: Charles M. Hopkins
Associate Publisher: Douglas A. Pfeiffer
Editorial Staff: Timothy W. Frew, Tricia Brown, Jean Andrews, Kathy Howard, Jean Bond-Slaughter
Copy Editor: Heath Silberfeld
Production Staff: Richard L. Owsiany, Joanna Goebel
Designer: Constance Bollen
Cartographer: Gray Mouse Graphics
Printed in Hong Kong

Front cover (clockwise from top right): *Harris Beach State Park near Brookings; Leslie Gulch in Malheur County; Elk Cove Creek in Mount Hood Wilderness; Eagle Cap Mountain in Eagle Cap Wilderness; Grant McOmie.*
Back cover: *Eagle Cap Mountain soars above Moccasin Lake in the Wallowa Mountains.*
Title page: *Entrance to the South Slough National Estuarine Research Reserve near Bandon, Oregon.*
Page 5: *Whitewashed granite and windblown spruce frame Matterhorn Mountain in Eagle Cap Wilderness.*
Page 6: *A popular destination on Oregon's central coast, Heceta Head Lighthouse is shrouded in early morning fog.*
Page 8: *The Roaring River sweeps past lush, colorful beauty through the Willamette National Forest.*

Contents

Acknowledgments 5
Photographer's Preface 6
Introduction 9
Mileage Chart 12
Map 13

Spring 15

COAST
1 Land of the Giants—
   Oregon's Redwoods 16
2 A Friend to the Critters—
   Free Flight 18
3 A Blizzard of Feathers—
   Shorebird Migration Survey 20

INLAND
4 Dizzying Heights, Quiet Byways—
   Marys Peak and the Alsea River 22
5 Know Your Trees and Forests—
   Valley of the Giants 24

COLUMBIA
6 Dinosaurs with Fins?—
   *Herman the Sturgeon and the
   Bonneville Fish Hatchery* 26

7 Climbing to New Heights—
   Horsethief Butte 28

CASCADES
8 Campsite with a View—
   Timothy Lake 30
9 The Road to Paradise—
   McKenzie River Scenic Drive 33
10 Trail of Ten Falls—
   Silver Falls State Park 36

CENTRAL/EASTERN
11 Oregon's Forgotten Corner—
   Owyhee Country 38
12 Oasis in the Desert—
   Malheur National Wildlife Refuge 41

Summer 45

COAST
13 Vanishing Wilderness—
   *South Slough Estuary and
   Bastendorff County Park* 46
14 A Ride as Smooth as Silk—
   Kingfisher and Supper from the Sea 48

15 Poor Man's Lobster—
   Trask County Park and Crawfishing 51

INLAND
16 Lions and Tigers and Bears,
   Oh My!—
   Wildlife Safari 53
17 Another Time, Another Place—
   Erratic Rocks State Park 55
18 Fickle Mother Nature—
   Fern Ridge Reservoir 56

COLUMBIA
19 A Byway Restored—
   Eagle Creek and Cascade Locks 58

CASCADES
20 Birth of a River—
   Metolius River and Camp Sherman 60
21 Watching the Clouds Roll By—
   Cloud Cap Inn 62
22 Volcano Views—
   Windy Ridge and Ape Cave 64

CENTRAL/EASTERN
23 Golden Nugget—
   *Sumpter Valley Dredge State Park
   and Railway* 67
24 Oregon's Swiss Alps—
   The Wallowas 69

continues

Fall 73

COAST
25 Whitewashed Wonder—
Yaquina Head 74
26 Gone, Never Forgotten—
Tillamook Air Museum 76
27 Secrets in the Sand—
Float Fairies 78

INLAND
28 Gaggles of Geese—
*National Wildlife Refuges
(Willamette Valley)* 80
29 Down by the Ol' Mill Stream—
Cedar Creek Bridge and Mill 82
30 Out 'n' Back—
*Bald Peak State Park and
Wheatland Ferry* 84

COLUMBIA
31 Poem in Stone—
Historic Columbia River Highway 86
32 Cool Retreat—
Ice Cave and Indian Heaven 88

CASCADES
33 Updrafts and Thermals—
Bonney Butte HawkWatch 90
34 Back Road without Numbers—
Aufderheide Scenic Drive 92

CENTRAL/EASTERN
35 Where the Antelope Play—
Hart Mountain 94
36 Treasures from the Earth—
Richardson's Rock Ranch 96

Winter 99

COAST
37 Lewis and Clark Slept Here—
Fort Clatsop National Memorial 100
38 Keep the Beacon Burning—
Heceta Head Lighthouse 102

INLAND
39 The Community That Flocks
Together—
Jackson Bottom Wetlands 104
40 In the Comfort of Your Car—
Ridgefield National Wildlife Refuge 106

41 Oregon's Niagara Falls—
Nestucca River Back Country Byway 108

COLUMBIA
42 A Wildlife Parade—
*National Wildlife Refuges
(Washington)* 110
43 A Home for Eagles—
Twilight Eagle Sanctuary 112
44 Eulachons or Hooligans?—
Cowlitz River Smelt Run 114

CASCADES
45 A Jewel Anytime—
Diamond Lake and Crater Lake 116
46 Away from the Crowds—
Wind River 118

CENTRAL/EASTERN
47 A Bull Elk Romance—
Elk Horn Wildlife Area 121
48 Into the Deep—
Wallula Gap near Pasco 123

Source Notes 126
Recommended Reading 126
Index 127

Acknowledgments

I have heard it said that "Our lives are but houses built of memories." If that's true—and it seems a fair mark of my life—I think people should make outdoor travel and adventures the bricks and mortar of their lives. I've tried to do that for more than twenty-five years as a teacher, television news reporter, and travel writer. *Grant's Getaways II* is a visible measure of my effort, but, importantly, it is a work neither conceived nor completed alone.

I continue to owe much gratitude to my partner in this project, Steve Terrill, who first suggested the idea of a book based upon my long-running KATU television segment and who continues to capture on film countless outstanding visions of the Northwest. I am proud to share the pages with him.

I also owe much appreciation to the videographers at KATU who joined me on many of the adventures herein. Thanks to Scott Hopkins, Mike Rosborough, Eric Spolar, Don Stapleton, Bryon Garvin, Tom Turner, Curtis Miller, and Bob Jaundalderis, and to KATU helicopter pilot Bob Smart.

The staff at Graphic Arts Center Publishing® continues to keep me focused, on track, and especially on time—and that's a very good thing. Thanks to Tim Frew, Kathy Howard, Lake Boggan, and my fine editor, Heath Silberfeld, who improved my text a thousandfold.

Thanks also to the many people inside the U.S. Forest Service, the Bureau of Land Management, the Oregon Department of Fish and Wildlife, the U.S. Fish and Wildlife Service, and Oregon Parks and Recreation, as well as special thanks to my friends at The Nature Conservancy and the Oregon Wildlife Heritage Foundation. All helped with advice, tips, background information, and other valuable resources whenever I called upon them for help in this venture.

As always, I thank my wife, Christine, and our sons, my finest and favorite travel companions.

Finally, I'll let you in on a little secret: I get a kick out of the traveling life! And I suspect you do, too, so I extend my sincere appreciation to all who find pleasure and satisfaction in the journey.

—Grant McOmie

Photographer's Preface: A Visit from Ruth

First, I want to thank all of you who enjoyed the first *Grant's Getaways*. Without your support, this second book would never have been published. To you, and to those readers who are picking up a copy of *Getaways* for the first time, I hope that this book will be a valuable guide as you explore the great outdoors with your families and friends. I had a great time traveling throughout the Northwest while I captured each of these destinations on film. As beautiful as these getaways are in print, they are even more breathtaking in person. You'll just have to go and see for yourself.

Not only is the Northwest filled with unique, beautiful places, but, like me, one day you may come across something that is quite out of the ordinary. One of the destinations in *Grant's Getaways II* is the Heceta Head Lightkeeper's House, where a few years ago, I had an experience that could only fall into the "Believe It or Not!" category.

Photographer's Preface

Early one December I received a call from my friend and colleague, Larry Geddis. He asked if I wanted to join him for a photographic trip to the coast for a few days. His plan was to visit the Heceta Head Lighthouse to photograph the sunset and holiday lights gracing the Lightkeeper's House. I took him up on the offer.

At Heceta Head, we were pleasantly surprised to see that the holiday lights were all in place. I visualized what it was going to look like at dusk. That afternoon, Larry and I agreed that we should stay at the B&B there so we could shoot in the early morning hours, too. We checked with the innkeepers and learned that they had rooms available. In fact, no other guests were staying the evening. We'd have it to ourselves. As the innkeepers gave us our keys, they told us that they were going out for the evening and wouldn't be back until after midnight.

As darkness approached, Larry and I set up our photographic positions in hopes of capturing the holiday lights that were beginning to glow against the stark, white house. Just a few feet apart, we chatted as we waited for the right lighting conditions.

Then, as my eyes scanned the house, I saw a light glowing from the ceiling in a small upstairs room. Furthermore, I saw a person standing in the window, just a bit off to the side. *No big deal*, I thought. *Someone was just looking for something in the room.* Then it dawned: *Wait . . . no one is supposed to be in the house!*

"Um, Larry? Do you see anything in any of the windows?" I asked.

"No," he mumbled at first, his eyes sweeping the house. Then he did a double-take at the same window where I had witnessed the figure a few seconds earlier.

He turned to me. "I thought I saw a person standing at that window up there, but when I looked again, it disappeared."

"Maybe it was 'Ruth,' " I said, referring to the ghost that is rumored to dwell in the house. For good measure, I had to add: "And don't forget, your room is right below that one—maybe we'll get a visit from Ruth while we're here . . . "

Finishing up our shoot, we headed indoors. We sat in Larry's room and talked for a while about our sighting that evening, then sheepishly looked around in hopes of finding some signs of Ruth, but turned up nothing. Back in my room, I fell asleep quickly and the night passed quietly except for the sound of the crashing waves against the cliffs below. No visit from Ruth.

In the morning I got up and heard Larry rustling about the same time. I walked into his room and flopped down in the same chair as I had the evening before.

"Well, did you have a sound sleep? Any sign of Ruth during the night?" I asked.

"Nope," he said. "I had a very restful, uneventful night."

Then I glanced toward the table next to me. There I saw a book that had not been there the previous night.

"Where'd this book come from?" I asked Larry.

"What book?" He had a bewildered expression on his face.

Chills came over me as I opened it and started to read. It appeared to be a journal of people who had stayed at the house, each telling an account of sighting Ruth during their visit.

"Okay, Larry. Joke's over," I said as I slapped the book shut. "Really, where did you find this?"

"Very funny," he answered. "I didn't put it there, but I'm not so sure about you."

Soon we realized that neither of us was joking. Neither had seen the book before that morning and we were certain that it was not there the previous night.

When we packed up and headed off to our next photo destination, we still didn't have any answers.

I'm here to tell you, that was a true story, even though some of you might not want to believe it. It was an exciting, strange adventure that I will remember for a lifetime.

And I guess the same could be said for my part in this book: an exciting adventure that I will remember for a lifetime. I hope that one—or many—of these getaways will direct you to adventures and memories that will last a lifetime. I can't promise any ghost sightings or supernatural happenings, but if you are looking for unbelievable scenery, great activities, or family fun, then this is the book for you.

One last thing. If you ever find yourself overnighting at the Heceta Head Lightkeeper's House, and you just happen to see Ruth, tell her Steve says hi!

— Steve Terrill

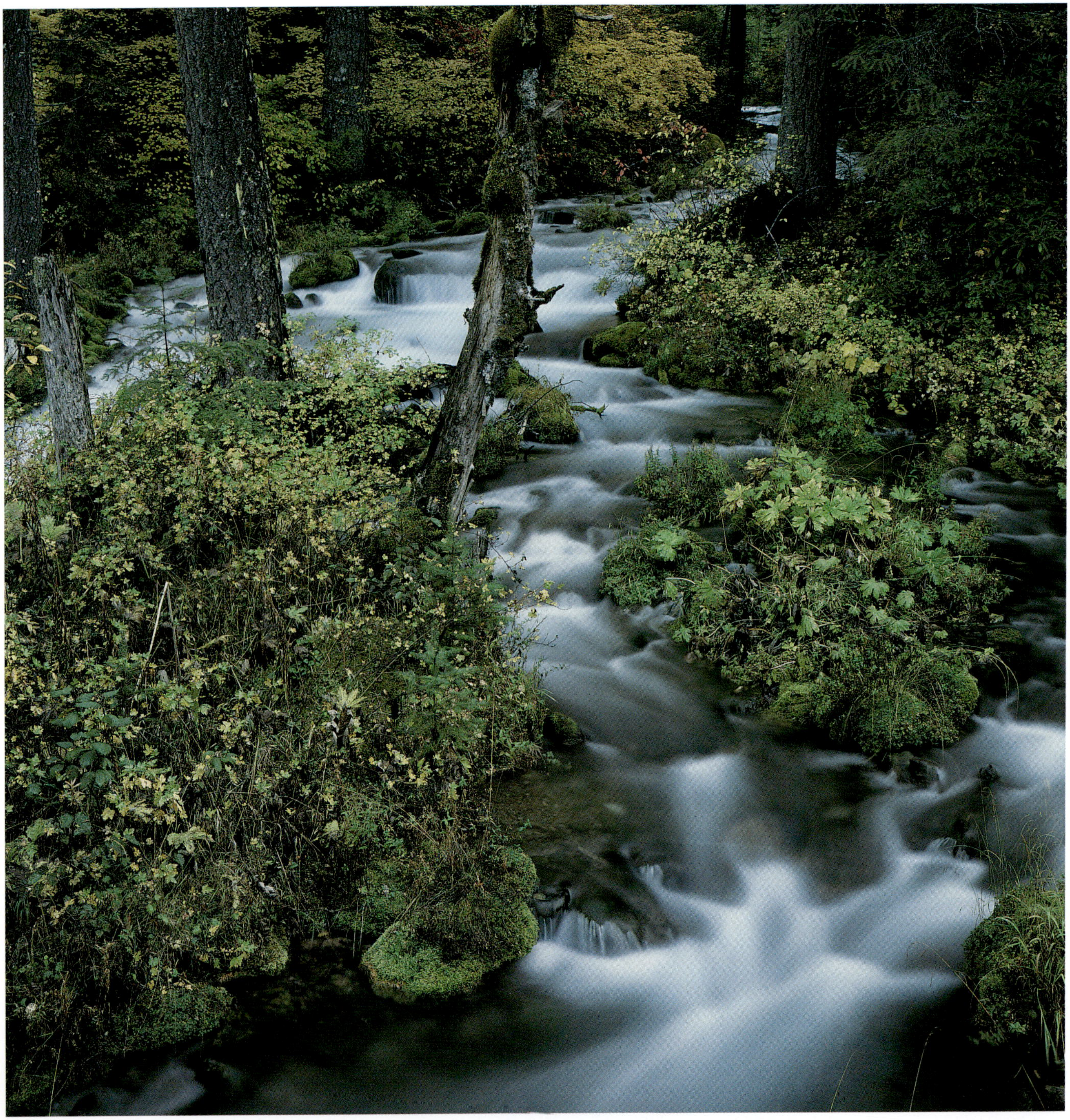

Introduction

Afoot and light-hearted I take to the open road,

Healthy, free, the world before me,

The long brown path before me leading wherever I choose.

"Song of the Open Road," Walt Whitman

~

Ohhhhh, Graaant! We've got a plum assignment for you! A reeeeaaaal juicy plum, too! Graaant!!!"

Rob, a young television producer, was far too excited and far too enthusiastic—even for a Monday morning—as he sprinted past my cozy newsroom cubicle, shouting and scanning the narrow hallway for signs of life. Eagerness had the best of this twenty-something news producer, who continued on his search-and-capture mission, not realizing I was standing but ten feet behind him.

"Yes, Rob?" I answered coolly. "I've already had my breakfast. What is it?" Perhaps I was a bit too unflappable for the first day of a new week in a major-market news operation (KOMO in Seattle), where I had begun my television career just eight months earlier. Granted, Mondays were always charged with higher energy and anticipation than other days, given that a full week of news stories was set to start. But I could tell by Rob's high-pitched giggles of delight that he had an assignment that was out of the ordinary and that something very special was about to come my way.

"Grant, we've got a reeeeaaal plum for you—seriously, a good story! Guess who's coming through town, just guess—one of your favorites—you're not gonna believe it—and we want you to interview him. Charles Kuralt! Man—it's gonna be fantastic!"

With those words, Rob had me hooked like a hungry salmon flopping on the water's surface with juicy bait firmly set in its jaw. Charles Kuralt! The man was a news icon and a hero to me. Like millions of admirers, for decades I had enjoyed Kuralt's stories and envied his career. His sincere passion and unmatched skill at crafting great stories that never made the headlines were legendary. Kuralt could weave a television story with power and grace, and his stories always cut to the heart of humanity. More important, he was my kind of storyteller because he prowled the back roads of America. At that time, nearly twenty years ago, the well-traveled Kuralt was passing through the region and making time for news folks who wanted to chat about his books, his shows, and a life made famous by his CBS *On the Road* segments about common people doing uncommon things. He was unrivaled in the business and now I was going to interview him!

But what do you ask a man who's seen so much of life across the planet—from deep sorrow in war-ravaged countries to the exquisite happiness of small-town life in America? I struggled for more than a week, crafting just the right list of questions—my perfect list—one that would spawn deep, insightful answers.

Easy "yes" or "no" responses wouldn't do for this interview. Rather, my list of ten questions would be superb—well-constructed, deeply thought out, and expertly typed queries about the meaning of his job, his life, the power of TV, and how he thought each had influenced people.

On the day of Kuralt's visit, I was petrified! After all, I was a mere rookie—learning and earning my way in the news business one story at a time. Fact is, my fear must have shown, too, for I was scared out of my wits and I tightly clutched my list—my perfectly researched list, indelibly linked by numbers one through ten, and composed with a logic that flowed naturally from one question to the next. As we sat for the interview, while lights and camera were adjusted, we made small talk. Kuralt was gracious, polite, and simply himself. But I also suspect he was a wee bit alarmed by the white-knuckle death grip with which I held my plain brown clipboard with its crisp sheet of paper, perfectly taped at each corner to keep the page from falling to the floor. It must have been obvious that I treated that list like a life vest—as though my very survival in the television news game was at stake—because within moments Kuralt asked if he might take a look. What could I say? Was this a compliment or criticism? I handed over my clipboard, and he politely glanced down my lineup.

"Why, this is mighty nice!" he noted in his distinctively deep tone. "Do you mind?"

Before I could answer, he gently pulled at the taped corners. In a flash, my oh-so-perfect list was set free. Then he neatly folded the paper not once, not twice, but three times and placed my list inside his coat pocket.

"There," Kuralt smoothly offered. "Now, Grant, why don't we just talk a little?"

And talk we did! Or rather I listened as he spoke of television, travel, and a career that hadn't let too many roads go unexplored. He also offered advice that has since helped guide me through my career.

"First," he mentored, "lists are fine—and you do have a dandy—but don't let them be gospel. There are far too many lists in this world made up by people who don't make enough conversation. Prepare for your stories, research your topics, and organize your thoughts. But (and here's the really important point) try to let your heart into your stories. If you like to travel the back roads and byways of this region and enjoy meeting new folks as much as you say, listen with your heart as much as with your head to what they have to say. And listen carefully. Then figure out a way to let your heart ask more questions. And then go figure out a way to bring more heart into your story. If you do this, I don't think you'll ever go wrong."

With that—and an hour's worth of his time—we were done, and I was amazed. In fact, I'm still amazed that I was able to "just talk" with one of America's finest journalists, who I also discovered was a fine and patient gentleman: a man who just happened to be famous because he listened with his heart and told stories that made people smile.

It's always been my hope that *Grant's Getaways* makes people smile, too. But I must say it's not been until recent years that I have recognized how deeply my meeting with Charles Kuralt influenced my desire to travel, write, and report about interesting people and places. I suspect his advice blended well with my recognition that most of my TV newsroom colleagues were far more interested in everyday breaking-news events—and much better at reporting them—than I ever was. My passion has always been for unexplored horizons, and in large measure that's carried over to both editions of *Grant's Getaways*.

As in the first edition, in this sequel I've assembled forty-eight adventures that span the varied geophysical regions of the Northwest and the four seasons. Together, we'll journey to a little-known corner of Oregon where you can stroll through a lush rain forest marked by a rare and towering stand of ancient giant redwood trees. We'll ride the rails back into history to one of the mother lodes of Oregon's gold mining past. We'll saddle up and join a horseback trip into the Eagle Cap Wilderness in Oregon's high country, where we'll lie under the stars in an alpine

Introduction

meadow along a pristine lakeshore. I'll take you where animals rule the grounds and the visitors are in "cages" at the unique drive-through wildlife viewing experience of Wildlife Safari. Your kids will love digging for buried treasure in the form of geologic gems called thunder eggs, and I'll show you where to find them. We'll tour the Northwest's snow country on a little-traveled cross-country ski trail in the Columbia River Gorge, then we'll speed aboard snowmobiles across snowfields to a scenic overlook at spectacular Crater Lake. We'll put on swimsuits and dive into a cool, refreshing stream on a sweltering summer's day and gather crawfish—and then I'll show you how to prepare them in a feast fit for kings.

Speaking of feasts, readers have encouraged me to offer more recipes, and in this edition I have. Not only will you learn about a premier place to pick baskets of huckleberries, but I'll also share a favorite recipe for huckleberry cobbler that is out of this world! In addition, I've included lip-smacking fish recipes that will impress your friends with true Northwest taste and flair. Perhaps you've heard about those millions of tiny, wiggly smelt that migrate to the Northwest each winter—maybe you've even thought you'd like to dip a bucket of them from shore, but then wondered what you would do with them. I've got the perfect recipe for a smelt cookout—and much, much more.

My getaway selections are a start for your own adventures, with or without your family, mostly in or around the Portland-Vancouver region. Most are accessible on a tank of gas, though others do require more planning and time. They offer some stand-out features, such as an inspiring viewpoint, a unique hike to a secluded campground, or a spectacular wildlife moment. I also describe interesting side trips and provide specific driving instructions, as well as more natural history and travel strategies. I mention wheelchair accessibility where available, though there is almost always a path or trail nearby that can be navigated in a wheelchair. Each getaway concludes with contact names and phone numbers for further information.

Not long ago, a friend and television colleague asked, "Why don't you go back to Alaska, Grant? Now those were some of your greatest shows!" The question caught me a bit off guard and my response was quick and instinctive: "Because there are so many more great places right here, and my time is short." It's true, isn't it, I mean, about the passage of time? There's so little time and so many sights and sounds for each of us to experience. I've often shunned distant, exotic ports of call for the allure of that which waits just off my doorstep. I often ponder the Northwest's hidden nooks and crannies: the diversities of habitats, from wringing wet and soggy to flat, endless, and arid. Ah, for those unexplored vistas! Curiosity is a part of it, too: to seek out what's around the next bend or up the road apiece. And perhaps I travel to learn what it is that sets Northwesterners apart! So lace up your hiking boots and buckle up your seat belts, too. We're traveling toward adventures that make the Northwest corner of the United States so special. I hope *Grant's Getaways II* helps guide your way.

◣ **Vineyards rise and fall like the tide on the rolling hills of Washington County.**

	Astoria OR	Baker City OR	Bend OR	Burns OR	Coos Bay OR	Corvallis OR	Dallas OR	Eugene OR	Grants Pass OR	Klamath Falls OR	La Grande OR	McMinnville OR	Medford OR	Pendleton OR	Portland OR	Roseburg OR	Salem OR	The Dalles OR	Tillamook OR	Longview WA	Olympia WA	Seattle WA	Spokane WA	Yakima WA
1—Oregon's Redwoods	346	653	369	424	114	286	322	243	105	209	609	335	133	559	349	173	305	434	281	400	482	542	704	535
2—Free Flight	255	545	261	390	24	164	214	132	143	244	501	197	173	451	243	85	199	327	190	292	356	415	594	427
3—Shorebird Migration: South Beach State Park	136	439	182	310	96	54	75	111	249	270	395	78	277	345	131	143	93	220	71	181	253	313	484	315
Cape Meares Beach	74	385	215	344	175	99	73	149	284	318	341	75	314	291	82	217	83	167	10	130	194	254	434	267
Trestle Bay Wetlands	10	399	263	392	231	171	148	198	333	367	355	105	363	305	95	265	134	181	65	36	123	184	447	228
4—Marys Peak and the Alsea River: Marys Peak	149	449	191	320	82	63	89	95	196	267	404	91	224	354	145	129	102	229	84	193	267	326	497	328
Alsea Falls	199	418	166	295	131	33	63	39	178	212	377	78	208	327	116	111	72	203	123	181	238	298	470	300
5—Valley of the Giants	154	376	157	285	164	30	10	80	215	245	332	35	241	282	71	147	25	158	75	133	193	243	425	255
6—Bonneville Fish Hatchery	132	260	162	291	261	126	103	152	287	321	216	80	315	166	43	220	91	41	116	85	149	208	309	143
7—Horsethief Butte	130	222	133	262	304	166	146	197	332	269	178	123	560	129	86	266	134	3	159	127	191	250	271	104
8—Timothy Lake	103	322	163	292	207	71	48	97	232	266	278	24	262	228	20	165	33	104	85	82	133	192	371	204
9—McKenzie River Scenic Drive, Paradise Campground	248	263	37	170	163	102	136	55	193	187	323	153	223	273	165	126	121	202	195	228	288	347	416	250
10—Silver Falls State Park	142	362	117	246	184	48	30	74	209	243	318	43	237	270	60	142	16	145	90	109	172	232	410	244
11—Owyhee Country	546	155	267	137	502	394	412	394	475	371	198	494	447	249	457	462	502	374	593	499	562	532	453	382
12—Malheur National Wildlife Refuge	454	217	198	67	426	324	342	317	334	229	262	356	305	264	372	385	328	319	402	393	457	516	464	392
13—South Slough Estuary and Bastendorff County Park	242	532	248	376	14	167	201	119	157	259	488	213	185	437	230	99	186	313	177	279	352	411	583	414
14—Kingfisher and Supper from the Sea: Kingfisher	134	438	180	318	98	52	73	99	234	268	394	76	264	344	129	166	83	219	69	117	248	308	486	319
Tradewind Charters at Depoe Bay	121	418	202	331	111	65	60	111	272	305	377	63	299	326	116	180	71	199	56	165	229	298	469	300
15—Trask County Park and Crawfishing	73	384	214	343	174	98	72	148	300	317	340	75	328	289	80	234	83	165	8	115	193	252	432	266
16—Wildlife Safari	268	415	204	333	76	122	156	79	67	170	443	169	95	393	186	9	141	271	215	234	298	357	538	372
17—Erratic Rocks State Park	119	358	165	299	168	56	28	104	233	269	314	19	267	267	56	172	38	139	61	105	169	228	406	240
18—Fern Ridge Reservoir	197	419	132	262	113	51	85	5	143	177	372	100	171	322	115	76	71	200	144	163	228	287	465	299
19—Eagle Creek and Cascade Locks	151	242	143	271	281	145	122	171	309	279	198	99	337	147	62	242	110	23	135	104	168	227	290	124
20—Metolius River and Camp Sherman	228	249	37	165	208	98	117	99	234	173	310	130	262	260	147	167	102	148	176	195	268	328	402	236
21—Cloud Cap Inn	190	281	182	310	320	184	161	211	348	318	237	138	376	186	101	281	149	61	174	143	207	266	329	163
22—Windy Ridge and Ape Cave: Windy Ridge Ape Cave	156	333	235	364	371	235	212	262	399	433	291	193	428	241	124	331	200	117	225	182	156	136	318	119
23—Sumpter Valley Dredge State Park and Railway	407	351	210	339	281	145	122	172	310	354	307	99	338	257	70	240	108	113	133	59	123	183	381	163
24—The Wallowas	421	29	208	126	425	415	392	317	451	343	74	369	379	124	332	385	377	249	405	374	438	407	329	266
25—Yaquina Head	425	120	369	269	557	419	396	445	579	505	76	402	541	128	336	513	381	252	408	377	441	381	204	269
26—Tillamook Air Museum	136	460	183	312	101	55	76	102	254	271	396	79	265	346	133	170	94	221	71	181	254	313	491	322
27—Float Fairies	65	376	205	334	166	90	65	140	292	310	332	69	320	281	72	226	75	157	-	107	185	244	424	258
28—National Wildlife Refuges, Willamette Valley:																								
William Finley National Wildlife Refuge	109	407	190	319	123	75	49	125	260	294	365	51	287	312	105	193	59	187	44	154	217	277	455	289
Ankeny National Wildlife Refuge	180	400	142	284	156	14	45	61	196	230	356	60	224	305	98	129	54	181	105	144	208	267	448	282
Baskett Slough National Wildlife Refuge	145	367	142	271	166	30	32	56	191	225	322	47	221	272	62	125	18	149	93	128	185	244	416	247
29—Cedar Creek Bridge and Mill	142	365	145	274	189	30	6	80	215	249	320	23	245	269	60	147	14	146	64	125	182	141	413	144
30—Bald Peak State Park and Wheatland Ferry:																								
Bald Peak State Park	76	350	191	320	256	120	97	146	281	315	288	74	309	237	37	214	83	113	108	29	93	152	380	214
Maud Williamson State Park, Wheatland Ferry,	91	342	179	308	223	69	47	114	249	283	297	23	279	247	42	181	43	123	66	90	154	213	390	224
and Willamette Mission State Park	114	350	144	273	188	52	24	78	213	247	306	16	243	255	45	456	12	129	73	94	165	224	398	229
31—Historic Columbia River Highway	129	266	168	296	261	125	102	152	287	321	220	77	317	172	40	219	88	48	113	82	146	205	314	148
32—Ice Cave and Indian Heaven	176	264	166	295	308	172	149	198	333	302	220	125	363	170	86	266	135	46	160	128	193	252	313	146
33—Bonney Butte HawkWatch	155	100	282	229	276	140	114	166	301	236	238	97	331	188	66	234	100	64	139	101	172	231	331	164
34—Aufderheide Scenic Drive	236	331	101	226	149	89	123	46	171	135	411	138	201	361	153	104	109	237	183	211	275	334	503	337
35—Hart Mountain	462	271	204	122	380	350	350	280	239	135	316	365	212	318	365	307	335	334	410	407	471	531	521	422
36—Richardson's Rock Ranch: Richardson's Rock Ranch	219	235	54	180	272	162	181	163	198	190	261	162	228	210	130	230	166	99	203	172	136	296	353	187
Deschutes River State Park	196	205	141	245	329	193	170	219	354	277	161	145	384	111	107	287	156	25	180	179	214	228	253	87
37—Fort Clatsop National Memorial	6	397	262	391	229	170	147	196	331	365	353	104	361	321	94	264	132	179	63	55	122	181	441	223
38—Heceta Head Lighthouse	171	486	201	330	61	86	111	72	174	247	442	113	204	392	184	107	140	268	107	232	297	356	534	368
39—Jackson Bottom Wetlands	79	322	186	315	230	94	71	120	255	289	227	31	285	227	18	188	57	103	60	66	130	190	204	370
40—Ridgefield National Wildlife Refuge	78	320	179	308	244	108	85	134	269	303	276	63	299	226	25	202	70	102	96	30	95	154	368	202
41—Nestucca River Back Country Byway	106	350	165	305	182	65	44	119	245	268	295	20	275	256	49	178	44	133	81	98	162	220	233	398
42—National Wildlife Refuges (Washington):																								
Steigerwald Lake National Wildlife Refuge	117	284	172	301	246	110	87	136	272	306	240	63	301	190	25	204	74	98	57	121	181	333	166	
Franz Lake National Wildlife Refuge	117	272	173	302	259	123	100	149	284	318	227	76	314	177	37	217	85	53	111	70	134	193	320	153
Pierce Lake National Wildlife Refuge	122	277	178	307	264	128	105	154	289	323	232	81	319	182	42	222	90	58	116	75	139	198	325	158
Beacon Rock State Park	122	267	169	298	270	133	111	160	295	329	223	85	325	173	48	227	96	49	121	74	139	198	316	149
43—Twilight Eagle Sanctuary: Scappoose Bay	68	329	202	331	246	110	87	136	271	305	285	60	301	235	26	203	73	111	81	26	93	151	378	211
Trojan Park Wetlands and Pond	53	353	212	341	261	125	102	174	311	320	309	76	341	259	42	244	88	135	97	11	78	138	401	178
Twilight Eagle Sanctuary	8	385	244	373	239	173	150	199	334	368	340	108	364	290	90	266	135	166	73	182	110	169	431	210
44—Cowlitz River Smelt Run	51	344	203	331	267	140	109	167	302	327	299	85	332	249	49	234	94	125	120	2	67	126	392	167
45—Diamond Lake and Crater Lake	322	327	97	222	162	176	210	132	102	84	388	224	86	338	239	79	195	226	269	288	352	411	481	314
46—Wind River	126	294	187	316	296	160	137	186	321	355	241	113	351	191	74	254	122	67	147	78	143	162	333	167
47—Elk Horn Wildlife Area	368	22	313	214	501	365	342	391	526	449	22	357	556	72	279	459	328	197	353	301	365	334	256	193
48—Wallula Gap near Pasco: Hat Rock State Park	285	132	230	232	418	282	259	308	443	366	88	274	473	38	196	376	245	114	269	238	302	252	169	110
Sacajawea State Park	311	170	255	270	443	307	284	334	469	392	125	299	499	75	222	401	270	139	295	264	290	230	138	89

mileage is approximate

12

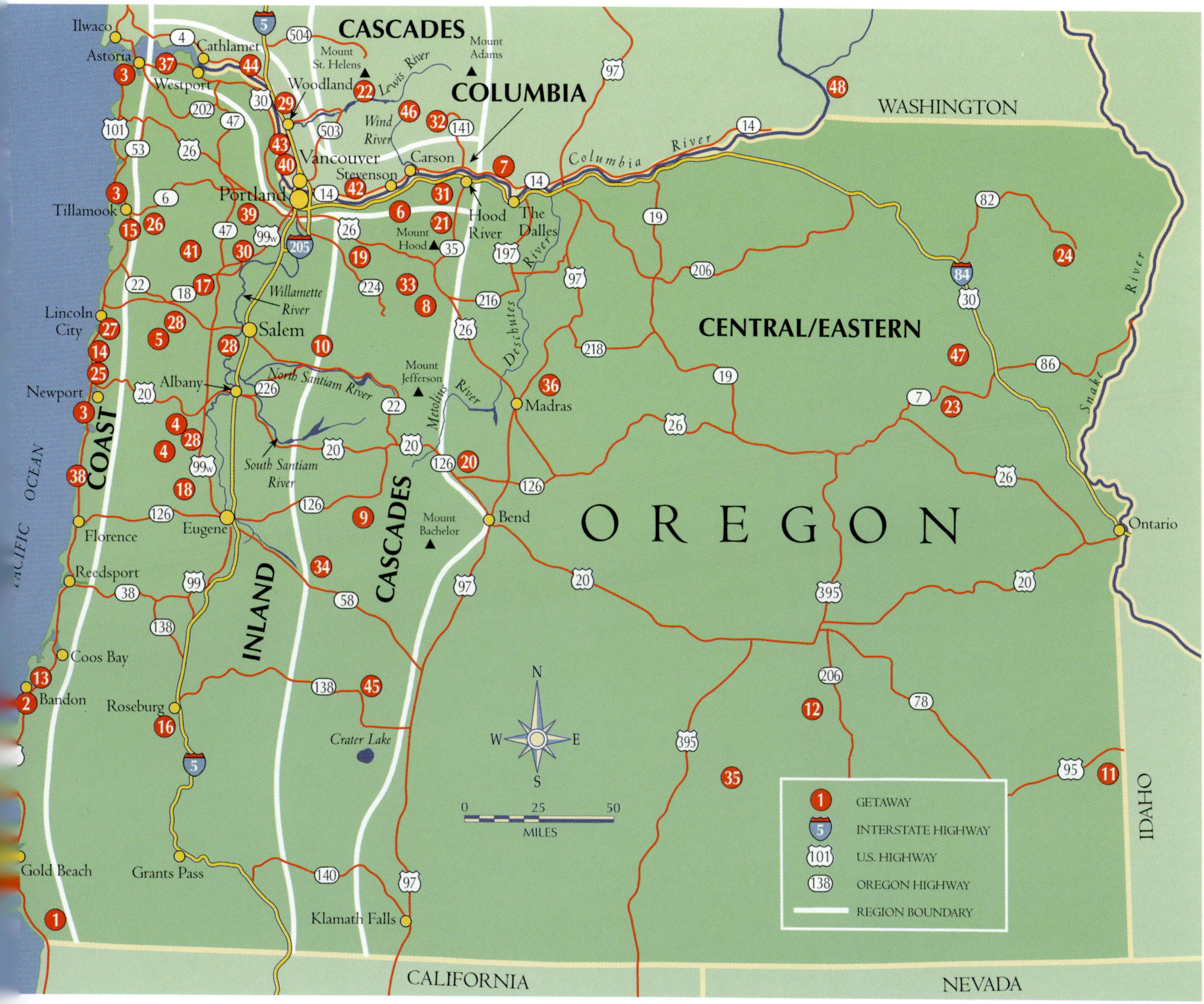
CASCADES
COLUMBIA
CENTRAL/EASTERN
OREGON
COAST
INLAND
CASCADES
WASHINGTON
CALIFORNIA
NEVADA
IDAHO
PACIFIC OCEAN
Ilwaco
Astoria
Cathlamet
Westport
Woodland
Vancouver
Portland
Carson
Stevenson
Hood River
The Dalles
Tillamook
Lincoln City
Newport
Salem
Albany
Madras
Bend
Eugene
Florence
Reedsport
Coos Bay
Bandon
Roseburg
Gold Beach
Grants Pass
Klamath Falls
Ontario
Mount St. Helens
Mount Adams
Mount Hood
Mount Jefferson
Mount Bachelor
Crater Lake
Lewis River
Wind River
Columbia River
Willamette River
North Santiam River
South Santiam River
Metolius River
Deschutes River
Snake River
N
S
E
W
0 25 50
MILES
GETAWAY
INTERSTATE HIGHWAY
U.S. HIGHWAY
OREGON HIGHWAY
REGION BOUNDARY

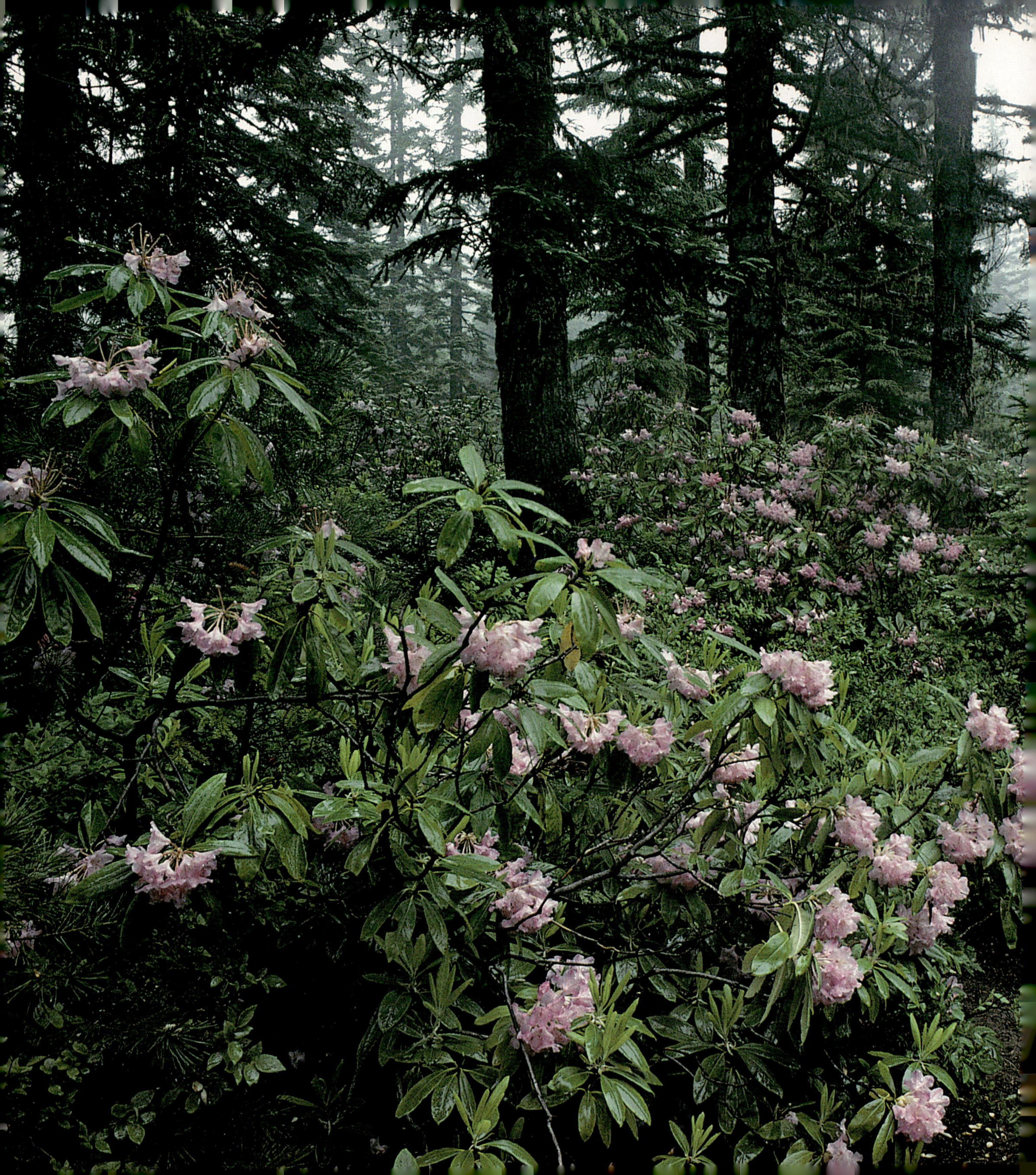

SPRING

Something hidden.

Go and find it.

Go and look behind the Ranges.

Something lost behind the Ranges.

Lost and waiting for you.

Go!

RUDYARD KIPLING, "THE EXPLORER"

◄ Colorful bursts of wild rhodies spice up the scene in the Mount Hood National Forest.

COAST

Land of the Giants

Oregon's Redwoods

Oregon has a "banana belt"? Oh yes, it's true! A near-tropical land, but not for fruit! For those in the know, Oregon's banana belt offers a pleasant setting with the mildest climate on the coast near the community of Brookings, approximately six miles north of the California border on coastal highway U.S. 101. Whether it's July or January, seventy-degree temperatures rule the scene, and while you won't find any pineapples, mangoes, or papayas growing in these parts, the Brookings area is famous for producing nearly 90 percent of America's Easter lilies. In the nearby hills, where the soft blankets of fog hint at a certain beauty that only springtime delivers, you can explore a stretch of coastal rain forest along the Chetco River—marked by weak light, high humidity, and lush growth—and discover an astonishing trail leading to a grove of redwoods, the largest and oldest trees in North America.

While redwoods (*Sequoia sempervirens*) reach their greatest size along California's northern coast, it's a little-known fact that Oregon is also home to magnificent redwoods. They are found on public lands managed by the Siskiyou National Forest and are the tallest trees on Earth, sometimes living more than two thousand years.

According to my hiking partner Tom Adzik, a U.S. Forest Service ecologist who guided our way on a relaxing trek through a fifty-acre grove along the Chetco River near Alfred A. Loeb State Park, "Redwoods are properly characterized as the 'ultimate' old-growth trees." He told me that no more than 1,350 acres of ancient redwoods remain standing in Oregon—including some small, isolated groves. The majestic redwoods along the Redwood Trail range from three hundred to eight hundred years in age, and Tom noted that Oregon's redwoods are unique because they are northernmost within the giants' range.

"Redwoods require high humidity," he explained as we paused along the trail to take in the lushness of the experience. This was a scene out of *Jurassic Park*, including dim, diffused light from an otherwise opaque sun and ferns of all sizes and shapes—sword, deer, lady, licorice, maidenhair—carpeting the ground before us. "And high humidity," Tom continued, "means constant atmospheric moisture, like fog, accompanying even moderate temperatures. Oregon's redwood range is limited by the occurrence of freezing temperatures. That is, redwoods don't like to get too cold."

We gazed across a glorious stand of gigantic trees, some towering more than 350 feet above us with diameters exceeding

◤ **A gentle trail leads you through ancient natural history near Alfred A. Loeb State Park.**

◢ **Some redwoods date back over a thousand years and are worth a pause to consider!**

16

25 feet. I learned that redwoods are resistant to insects and disease and have been growing in warm coastal zones like this ever since the Ice Age. Tom added that even though Oregon's redwoods are eight hundred years old, they can live twice that long. "In terms of their size—both height and diameter—there's nothing like them anywhere in the world." Their majestic scale will provide you with much to ponder as you head down the well-maintained gravel trail that leads through the grove and forms a mile-long loop with a few steep sections.

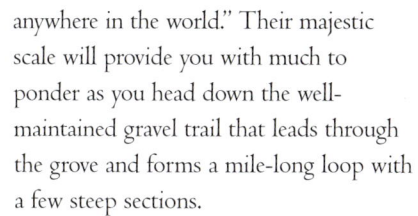

While you're in the area, see the grove of big Oregon myrtle that is protected at nearby Alfred A. Loeb State Park. You'll likely smell the park before you see it, for the scent of the myrtle forest—a crisp, bay-leaf aroma—dominates the air. The park is nestled in a 320-acre grove of myrtles that are well over two hundred years old. The Chetco River swirls and dances just beyond this state park, which offers many campsites plus three rental cabins that face the river. Depending on the season, you can fish, swim, raft, or walk a self-guided streamside nature trail. This oasis provides a wonderful escape any time of year.

All campsites at Alfred A. Loeb State Park are first-come, first-served. Three cabins and forty-eight electrical sites (maximum fifty feet) are reservable by phone.

■ Getting There

From U.S. 101 in Brookings, drive eight miles east on North Bank Chetco River Road. The Redwood Trail is on the left, about three-quarters of a mile past the entrance to Alfred A. Loeb State Park.

■ For More Information

Alfred A. Loeb State Park (reservations), (541) 469-2021, (800) 551-6949

Reservations Northwest (campsite reservations), (800) 452-5687

COAST

A Friend to the Critters

Free Flight

2

Throughout my travels over the past two decades, few people have impressed me more with their passion and sense of purpose than the kindhearted gentleman who found his life's calling at his home, perched on the cliffs in Bandon, Oregon, on the southern Oregon coast. Dan Deuel has been called the "Birdman of Bandon," a title suggesting a soul charitable toward wild creatures. That much is certainly true, but the road he traveled to find peace of mind and clarity of mission has been marked by more pain and misery than most of us might bear in twenty lifetimes. Yet we and countless wild critters that include seals, hawks, eagles, owls, murres, gulls, and even little hummingbirds are the better for Dan's knowing way of repairing, rehabilitating, and curing the sick and injured animals that come through his doorway at the not-for-profit Free Flight Bird and Marine Mammal Rehabilitation Center.

I first journeyed to Bandon to meet Dan for a special KATU television program in 1988 (following many positive reports I'd heard about his successful wildlife-care efforts), only to arrive in the midst of a surprising and terrible early spring storm. A powerful cold front aimed straight at Oregon had raced out of the Gulf of Alaska. It was staging a relentless March attack on the coastline near Bandon with ninety-mile-per-hour winds building massive, endless breakers that rolled and exploded onto the rugged shore. This was a time when nature was at its spectacularly roughest, and yet it was against that backdrop of coastal wildness that I found a remarkable back eddy of calm at a small wildlife hospital. With a whooshing blast of arctic wind accompanying my entrance, I hurriedly closed the door behind me and introduced myself to Dan—who had his hands full with a wounded red-tailed hawk.

"Oh—nice to meet you, too—uhhh—well, we're going to get a bite to eat. Care to cut some meat?" And with that, he put me to work. Trading my notepad for a razor-sharp boning knife, I set about carving bite-size pieces of venison from a carcass that had been brought in by the local game warden. (I'd later learn that roadkill deer is a reliable food source for Dan's many raptors.) As we talked, I offered the chunks of meat to Dan, who carefully offered them to the young raptor, who in turn eagerly gobbled them down.

"Juvenile bird," he explained. "You can see she doesn't have a red tail yet. It'll take a full year before she gets her telltale red tail. She's also considerably larger than her male counterpart of the same age, who's about a third smaller. Unfortunately, her soaring days were done before they really got started. Too many shotgun pellets in her wings."

I would learn that "raptors and rifles" constitute a common theme at Free Flight. In fact, scores of wounded birds are brought to the clinic each year, and Dan is able to patch up many of them for release back to the wild. But for a not-so-lucky few, fate has determined another path. The otherwise healthy birds become ambassadors of sorts for wildlife education programs.

As we walked and talked, Dan proudly described his many resident birds, including another mature red-tailed hawk whose right wing was but a mere stub of its former self—another gunshot wound, this one leading to amputation.

"This bird still attempts to fly when I go into its cage. It usually goes straight up and straight down, landing on its head—a sad story, since it was robbed of its ability to fly. But this bird has value as a teaching aid for showing kids what shooting does to wildlife. Plus, it's something important I can do with the animal rather than just euthanize it."

Without a hint of irony or sarcasm in his voice, Dan gestured to the dozen raptor cages lined up outside the clinic and proclaimed, "Veterans of warfare!"

◣ Dan Deuel has been called the "Birdman of Bandon," and he has dedicated his life to healing sick or injured wildlife like this red-tailed hawk.

You see, Deuel has his share of personal war stories and lasting wounds as well—from a distant time in America's past when a draft notice became his ticket to Vietnam. Dan was part of the First Air Cavalry and was assigned to do combat intelligence work. It was dangerous and deadly work, and land mines, helicopter crashes, and dead friends scarred Dan's body and mind. The combat experience also rewarded him with a chest full of medals, including two bronze stars, but that's something he won't talk about much.

"I got rewarded for my actions because I was a white face and because someone happened to be watching me. It's when they weren't watching that the worst happened. You know, when I arrived in 'Nam, I was young, eager, and a born killer—a real stud! But I grew up in a hurry, and when I was done I had no idea why we were there in the first place."

To be sure, Dan struggled for many years with lasting physical and emotional wounds, but the worst was to follow on his return home. On a lonely night when he came to the aid of a stranded motorist, Dan Deuel took a direct hit from a drunken driver who shattered his body again. His pelvis and hips and legs were crushed; internal injuries included heart damage, plus a coma that lasted for weeks. His body weight dropped nearly ninety pounds and yet—somehow—he survived! Today he lives with constant pain, lifetime medications, and a leg brace that results in a permanent step-and-a-half gait.

Dan told me he had seen it all—the worst that humans can do—yet he also admitted that when he was on the edge, when he was at his absolute worst and unsure if he would see the next light of day, a chance encounter with an Audubon rehabilitation doctor revived something he'd known as a kid: caring for birds. As a result, Dan reconstructed his own life from many shattered pieces, went back to school, learned how to care for wildlife, and opened Free Flight in 1978.

Dan and the many Free Flight volunteers provide daily care for the varied birds and mammals at the center. In addition, Dan tells all who will listen that too many coastal animals are wounded by gunfire, or from oil on the beach, or—increasingly—from being bound up in plastic trash, like six-pack rings, Styrofoam, and fishing line. He visits with groups, especially schoolchildren, whenever and wherever he can in order to spread his message: that each day he sees wild animals suffering for no good reason except they encountered humans.

"You know, I can't go out and save the whales, and I can't stop war across the planet or be against this or that. I can do one thing—one thing in a positive way—and that is put creatures that have been injured by humans back in the wild. That's the little bit I can do for peace on this planet."

■ Getting There
Directions and appointments available by phone.

■ For More Information
Free Flight Bird and Marine Mammal Rehabilitation Center, (541) 347-3882

COAST

A Blizzard of Feathers

3
Shorebird Migration Survey

Some people can watch wildlife in meditative silence. I, on the other hand, can be an unabashed top-o'-my-lungs screamer.

"Oooooh!" I screeched on a recent spring birding trip to the central Oregon coastline. "That flash of white there—oh, it's just fantastic! Ohh! Look at the way all those shorebirds twist and turn in a swarm!" I am certain I must irritate my news photography partners to no end as they strive to capture as much natural outdoor sound with their microphones as they can, and there I am, often going on and on about this dunlin or that dowitcher or whatever fanciful feathered shorebird streams past us.

A couple years back, we joined U.S. Fish and Wildlife biologist Roy Lowe to chronicle his springtime birding survey near South Beach at Newport in Lincoln County. Roy relies upon a "quad," a four-wheel-drive all-terrain vehicle, to get up and down miles and miles of sandy beach in a speedy manner. Speed is of the essence during the last week of April—when an annual West Coast bird survey is conducted. Roy's procedure is simple enough: travel a quarter mile, stop, gaze across the sand for a few moments, document on a notepad the bird species seen and their numbers, then move along and repeat the same procedures again and again over a five- to ten-mile stretch.

As a restless flock of semipalmated sandpipers rose from the distant shore, swept out over the ocean surf, then steered a course toward our position, I was overwhelmed by the beauty of the moment. Like a distant, dreamy mirage, the flock appeared, undulating in the warm heat waves above the sand. The birds bounced and bobbed their way on the air as a single unit that became clearer as it came closer. "There's a fair-sized flock," Roy noted matter-of-factly. "See way up there, past that group of people, maybe a quarter mile? There could be a couple hundred or so birds. They're heading our way, so we need to be patient for a moment to get quite a show."

The tiny sandpipers charged through the air! Their high energy and sleek bodies seemed built for speed, and that's critical for shorebirds. They are among the greatest long-distance migrants in the avian world. As Roy pointed out to me, of the species of shorebirds that breed in North America—plovers, sandpipers, yellowlegs, dowitchers, avocets, stilts, and the like—most of them fly more than seven thousand miles round-trip, and many

◣ **Oregon estuaries like Siletz Bay offer wonderful and unexpected wildlife moments.**

SPRING ~ Shorebird Migration Survey

exceed fourteen thousand miles. "My little part here at South Beach and two other sites is to conduct a snapshot survey of sorts—there are scores of others who are doing the same across a four-day period, so we get a window in time, so to speak, of the overall numbers of birds traveling the West Coast flyway of the United States." Roy added that, in the coming weeks of spring, more than a million dunlins and sandpipers, dowitchers, and plovers will stream along the Oregon and Washington coastlines in an epic journey. The birds have little time to waste, so they are in constant motion, searching for food in the sand and moving on along the seashore.

Not only are beaches keen sites to see shorebird migrations, but so are estuaries, bays, and other freshwater inlets where the birds will often stop and congregate to rest and feed for a time. High tide is the best time to watch. At low tide, the birds seem spread out, but as the tide moves in the birds are compressed into narrower strips of shoreline. Western sandpipers, the most common of the shorebirds in the migration, fly two hundred to five hundred miles at a time, then rest and feed for two to four days.

The best show is the grand sweep of sandpipers and dunlins on the wing. Birds fly and turn in tightly packed flocks, streak past you in a nearly camouflaged blur, and then veer suddenly. Bird-watchers and researchers have long wondered how the birds coordinate their movements to avoid each other in flight. Roy told me that biologists studying slow-motion film of moving birds have suggested that the birds move like a chorus line. Roy explained, "No single bird leads the flock, but which birds lead it and how remains a mystery. It's a pretty amazing and broad-based bird behavior that's been pretty much ignored until the past decade. We still don't have much baseline data on many of the species, but ten years from now we'll know much, much more because of the work we're doing today."

■ Getting There

South Beach State Park: Travel south on coastal highway U.S. 101 approximately two miles past Newport. The park entrance is on the west side of the highway.

Cape Meares Beach and Bayocean Spit: From Portland, travel west on U.S. 26 to the junction with Oregon 6 (Wilson River Highway). Follow Oregon 6 to Tillamook and travel west on the Three Capes Scenic Drive for approximately two miles to the junction with Cape Meares Road. Travel west on Cape Meares Road for four miles until you reach the small beachside community of Cape Meares, where you will find a parking area and beach access.

Trestle Bay Wetlands: From Portland, travel west on U.S. 26 to Astoria and coastal highway U.S. 101. Approximately two miles south of Astoria on U.S. 101, follow signs for an additional eight miles to Fort Stevens State Park. At the park, follow signs to the South Jetty lookout tower. From the tower, follow the road one mile east to the parking area for the Trestle Bay Wetlands wildlife boardwalk and viewing area. Note: The boardwalk trail is wheelchair accessible.

■ For More Information

Oregon State Parks (campground information), (800) 452-5687

LEAVE THE BABES ALONE

Roy Lowe and many other wildlife experts say that people's best intentions in spring can lead to the worst disasters for newborn wildlife. Biologists warn that deer fawns, seal pups, fledgling birds, and elk calves need a break to thrive. As Roy explained, people too often seem to feel that spring is animal-rescue season.

"People will see a seal pup or a deer fawn and assume that, because it's alone, it's been deserted by its parent. So they pick it up and bring it to us or some other agency or a wildlife rehabilitation center. Their efforts may be well-intentioned, but they are uninformed. They've just created an orphan."

The truth is that most often the parent is busy hunting or foraging for food and will soon be back. Does often leave fawns alone temporarily to avoid drawing predators with their own body scent, and seal mothers behave the same with beached pups. Fledgling birds often land on the ground, where they beg for parent birds to feed them and coach them to safety.

Anglers and other outdoors folks would do better to pick up discarded nylon fishingline, plastic six-pack rings, and other nonbiodegradable trash that often entangles ducks, geese, raptors, songbirds, and other animals. Many trapped creatures die from starvation or their inability to escape predators. Roy's message is simple: If you find a wildlife babe in the woods or on the beach, back away and leave it alone. Chances are good its mother will return shortly.

INLAND

Dizzying Heights, Quiet Byways

4

Marys Peak and the Alsea River

When my family's in the mood to rise above dreary winter weather in order to welcome the early days of spring, we pack up and head south from our Portland-area home to see the sights in the heights—in fact, the greatest heights in Oregon's Coast Range! It's the promise of a bird's-eye view of the grand Willamette Valley with some secluded streamside campsites that keeps my family enthused about this adventure. They simply love to get away from it all! Admittedly, the Coast Range may not offer the magnificence of the snowcapped Cascades and most people aren't screaming "Give me scenery!" while they are driving from the valley to the coast. But that's unfortunate, because one particular Coast Range mountain really steals the scene in western Oregon. Perhaps Marys Peak will steal your heart, too, as you leave the pastoral Willamette Valley behind. Just twenty-three miles southwest of Corvallis, a winding, rising trek can take you to this highest point in the Oregon Coast Range north of the Coquille River.

The Marys Peak experience begins with Marys Peak Road: A curvy nine miles forces you to slow down and enjoy dramatic scenic surprises at every turn. Tree-clad hills seem to rise and rise higher and higher along this roadway with its many awesome viewpoints with waysides. At 4,097 feet, Marys Peak is highly regarded for providing one of western Oregon's most dazzling panoramas. On a clear day, the summit offers mountain views that include all of the Cascade favorites: Rainier, Adams, St. Helens, Hood, Jefferson, Bachelor, and the Three Sisters. Even the breaking surf along the central Oregon coast near Newport can be seen on a sun-kissed day.

The Observation Point Summit area provides additional reasons for exploration via hiking trails that branch in many directions for many miles. These trails crisscross forests and meadows on and alongside the peak, yet each of them loops back to the summit parking area for easy access and return. To enjoy the finest vistas, hike the Summit Trail from the parking area to the top of Marys Peak. Also try the 1.6-mile Meadow Edge Trail, which begins in an old-growth forest and sports many information posts along a self-guided tour that will teach you more about the local ecosystems.

Are you wondering how the peak was tagged with the moniker of "Mary"? The simple answer is that it's a mystery. My friend and local historian Bill Burwell says the mountain is shrouded in an ancient mystique. It seems that local Native American tribes considered it a magical place and called it "Tcha Teemanwi," or "Home to Spirits." While Marys Peak showed up on pioneer maps and logs of the region long ago, exactly who Mary was remains a mystery.

Marys Peak is a fine destination for sure, but make it only part of this daylong excursion. In fact, if you had the foresight to pack a tent and sleeping bag, you'll not be disappointed when you drive west from Marys Peak on Oregon 34 toward the small coastal village of Waldport and into the Alsea Falls Recreation Area and campground, which is open May to late September. There are twenty-two single-family units in the park's campground, and drinking water, vault toilets, grills, and fireplaces for wood and charcoal are available.

This area is also immediately adjacent to the South Fork Alsea River National Back Country Byway. The byway is a recreation destination that offers many campers' delights as the big-leaf maples bud to leafy life and the Alsea River whirls on its way to the sea. The byway offers the traveler a leisurely route through a coastal rain forest and its varied attractions, with picnic facilities, hiking trails, an outstanding view of Alsea Falls, drinking water, restrooms, and campgrounds.

The Alsea Falls Recreation Area was developed by the Bureau of Land Management and was named after its original inhabitants, the Alsea Indians.

❯ **You'll enjoy the bird's-eye view of the Willamette Valley atop Marys Peak.**

SPRING ~ Marys Peak and the Alsea River

The first white settlers had arrived here by the mid-nineteenth century, and it wasn't long before logging dominated the scene. Like many sites across Oregon, timber provided the area's economic lifeblood, so keep your eyes open for the many remnant old-growth fir and hemlock stumps scattered throughout this park. Some of these giants measure more than six feet in diameter.

The Alsea River area is one of the wettest places in the Northwest, receiving more than a hundred inches a year. That's good news for waterfall fans because Alsea River Falls slips and slides down smooth basalt rock for more than 125 feet and provides the scenic centerpiece of the area. Please bring your camera!

■ Getting There

Marys Peak: From Portland, travel Interstate 5 south to exit 228. Exit and drive on Oregon 34 west toward Corvallis. Follow Oregon 34 through Corvallis to Philomath. Follow signs for Oregon 34 toward Waldport for approximately eight miles until you reach the Marys Peak access road (on the right). The parking area and summit views are wheelchair accessible.

Alsea Falls Recreation Area and Campground (from the east): From Corvallis, take U.S. 99W south fifteen miles. Turn left on County Road 45120 and drive five miles to Alpine Junction. Continue nine miles along the South Fork Alsea Access Road to the Alsea Falls Campground.

Alsea Falls Recreation Area and Campground (from the west): As you enter the town of Alsea, take Oregon 201 (not marked, but on the west side of Alsea as you enter the town) to County Road 48200, which connects with the South Fork Alsea Access Road. Continue nine miles to the Alsea Falls Campground.

■ For More Information

Bureau of Land Management, Salem District Office, Alsea Falls Campground, (503) 375-5646

INLAND

Know Your Trees and Forests

Valley of the Giants

5

"If you find someone who really cares about trees, why then, Grant, you've found someone who's probably worth knowing!" So began my encounter with Maynard Drawson, one of the most interesting and enthusiastic documenters of regional history. I had known of Maynard's efforts to identify and protect Oregon's really old and really big trees for many years, yet surprisingly our paths never crossed until 1999, when the Oregon Travel Council published a new brochure, largely a result of Maynard's work, showcasing fifteen Oregon "Heritage Trees."

The Heritage Tree Program had been established in 1995 to increase public awareness of the important contribution of trees to Oregon's history and the significant role they still play in the quality of life. It is the only state-sponsored program of its kind in the nation. I had wanted to meet the man who had intimate knowledge of Oregon's back roads, history, mountains, rivers, and trees.

Eventually, I did meet and enjoy the company of a fine, gracious gentleman and purveyor of facts about our past who has a passion for holding on to heritage trees as though they are members of his family. Despite being seventy-something years old, he is as sharp and active as a person half his age and his enthusiasm is infectious. He can recite historical facts and names of people, places, and trees at the drop of a hat, so it can be said that he's Oregon's "Ambassador of Trees," a spokesperson for the magnificent, stately, and significant trees that have survived through the years. On a warm, overcast April afternoon, he offered to show me around some of the impressive trees near his Salem, Oregon, home.

We began our daylong adventure in downtown Salem at the Waldo City Park and Redwood. Although small in acreage (the park measures just twelve by twenty feet), the Sierra redwood there stands huge next to the state capitol building. This giant was originally planted in the late 1800s, and in 1936 its location was designated a city park by the Salem City Council. Today the eighty-two-foot-tall tree, whose trunk measures six feet in diameter, soars above Summer Street, with a fine backdrop of the state capitol just beyond its branches.

▶ **The many towering Douglas fir trees in the Valley of the Giants will make you feel small.**

On we motored toward Interstate 5, where the traffic roars by at a shattering pace at its junction with Oregon 22, and where the Hager Pear Tree grows. It's too bad more folks don't slow down here, for if they did, as Maynard explained to me, "they might just learn a bit about Oregon history." Protected by a chain-link fence, with Canada geese often seen lounging near its base, this lovely tree, planted in 1848, was once part of a huge grove of pear trees that supplied fruit up and down the Willamette Valley and beyond. Maynard noted that, for its kind, this is one of the giants of the tree world and it is especially spectacular when its blossoms are at their peak display, as they were on this fine spring day.

But size isn't everything. When it comes to remarkable trees, sometimes it's age or even appearance—like the cottonwood tree at nearby Willamette Mission State Park, tree stop number three on our busy day. This oldest cottonwood in the United States measures almost twenty-eight feet in circumference, but its thick, chunky bark, deeply furrowed like a freshly plowed field, is amazing to touch. Access is readily available on a well-used trail, and as we stood and gazed up at its branches—which appeared to me to be the size of most of the surrounding trees' trunks—I asked Maynard if he ever got tired of just looking and wondering about the stories these big old trees might tell.

"Nope—absolutely not! How could I? I mean, it's amazing that these trees have survived as long as they have. And can you imagine what events have occurred around these sites? And they're still here with us. But if you want to see something really special, Grant, you need to go where a lot of giants grow—the 'Valley of the Giants,' that is."

Maynard's message reminds us to examine the important links that these trees provide, and that is perhaps more true in the Valley of the Giants. It's a fifty-one-acre parcel of public land deep in the Oregon Coast Range where you can walk among four-hundred- and five-hundred-year-old Douglas firs and western hemlocks. Set aside by the Bureau of Land Management (BLM) more than twenty-five years ago for scientific research and education, the stand is a protected Outstanding Natural Area.

On a bright summery day in May, I joined BLM scientists Scott Hopkins and Trish Hogervorst for the long, arduous ninety-minute drive west of Falls City to see an incredible tract of old-growth timber that had somehow escaped logging over the decades. I discovered that the Valley of the Giants makes you feel small—actually tiny! The grandeur of the watershed (within the North Fork of the Siletz River basin) is unmatched, and it is unlike any forest you will visit in northwest Oregon. As the three of us made our way slowly down the moderately steep though well-maintained trail, I felt as if I were in a cathedral, the sun's rays filtering down to the trail, still soft and muddy from a recent rain. Trish told me that many of the "giants" are more than twenty feet in circumference and nearly two hundred feet tall—so tall, in fact, that we could not see the tops of the trees without lying on the ground. We paused often to look at the trailside oxalis, monkeyflower, rhododendron, salmonberry, and salal. Trish added that the remote nature of the stand contributed to its protection. "Several years ago we designated it as an Outstanding Natural Area and an area of critical environmental concern. So it's protected about as much as possible for research, and we hope to keep it that way for the long term."

The Siletz River Basin is one of the wettest in the Coast Range, getting an average of 180 inches of rain per year, and up to 300 inches in the Valley of the Giants. The giant forest canopy shades and cools the small creeks and larger streams, while the forest floor acts as a sponge to moderate the flow into the nearby North Fork Siletz River.

"Things grow fast here," Scott said. He added that this place is a remnant of what much of northwestern Oregon once looked like and provides habitat for many species of wildlife, including the northern spotted owl, bald eagle, and marbled murrelet. "It seems like every year a new piece of biological information that comes in from this site helps us understand where we're going and what more we might discover out here. There are more species of plant life than I recognize here. The place is so special!"

Please note the following:
  Valley of the Giants is a day-use area.
  The 1.5-mile loop trail is mostly

25

moderate, steep in places, and well maintained.

Camping and fires are not allowed.

Park only in the established area and stay on trails; wildlife and vegetation will be disturbed if you stray off the trail.

Toilets are not available.

Private lands surround the access to the Valley of the Giants and can only be accessed with permission from the landowner. Roads with gates are closed to public access when the gates are closed. (Road closures are common during periods of high fire danger, usually the late summer and fall.)

The area is about fourteen air miles west of Falls City, but due to the circuitous, rough, unpaved access roads, the drive is some thirty-one miles and takes well over an hour.

■ Getting There

If you are a first-time visitor, do not travel without directions. Call first for road conditions.

You can get close to fifteen of Oregon's Heritage Trees through a new brochure from the Oregon Travel Council. It is available through Oregon State Parks and Recreation Department in Salem and also at information outposts.

■ For More Information

Oregon Heritage Trees brochure and map: Oregon Travel Information Council, (800) 574-8397

Valley of the Giants brochure: BLM Salem District Office, (503) 375-5646

COLUMBIA

Dinosaurs with Fins?

6

Herman the Sturgeon and the Bonneville Fish Hatchery

Oh, come on, Dad, there's no such thing as a dinosaur these days! I know all about dinosaurs and they died out sixty million years ago. I learned that in class!" My ten-year-old son had insisted on this point for more than an hour as we cruised east of Portland on Interstate 84 toward Bonneville Dam. In fact, he was unwavering to a degree I'd not seen since Christmas a couple years earlier, when the topic of "Santa" had come up for family discussion. Youngsters can be pretty determined in their beliefs—"Of course there's a Santa, and a Tooth Fairy, and an Easter Bunny"—but this topic was different. Eric was strongly convinced that there couldn't possibly be ("No way, no how") any living prehistoric animal species in our corner of the world. His determination was engraved upon an ever-deepening furrowed brow, and this was going to be a very tough sell for me.

"Well, son," I slowly, politely, offered. "Fact is there is an ancient critter living here in the Northwest that is pretty well known in some circles. It's a species whose history reaches back two hundred million years. That's way before T-Rex's time, huh?"

"No way, no way, no way," he chimed. "There are no more dinosaurs!"

Eric was stumped for a research topic for a science class assignment, and I had an idea that might help him—and perhaps surprise and teach many of his fellow students, too. As we pulled into the parking area of the Bonneville Fish Hatchery, adjacent to the sprawling, monumental complex at Bonneville Dam, I had a plan to teach the youngster that there really was a dinosaur of a species alive and well in Oregon.

I love to visit the largest and most tourist-friendly fish hatcheries in Oregon each spring. We strolled past several gorgeous and glorious flower beds decked out with spectacular roses, marigolds, and impatiens whose blossoms were peaking like some colorful parade.

"Well," I hinted, "this animal swims," hoping my clues might pique his youthful curiosity. "And it lives in rivers, but it also migrates to the ocean. It doesn't have scales, but it does have fins, and it can grow to a gigantic size, say ten or eleven feet long. Any ideas?"

"Oh, Dad, I can't think of any." He was puzzled. I smiled, and together we ambled to the newest feature of the six-acre facility: the home of "Herman the Sturgeon."

▶ **Everyone can lend a hand feeding the fish at the Bonneville Fish Hatchery.**

SPRING ~ Herman the Sturgeon and the Bonneville Fish Hatchery

"A sturgeon!" he exclaimed. "Wow!"

Two 1-inch-thick Plexiglas windows are all that separate 450-pound Herman the Sturgeon from his adoring fans at Bonneville Hatchery in the Columbia Gorge. Herman is a nine-foot, ten-inch-long white sturgeon, probably seventy years old, and a member of a fish family dating back some two hundred million years. The Oregon Department of Fish and Wildlife, working closely with the Oregon Wildlife Heritage Foundation, had designed the "Home for Herman" to give him room to move about in a natural setting and allow visitors to stay dry while watching him below water level.

The pond measures thirty feet by one hundred feet and is about ten feet deep, and unless you're a Columbia River fisherman, you've never been able to see a sturgeon so well, or to learn about their biology from well-designed information panels located near the windows. For the most part, these giants of the Northwest are bottom dwellers, and their pea-size eyes don't allow them to see much in the murky depths of a river, so they rely upon four hairlike projections called "barbels" that are located at the ends of their snouts. These help the fish find food and feel their way along the river bottom. Instead of scales, sturgeon have tough skin and rows of bony, diamond-shaped plates along their lateral sides and down their top sides or dorsals. The plates are called "scutes" (pronounced "skoots"), and biologists think of them as a sort of fish armor. It seems that in prehistoric times sturgeon were entirely covered by these scutes for protection against even larger predator fish. Sturgeons also have upturned, sharklike tails and skeletons largely made of cartilage and less of bone. Sturgeon historically migrated throughout the Columbia River Basin to the Pacific Ocean and can grow to twenty feet, weigh a thousand pounds or more, and live for more than a hundred years.

The first reference to a sturgeon named "Herman" occurred in 1925 at either the Bonneville or the Roaring River Hatchery near Scio. The very first report of a sturgeon named "Herman" occurred in 1935 when a former game commissioner raised the fish to be shown each year at the Oregon State Fair. This Herman was stolen from the Roaring River Hatchery in the middle of the night. Other "Hermans" have fulfilled the role since then.

The current facility features interpretive signs and displays and is open to the public throughout the year. The department also makes it available to school groups as an educational destination. As we gazed through the windows, Eric was not only impressed by Herman's length and girth, but also by the fact that even larger Hermans are alive and well in the Columbia. "Wow! That's pretty cool, Dad!" Eric snapped photos of Herman through the glass and then scrambled for another view. "A living dinosaur! I've got something really special to write about for my science project now."

Herman is not the only attraction at the hatchery. A nearby viewing room allows visitors each fall to watch hatchery staff spawn chinook and coho salmon, and visitors can walk along the dozens of raceways where the department rears millions of tiny salmon and steelhead for release each spring. For a quarter, visitors can feed brood trout and other fish.

Bonneville is one of thirty-six operating fish hatcheries in Oregon, many of which also offer fish and wildlife viewing opportunities.

■ Getting There
From Portland, travel east on Interstate 84 to exit 40 at Bonneville Dam. The Bonneville Fish Hatchery parking area is adjacent to the entrance. The property is wheelchair accessible throughout.

■ For More Information
Bonneville Fish Hatchery, (541) 374-8393

COLUMBIA

Climbing to New Heights

Horsethief Butte

7

"On belay?" I nervously asked my climbing instructor, Gary Peterson, who was gripping my safety rope.

"On belay!" followed his quick and certain reply—with a curt query: "Ready to climb?"

"Climbing!" I snapped back.

It was a simple yet critical series of questions and answers that left little room for error. After all, I did want to be safe and secure on this entry-level rock-climbing lesson.

"Ohhhh, man—that's a tight fit," I said as I reached up, slid my hand sideways, and slipped three fingers into a tiny rock crevice for a bit of a hold on a knob of basalt. Then, with a bit more effort, I pushed up with my legs.

"Reach, pull, and push yourself up" is the name of the rock-climbing game according to Gary, a professional guide with the Portland Mountain Guides Alliance. His confident tone assured me that all was well and I was learning the ropes—err, make that the ropes and the rocks—in the fun, challenging sport of rock climbing at Horsethief Butte in the Columbia River Gorge.

Horsethief Butte rises above the Columbia River like some ancient fortress, but the fact is that, like the surrounding Columbia River channel, the butte was carved out of basalt rock by floods that followed the last ice age. Today, Horsethief Butte is something of a mecca for beginning climbers because, in the jargon of climbers like the accomplished Peterson, it is so well suited for "top-roping" and "bouldering." Gary and hundreds of other climbers find tremendous challenge in Horsethief's nooks, crannies, and boulders with a rope, a climbing harness, and good friends to share the day. Even though the pursuit of the sport has led him across the planet, the forty-something Gary told me Horsethief Butte is special. "Everything you find here, Grant, from face climbing to crack climbing to bouldering, is applicable to climbing sites across the country, so it's a great starting point that isn't very far from Portland."

Snug in my climbing harness, and secured by Gary's belay, my challenge was simple, straightforward, and smack in front of my face in the thirty-foot-high wall of basalt. Now all I had to do was climb to the top. Gary coached and prodded and cajoled me: "Nice—good job—that's it—stay with it—slowly—and don't forget to breathe!" Gary's words followed me as I inched up the relatively simple route. Yet it didn't seem so simple to me, a fellow who's a bit nervous and

SPRING ~ Horsethief Butte

◤ "She Who Watches" is an ancient and awesome petrolgyph at Horsethief Lake State Park.

"Uhh, Grant—that's quite a smile you're wearing!" he shouted.

"Oh yee-aah, Gary!" I was ecstatic as I rose, twisted, and parked myself on the top rock. I'd gained a valuable lesson in trust and confidence. Then I shouted for all to hear, "This feels greeeeat!"

The feeling of sitting high on the ramparts of Horsethief Butte was exhilarating, if only for the awesome view of nearby Horsethief Lake State Park. The park sprawls across 338 acres and offers more than seven thousand feet of Columbia River shoreline. The lake covers about ninety acres and is a popular destination for all sorts of recreation—from hiking to camping to boating.

Horsethief Lake is a National Historic Site, and guided tours of the area's rock art occur each Friday and Saturday. Included on the tour are many pictographs (rock paintings) and petroglyphs (rock carvings), including some of the oldest in the Northwest, like the well-known petroglyph "She Who Watches." Many signs are posted advising visitors to respect these sites and to remember that archeological sites and artifacts are protected by both federal and state laws and that their disturbance and/or removal are illegal. The tours begin at 10:00 A.M. on Fridays and Saturdays from April to October. Reservations are required.

The park includes thirty-five unsheltered picnic tables in the day-use area and

shaky during a shingle repair on a roof. Somehow, looking up from the bottom of this wall, the ascent appeared much easier. Now, face to face with it at eye level, the sun-browned rock seemed flat, devoid of character, and I had to search carefully for any sort of hold—a crack to grab or a thin ledge on which to rest.

"Grant, you need to lean in a little more," Gary encouraged. "Feel the gravity. There you go. Now step up and onto that lip there." Thirty minutes later and twenty-five feet up the rock wall, the top was in sight. I suddenly began to enjoy the little successes that were measured by rising inches, feet, and then yards. Climbing offers so many internal rewards, including a sense of accomplishment that's earned by each grasp, pull, or push along the way. As I neared the top, I peered down at Gary, who'd been keeping a tight belay, pulling in the slack rope as I moved upward.

two boat ramps. Motorized boats are permitted on the lake, with a posted speed limit of five miles per hour for the entire lake. A watercraft launch permit is available at the park.

Caution: Watch out for rattlesnakes and for the poison oak in the rock-climbing areas of the butte. Also, spring is tick season, and these tiny insects can be a real nuisance, so be sure to check for them after hiking through the park's remote areas.

Note to climbers: Climbers are directed to limit their use of chalk at Horsethief Butte, and two areas are signed "No climbing" for cultural resource protection.

■ Getting There
From Portland, drive east on Interstate 84 to The Dalles. Drive across the Columbia River on The Dalles Bridge and take Washington 14 east for another 1.1 miles. Near milepost 85, turn right (southeast) onto the paved entrance road to the state park. Proceed about another mile east on Washington 14 to Horsethief Butte, on the right. Parking is often along the shoulder of the road here.

■ For More Information
Horsethief Lake State Park (general information), (360) 902-8608

Horsethief Lake State Park Natural/Cultural History Tour (reservations), (509) 767-1159

CASCADES

Campsite with a View
Timothy Lake
8

"Who wants to go camping?" I roared, trying my best to suppress a sly grin on a sun-blessed summer morning. Perhaps a half second passed before an ecstatic chorus erupted from my three young boys standing nearby. They chimed in at once:

"Me, me, me!"

"Yeah, yeah, yeah!"

"I do, I do, I do!"

Overjoyed that vacation time had finally arrived, my sons' anticipation was at an all-time high. But then I had been building the suspense for weeks about just where we might make our first-of-the-season spring campout. Now everyone wanted to know where we were going. Fact is, we McOmies are not ones to let the grass grow under our feet; we're a family on the move when the warm season strikes, bound for new adventures, places to see, people to meet, and activities to enjoy as we build memories of family time together.

I am a big believer that some of the best adventures can be found right in our own backyards, so we were on the fast-track into the Mount Hood National Forest, a little less than two hours from Portland, to enjoy a quiet midweek break at a most delightful lake in the forest. Timothy Lake is certainly close to the Portland metropolitan area, yet it remains a distant world away from urban pavement and noise.

We headed into the Cascades on U.S. 26 and veered right at the junction just past Government Camp with Skyline Road (also known as Forest Service Road 42), which zips through woods with nary a house or meadow to be seen. Skyline Road is a major artery for recreation travel and is one of many Forest Service roads that lace the Oregon Cascades. Before long, we arrived at the 1,500-acre lake that offers four campgrounds: Gone Creek, Oak Fork, Pine Point, and—our favorite—Hoodview. Collectively, these campgrounds provide more than two hundred campsites and several picnic areas along the lakeshore.

Timothy Lake is really a reservoir that was formed in 1956 when Portland General Electric dammed the Oak Fork of the Clackamas River for electric power generation. According to one of the U.S. Forest Service district rangers, Cathleen Walker, the entire area was once the historic site of Timothy Meadows, which had been a favorite area for summer grazing of sheep. Cathleen told me that

▶ **Your family will enjoy a paddler's paradise at Timothy Lake in the Mount Hood National Forest.**

SPRING ~ Timothy Lake

sheepherders spread Timothy grass to enrich the native grasses that grew on the meadows, hence the name Timothy Lake. The circular lake rests behind a 110-foot-high, 740-foot-long dam and is primarily popular for its camping and fishing opportunities. In fact, on this early June adventure I had arranged to connect with my longtime fishing partner, Trey Carskadon, who enjoys exploring all the Cascade watery nooks and crannies that hold hungry trout. He's made a summer pilgrimage to Timothy Lake ever since he was a young boy, and he was anxious to show us around the lake. Once our family trailer had been set on its camping site at Hoodview—with a spectacular overlook of the lake and surrounding forest—we couldn't get tackle boxes, rods, reels, and bait unpacked fast enough. After all, I had three eager anglers leading the charge, and it was all I could do to grab a cooler full of lunch, rein in the boys, then race ahead fast enough to prevent a McOmie stampede onto Trey's twenty-two-foot fishing boat. He had been standing by, his boat warmed and ready to troll all of us across the lake. He said he had just the ticket to help us catch our dinner. But as I stepped aboard, I noticed how quickly the weather had changed: stunning sunshine disappeared and played peekaboo as milky white wisps washed in from the west to skirt the top of the forest.

A light breeze carried a late afternoon chill that joined our fishing adventure.

"Mighty cold weather for June, my friend," I remarked as I shivered and Trey set the boat's course to parallel the lake's shoreline.

"Yes, yes, it is." With a chuckle he added, "And this is the banana belt of the Cascades. We're only at three thousand feet in elevation! But at this time of year the weather can change in a heartbeat, so you have to be prepared with warm clothing. Now, the upside is that the fish are definitely biting. In fact, today it's been red hot!"

That's exactly what I was hoping to hear, and it warmed my heart as we

31

joined Trey and his partner Eric Aronson. They were using lightweight fishing rods, reels, and small spinners called "rooster tails," which are available in a variety of colors. (Trey prefers brown, black, and green.) As an added bonus to attract the trout, Trey placed a small night crawler on each lure's hooks. He called it a bit of "extra insurance" that always guarantees a bite.

Timothy Lake is a favorite recreational site, particularly for Portland-area residents, because tens of thousands of rainbow trout are stocked annually by the Oregon Department of Fish and Wildlife. You may also catch brook trout, cutthroat trout, or kokaneee (a smallish, landlocked sockeye salmon) from the lake's cold waters. Within moments, my young Eric, always anxious to catch a fish, had a silvery fourteen-inch rainbow trout hooked, splashing, and ready to net. As I admired the darting flashes reflected from the fat and sassy trout, I also noticed the telltale crimson marks along its deep-bodied sides. I asked Trey about the rainbow trout stocking program at Timothy.

"That's really a nice trout, Trey, and you say this size is typical of Timothy trout?"

"That's correct, Grant. The Oregon Fish and Wildlife Department does a great job keeping this lake stocked with trout all summer long. Thousands will be planted, and, interestingly, anglers will catch most of the fish by season's end in September. People come from all over the Northwest to fish this lake. And by the way, Grant—you've got one on!"

Yikes! I did—a gorgeous trout easily pushing the tape at fourteen inches or more. And with that, as though some god of the trout bite had pushed a "fish on" button, each of us in turn grabbed our rods that had been bent into horseshoe-shaped pretzel affairs by the strong diving pulls of the fighting fish. Fins and tails were splashing, as the trout went dashing while the kids were laughing—and all of it was marvelous! We were in the midst of a trout feeding frenzy, and we were the special guests. Trey really knew the lake and the trout and offered some quick tips for the novice visitor.

"Probably the best tip that I can give someone," he offered, "and it applies to any of the high Cascade lakes in the Mount Hood National Forest, is to pay attention to what other people around you are doing. It may seem obvious, but watch to see what the successful anglers are using to catch trout. Also, too many people who are new to these lakes say, 'Well, it's deeper out there in the middle of the lake, so that must be where more fish live.' Not true! My experience has been—especially early in the season like this—just the opposite. Today, we're only trolling—what, twenty yards from shore in twenty to thirty feet of water. That's because the water's warmer here from the radiant sun. And it's where the fish are feeding. So stick close to shore and you'll catch more."

Within a couple of hours, our limits were filled and we'd arrived back at camp for a shore-side supper of grilled trout. Then we enjoyed the crackling warmth of a campfire, as my wife, Christine, passed cups of steaming hot cocoa all around. We told fish stories, exchanged jokes and spooky stories that left our sides sore from the giggling and laughing, and soaked up the scenery of a fading sunset that shone across a dazzling Mount Hood. I raised my cup in a toast to Trey for a job well done. He and I and my family were pleased to be so close to so much beauty, and I couldn't help but think that Oregon's summer season is really made for moments like this: precious time that's not to be wasted.

As Trey admired the setting sun, he noted, "When the sun finally breaks through, it does offer an unbelievable vista of Timothy Lake, the forest, and snow-covered Mount Hood dominating the entire scene. That's one of the things that strikes me the most about this area—plus it's a neat and pristine getaway, and such a short hop from Portland."

Timothy Lake is open from May until September.

■ Getting There

Follow U.S. 26 east from Portland to Sandy. Travel another 66.5 miles (continuing past Government Camp) and take a right onto Skyline Road (Forest Service Road 42). Travel south for nine miles. Turn right onto FS Road 57 and continue another two miles. Turn right at the Hoodview Campground entrance sign.

■ For More Information

General information, (541) 622-7674

Reservations, reserveusa.com, (877) 444-6777

CASCADES

The Road to Paradise

McKenzie River Scenic Drive

My family is destined to wander! It often seems we are unpacking our gear from one adventure, only to begin repacking a day or two later and heading down some other back road toward a new destination. I've given my loved ones little choice, really, but I think that's because the RV life makes travel and adventure so easy. I enjoy "getting away" for enjoyment and discovery across Oregon's varied and intriguing byways so much that I am often left wondering if we'll ever return home.

Just one spring season back, we were on course for a patch of the Oregon Cascade Mountains that I'd not visited in many years, and it was frustrating trying to find enough time to explore the many faces of this land. Our travel trailer was loaded to the gills as we meandered up the McKenzie River valley on U.S. 126, east of the Eugene-Springfield area.

From its headwaters at Clear Lake, high in the Cascade Mountains, the McKenzie is a swift and lively river. The scenic drive explodes with opportunities to partake in outdoor activities amid some of Oregon's most beautiful mountain landscapes.

▶ The view to Three Sisters Wilderness atop McKenzie Pass will stir your soul and capture your heart.

Our stops along this route included Goodpasture Covered Bridge near Vida. At 165 feet in length, it is the second-longest covered bridge in Oregon. It's also where spring busts out all over with dramatic, colorful backdrops from every angle, so it's a great photo stop. A second and equally scenic covered bridge is the Belknap Bridge, located in the community of Rainbow. Stop the car and stretch your legs with a short hike around the Delta Old Growth Forest. The half-mile interpretive trail provides interesting insight into this fragile ecosystem and close-up views of five-hundred-year-old trees nearly 250 feet tall.

If you like a campout, this is your byway, for there are many choices in many settings along the way. After a day of frenzied travel, our place to unwind is Paradise Creek Campground. It truly is a

33

wonder, one of fourteen U.S. Forest Service campgrounds within the McKenzie District of the Willamette National Forest. Paradise offers sixty-four campsites, and many of the sites are right along the stream, whether you stay in a tent or a motor home. Set in a classic Pacific Northwest semi–rain forest, Paradise Campground is cloaked in Douglas fir and hemlock trees. Rainfall is common throughout fall, winter, and spring, so do come prepared. The campground sits near the junction of Oregon 242 (leading to McKenzie Pass) and provides a convenient base camp from which to explore in many directions.

As you can imagine, the local folks take great pride in their corner of the Pacific Northwest. In fact, U.S. Forest Service Ranger Pam Navitsky told me, "We love the scenery, the history, and the quiet of this river—and we love to share its secrets with visitors. In fact, when you arrive, you quickly learn that the McKenzie River played a large role in Oregon's history as a lifeline for Native Americans, then trappers, then pioneer settlers, and now the locals." Today, the McKenzie River National Recreation Trail stretches along twenty-five miles of the banks of the river. The trail is flat and easy to walk for the most part, with few climbs or switchbacks, and it is open to bicyclists.

Whether hiking or driving along the river, you will encounter three scenic waterfalls—Sahalie, Koosah, and Tamolitch—that offer a nice break for relaxing a bit, plus each is spectacular enough for display in any Oregon calendar. After we pulled into the Sahalie Falls parking lot, my three sons raced from the car down the short and easy paved trail to an overlook that proved irresistible. We stood slack-jawed and spellbound for a half hour while admiring the plunge-pool falls dropping nearly a hundred feet. Nearby Koosah Falls drops about seventy feet top to bottom and is equally rewarding. (We were pleased that we carried our camera for a family photo, so don't forget yours.) Tamolitch Falls—just a short walk away—will delight your senses with beauty and drama as it falls into a lava-rimmed punchbowl.

When my youngsters first viewed Clear Lake, the headwaters of the McKenzie, they voiced countless comments about one of Oregon's most transparent bodies of water: "Dad, it looks as though it's only a few feet deep, look at all those trees." "They're standing straight up, too." "How deep is this lake anyway?" We usually drop a canoe in or rent a rowboat from the small resort (no motors allowed on Clear Lake) and paddle or row across the lake to another world formed thousands of years ago when an eruption of lava blocked the flow of the headwaters of the McKenzie

▸ **Stark yet compelling beauty is yours to enjoy along the McKenzie Scenic Highway.**

BEWARE OF FIRE

As the summer of 2002 proved, catastrophic fires can rule and ruin many vacation plans, so please heed this note of camping caution. Traditionally the centerpiece of any campsite, a campfire is also the most dangerous element on any camping trip if not planned and handled properly. The U.S. Forest Service encourages campers to adhere to the following guidelines when camping in national and state forests:

- If you are intending to camp in a dispersed area, wilderness area, or undeveloped forest or park, obtain the proper permits.
- Always abide by current fire-restriction information.
- When fires are allowed, most forests and parks in developed campgrounds do not require a campfire permit.
- Just before you depart on your camping trip, contact the nearest Forest Service district office, visitor center, or ranger or fire station to check on current fire conditions.

River near Santiam Pass. These headwater springs are cold—thirty-five to forty-three degrees year-round—and have preserved the trees that were captured underwater when the lake was formed. In fact, the trees are still visible in the lake, and yes, it is quite deep—up to a couple hundred feet.

The Santiam Fish and Game Association (SFGA) has operated Clear Lake Resort, located near the junction of Oregon 126 and U.S. 20, since 1929. Largely a group of local outdoor folk, the SFGA opens the lake each April, and according to Bud Barnes, chairman of the Clear Lake committee, the energy to run the resort is all volunteer. "It's a clean, friendly, relaxing place to be," he said. "We've always aimed at being family-oriented, too, so it's lights out by ten o'clock P.M. and back on at six o'clock A.M." It is also one of the few volunteer-run and -supported resorts in Oregon. Bud told me the association is doing well, with the resort collecting more than enough funds from visitors, so they hope to be around for many more decades to come. Clear Lake is open year-round for fishing, and the lake is stocked with trout throughout spring and summer.

An equally splendid scenic drive begins at the junction of Oregon 126 and 242 and leads east to McKenzie Pass and beyond to Sisters, Oregon. This scenic drive follows an 1860s wagon route and crosses the Willamette and Deschutes National Forests, first through Douglas fir, then ponderosa pine, and then stands of aspen. Scenic vistas along the byway provide beautiful views of the Three Sisters peaks as well as the surrounding wilderness.

When you reach 5,325-foot McKenzie Pass, you're surrounded by lava, so climb up to the nearby Dee Wright Observatory and savor the wide-screen panoramic view of six Cascades peaks. Dee Wright Observatory was named in honor of a Forest Service packer who served from 1910 to 1934 and was the foreman of the Civilian Conservation Corps crew that built the observatory. Nearby, enjoy the Lava River Trail, a half-mile loop and interpretive trail beginning at the observatory that winds through interesting lava gutters and crevasses.

Note: Oregon 242 is winding and narrow, so motor homes over twenty-two feet long and vehicles pulling trailers are discouraged from traveling. Depending upon snowfall, Oregon 242 is usually closed November to early July.

■ Getting There

From Portland: Drive Interstate 5 south to Eugene and the McKenzie River Highway (Oregon 126). Drive east on Oregon 126 approximately fifty-five miles to the Paradise Campground.

Koosah, Sahalie, and Tamolitch Falls: From Paradise Campground, drive approximately fifteen miles on Oregon 26.

Clear Lake: Drive approximately 17.5 miles from Paradise Campground on Oregon 126 to reach Clear Lake Resort and Campground.

Dee Wright Observatory: Drive approximately three-quarters of a mile from Paradise Campground on Oregon 126 to the junction with Oregon 242. Follow Oregon 242 for approximately fifteen miles to reach the observatory.

■ For More Information

McKenzie Ranger Station, (541) 822-3381

National Recreation Reservation Service, (877) 444-6777

Clear Lake Resort, 13000 Highway 20, Sisters, OR 97759 (no phone)

Santiam Fish and Game Association, (541) 258-3729

CASCADES

Trail of Ten Falls
Silver Falls State Park
10

"Rain, rain, go away, come again another day."

Have you ever found yourself humming this well-known ditty on a gray April afternoon? Never? Yeah, right!

Fact is, endless spring showers that are splintered only by occasional slices of sunshine is the way of life in the northwest corner of the West from March through May. And if you're new to this country, here's my best advice: Get used to it!

I threw in the towel long, long ago. So long ago, in fact, I cannot recall an April or May that wasn't wet, wetter, or the wettest—ever. Since there's little to do about it, why not find the beauty—no, make that the *delight*—in the Oregon outdoors when the rain seems to fall from above in buckets. I suggest you scoot into the hills near Silverton to a state park guaranteed to deliver huge, powerful, surging natural events that captivate your eyes, your ears, and perhaps your soul.

"I think Silver Falls calls to everybody!" roared Jim Bader, as the two of us paused just yards away from the full force of the majestic and loud South Falls. We held tight to the steel guardrail alongside the ten-foot-wide trail and were just about to duck behind the famous whopper waterfall that's on the Trail of Ten Falls at Silver Falls State Park. Jim, the park's manager, was getting our feet wet, so to speak, showing me around for a special KATU television program. He had just explained that mountain snowmelt accompanying the annual spring rains builds the south and north forks of Silver Creek to swollen threads of whitewater that race down canyon drainages all across the vast forest parkland. Thundering and roaring from recent downpours, the many cascading falls inside the park are immense spectacles to behold. Nestled in the lower elevation of Oregon's Cascade Mountains, Silver Falls is blessed to be located in a temperate rain forest. The park is Oregon's largest at 8,700 acres and boasts eleven waterfalls, as well as an array of other sights.

"They come in all shapes and sizes, Grant—whirling and rippling and seeming to shout for our attention. We have a little over seven miles of canyon trail in the park, with three different access points and several different hiking loops. You can choose how far you want to go and which falls to visit, so if you're looking for waterfalls, you can get the whole package right here—and we owe it all to prehistoric volcanoes."

Jim explained the geologic history behind so many falls in one location. It seems millions of years ago, successive and destructive lava flows covered the entire

➤ **North Falls seems to spill from the forest along the Trail of Ten Falls in Silver Falls State Park.**

SPRING ~ Silver Falls State Park

western region of Oregon. But over time within this parkland, the wind, rain, and ice eroded or cut through the lava to create tributary creeks and their falls—plus the mainstem Silver Creek. So much beauty from long-ago devastation is worth pausing to consider!

Much more recently, the Civilian Conservation Corps constructed South Falls Lodge in the 1930s. Deemed a "recreation demonstration site," and guarding the pathway entrance to South Falls, the rustic lodge is a scaled-down version of Mount Hood's Timberline Lodge. It stands large in the park, complete with rugged rock and timber construction. Following a recent remodel, it is now an interpretive center, equipped with a food vendor and a very welcome fireplace.

The pathway to each waterfall has a designation for degree of difficulty, and South Falls is designated as "easy access." It's a long, somewhat winding descent to the 177-foot-high waterfall, but this trail (as well as several others) allows you to walk behind the falls. There, as Jim and I discovered, the water sprays at you in varying degrees—like it would on a whitewater-rafting trip. It is indeed amazing and invigorating to stand next to the awesome power of this remarkable natural wonder.

Jim and I continued our hike along the Canyon Trail, and he pointed out the slow but certain descent along the trail to reach each falls. "That's important to keep in mind for the return trip, which is all uphill," he offered as we came to an intersection with a pathway leading to Frenchie Falls. This falls is tiny and hidden in comparison to most of the obviously gigantic falls in the park, but its seclusion is at the heart of its charm.

The next, Lower South Falls, also offers a hike behind a wall-of-water feature that gives you a unique perspective for enjoying the ninety-three-foot free fall. Lower North Falls requires a 1.5-mile hike to reach; it's more akin to a thirty-foot block or wedge of water, rather than the more typical long, cascading drop characteristic of most of the park's falls. Nearby Winter Falls is just the opposite: long and delicate at 140 feet from its base to its top. Middle North Falls is next in the lineup along the Canyon Trail; it's distinguished by another walk behind the falls, although it's on a side route that dead-ends just beyond the falls. Soon you'll come face to face with Drake Falls, which is the smallest of the entire park at just twenty-seven feet; here's a great photo opportunity because of the contrast between surging whitewater and black bedrock and river rock just visible under the surface.

It's 2.4 miles from South Falls to Double Falls, which is the only two-tiered falls in the park. One mile farther is Twin Falls, which takes a sharp ninety-degree turn on a bend in the creek and then splits into two falls around a protruding rock face. It's nearly another mile to powerful and hypnotic North Falls, which explodes out of a small slice in the bedrock and falls 180 feet into the canyon below; it's so loud that it's difficult to hold a conversation here with your travel companions!

Falls on Film?

Photographer Steve Terrill, my partner in this project, tells me that Silver Falls is like a photographer's buffet table offering a visual feast. "There's always something to see around each bend, but you have to slow down to enjoy it." Plus, he adds, "The more miles of hiking in the park, the better!"

He notes that the park is where the "shooter's bug" bites many photographers. "They see a scene and ask 'How can I take this home with me? Well, I better start taking pictures of it to have the memory.'"

As you might expect, when it comes to capturing waterfalls on film, Steve has a few tricks and tips, which he generously shares with us:

- Always use a tripod.
- Bring lots of film.
- Use a shutter release to prevent a shaky shot.
- Look beyond the object at hand. If you see great-looking waterfalls, be sure to see the layers of depth—the surrounding tree branches, leaves, grass, ferns, rocks, and the like—that help define the falls.

"It's like you're bringing a bit of the outdoors back home," says Terrill. "It's almost as if you can look at it and smell the smells, feel the wind, and hear the sounds of the water coming down. At least that's what it does for me."

You can also walk behind North Falls. Upper North Falls (about a half mile beyond North Falls) is a sixty-five-foot drop that offers a wide curtainlike affair that drops into a beautiful pool below.

When the sun gets through to Silver Falls State Park and sticks around for awhile, it's a scene where light and shadow are daytime partners, shifting and weaving among vine maples and Douglas firs. It's hard not to be impressed with so much whitewater thunder. It demands that you pause, gaze, and wonder at a getaway that fills the senses. Plentiful picnic and camping grounds invite longer stays, while the water tumbles and rolls and shimmers and whirls as it has for a very long time. Silver Falls will keep you coming back for more.

At Silver Falls, you will find unique group camping areas like the Old and New Ranch buildings, the Silver Creek Youth Camp, the North Falls trailer and tent areas, and RV, cabin, and tent camping in the overnight campground (fifty-four electrical sites, fifty-one tent sites, and showers, closed October 31 to April 15; fourteen rental cabins open year-round). Additional cabin rentals and complete group accommodations can be found at the Silver Falls Conference Center. Guided daytime horse trail rides for people of all abilities are available from Memorial Day to Labor Day for a fee. A small fee or annual pass is required for day use.

■ Getting There

From Portland: Take Interstate 5 south approximately twenty-five miles to the Woodburn exit. Take Oregon 214 approximately twenty-eight miles to the park.

From Salem: Take Oregon 22 east to the Silver Falls State Park exit. Follow Oregon 214 approximately twenty miles to the park.

CENTRAL/EASTERN

Oregon's Forgotten Corner

Owyhee Country

Rivers are liquid highways that, like their asphalt cousins, course through densely populated cities or remote and sparsely inhabited areas. A few years ago, I found myself on one of the most remote watery byways in Oregon, the Owyhee River. It runs through a corner of the state known as "I-O-N" country because of its close proximity to the state borders of Idaho, Oregon, and Nevada, which mesh together in a vastness covering more than ten thousand square miles.

Yet, if you mention the Owyhee to most folks, they stare back at you a tad bewildered and ask, "Did you say Ow-ya-hoo-ee? Or, Aw-ya-hay?" Well, it's pronounced "o-WAA-he," as in "Hawaii." The story goes that Peter Skene Ogden, who led a contingent of Hudson Bay trappers into the region in 1819, named the Owyhee River. Two Hawaiians had been sent to trap for furs on a tributary of the Snake River, where Ogden was camped. The trappers were killed by Indians, and Ogden named the tributary for them. Over the centuries, the "Hawaii River" name has been corrupted into the "Owyhee River."

Out of the way? It certainly is! This is a most secluded and pristine river, and with the sound of its water rushing through boulder-strewn rapids, it's just the kind of territory that stirs my senses and satisfies my soul. It's where I went looking for adventure with Gerald Moore, the owner and operator of Water Otters. We were slated to float the wild Owyhee over four days to produce a special outdoor program for KATU, so we joined Gerald's outfitting and guide company because it specialized in Oregon's hard-to-reach rivers. Also, unlike large whitewater rafts that seat up to six people, Water Otters (as the name implies) offers a flotilla of small, more intimate, inflatable kayaks. It's a cozy, self-sufficient experience, where you are your own skipper on a voyage of discovery.

Gerald floated his first river in 1948 and has been hooked ever since, and told me as much at our launch point near Rome, where we gathered to sort out plans, stow our gear, and prepare for the early June adventure. "The river runs brim full only in spring when the upstream snowmelt fills the Owyhee River canyon," he explained. "So the river's height depends upon snowpack, and you never know just how big it'll be. Naturally, your beginners are somewhere between apprehensive and scared as hell." He laughed and I chuckled and my photographer looked pensive.

▶ **The distant Owyhee River has been called Oregon's Grand Canyon for its sprawling and spectacular scenery.**

SPRING ~ Owyhee Country

Gerald proceeded with the loading and the lessons without missing a beat.

"Not to worry, though. This winter was a mild one, so most of the snow melted long ago, and the water's actually low. You'll love it! After the first day, you'll get the feel of things. Stick like glue to our guides and mimic their strokes. That's the quickest way to teach someone how to float a river in these boats. If you feel uncomfortable, you can walk around a rapid and we'll take the boat through for you." This sounded like my kind of voyage, but not so to my uncertain partner, Curtis Miller, a longtime newshound and a premier photographer. He, like many, was a fellow who hadn't spent much time in the far reaches of the high desert, where rattlesnakes and scorpions can be everyday encounters.

The Owyhee River country may be considered a forgotten corner of the West, where distances are great and people are few, yet it's also a landscape marked by beautiful, far-flung ranges of sage and tall grass and, just beyond, broken buttes and jagged canyons. A sprawling area, unmatched for its gigantic spectacles, it's little wonder this place has been termed Oregon's Grand Canyon for its multicolored spires, dramatic canyons, sculpted grottos, natural hot springs, and thrilling rapids. In 1984, Congress designated 120 miles of the

Owyhee River, from the Oregon-Idaho border to the Owyhee Reservoir, as "Wild" and included it in the National Wild and Scenic Rivers System. The Lower Owyhee may be wild, but not for its enormous, frothy, churning whitewater. Rather, we left Rome (marked by an ancient, colossal rock wall formation that's appropriately named the "Coliseum"), and our sixty-seven-mile downriver adventure to the Owyhee Reservoir and State Park was dominated by friendly rapids, extraordinary scenery, and all-embracing solitude.

The Owyhee River is what river runners call "classic pool and drop," with long stretches of calm, glassy water broken by short bursts of cascading whitewater. Mile after mile, the river winds and curls like a coiled spring, sometimes in the shade of steep-walled canyons, where freshwater springs seep down the vertical walls. Yet other springs are so hot it's necessary to cool them with bucket-loads of river water.

Then there are the petroglyphs chipped by ancient Natives into flat-faced basalt blocks, and also petrified trees with stumps frozen into rock.

The inflatable kayaks are a blast! Rapids with names like Artillery and Widow Maker hint of danger and demand a boater's respect. Artillery Rapids, a rolling riot of standing waves, make you feel like a kid on a roller coaster at the county fair. Widow Maker and other rapids are more technical and require some accurate alignment and hard paddling to get through safely. At Montgomery Rapid, the largest rapid on the Owyhee River, I paddled a passage and flew through a water-soaking hole. I flew out of my boat, too, and was very happy I was wearing my life vest—gear that I kept on throughout the river trip.

The payoff for the effort required to travel into the Owyhee River canyon is an escape from the hurried, harried hubbub of city life. That's something I really noticed our second night out, when we camped across a wide apron of sand that gently kissed the river. I could feel the quiet shout at me! Surrounded by steep rock towers, I was restless and couldn't sleep. As I gazed up from my snug sleeping bag, I was stunned by a sky stuffed with stars. Gerald heard me stir and whispered across our otherwise quiet group of drowsy fellow travelers.

"Magnificent, huh? This float combines so much into one trip, Grant. You're rafting, you have whitewater, the fishing, and wildlife viewing. But this is the reason I come here." In the dark I imagined his hand sweeping across the night sky to touch the stars. "Almost a religious feeling, as though you're closer to God and closer to nature. Virtually everyone I bring into this canyon feels the same way."

The final stretch is a transition—marked by miles of flat water. We tied our boats together, and an outboard motor—

> ## Owyhee Byways
>
> Lake Owyhee State Park lies next to a fifty-three-mile-long lake formed by Owyhee Dam. Breathtaking views of the Owyhee Mountains await. A boat trip up the lake is one of the many not-to-be-missed experiences in eastern Oregon. Look closely! Bighorn sheep and pronghorn antelope live here, as do golden eagles, coyotes, mule deer, wild horses, and (rarely) mountain lions. Use the park as your base camp to explore the badlands of Oregon. Campsites include thirty with electrical hookups, ten for tents (maximum site fifty-five feet), and two with tepees. (When you rent a tepee, you get free use of a canoe.) Campsites are open April to October 30 and are first-come, first-served. All tepees are reservable by phone at (800) 452-5687. More information is available at (800) 551-6949. Fuel, ice, and food are sold at the park's headquarters office.
>
> North of Jordan Valley on U.S. 95, look for a sign for the Leslie Gulch Succor Creek Byway. Leslie Gulch offers high, irregular, burnished orange and bright pink, angular rocks, arches, and spires that demand quiet contemplation and the clicking of cameras. It's a great place to climb and roam and wander and wonder. You probably won't see many other people because this is remote, dusty, even dangerous country. It isn't very well-known either. All of this combines to make Leslie Gulch (which was named for a cattleman who was killed there in 1882) a fascinating hiking area.
>
> Caution: Leslie Gulch is most popular in the fall and spring because it heats up like a simmering stove in summer.

CENTRAL/EASTERN

Oasis in the Desert
~12~
Malheur National Wildlife Refuge

hauled for this reason—gave us the extra power to move across thirteen miles of Lake Owyhee to the Leslie Gulch takeout. From there a gravel road returned us to civilization and home—and time for reflection. The Owyhee River owns a rhythm of its own, and once people discover it, they become unplugged from the pace and race of their daily lives.

■ Getting There
From Portland: Follow I-84 to the Oregon-Idaho border. Just past the border, turn south onto U.S. 95 and follow it to Jordan Valley.

From Bend: Take U.S. 20 to Burns, Oregon 78 to Burns Junction, and U.S. 95 to Jordan Valley.

From California: Take U.S. 97 or U.S. 395 to U.S. 20, U.S. 20 east to Burns, Oregon 78 to Burns Junction, and U.S. 95 to Jordan Valley.

■ For More Information
Bureau of Land Management, 100 Oregon Street, Vale, OR 97918, (541) 473-3144 (request the Vale District Recreation Map)

Jordan Valley motels and trailer parks: Basque Station Hotel (and gas station), (541) 586-9244; Sahara Motel (and gas station), (541) 586-2500, (541) 586-9239; two trailer parks (showers, laundry, RV hookups)

Rome campgrounds: Small BLM campground on east side of the river; Rome Station (cafe, small store, gasoline, cabins, RV park, and airstrip) on the west side, (541) 586-2295

Okay, fellas, seat belts are a must, 'cause on this lake at forty miles an hour anything can happen!" As U.S. Fish and Wildlife biologist Dave Paulin offered this terse warning, I gazed across the unbounded miles of smooth, shimmering water where only a sliver of land peeked above a distant horizon. It was far too beautiful and far too friendly an April daybreak to believe any danger might be waiting for us. But Dave had been at this for many years, so I took his warning to heart as I stepped aboard his unusual airboat for a unique wildlife adventure in Malheur National Wildlife Refuge in southeastern Oregon.

News photographer Mike Rosborough and I were there to document the incredible flood that had inundated ranchlands and homesteads alike during the late 1980s. Several successive years of heavy spring snowmelt in the high desert had caused three refuge lakes (Malheur—pronounced "mal-hewer"—the largest, and Harney and Mud) to merge into one vast, watery world. In fact, the new lake covered more than a hundred thousand acres with water six feet deep. The water had risen so fast and remained high for so long that the area's families could do little but pack their belongings and leave their homes while hoping the floods would recede—

someday. We were there to report on the millions of dollars of damage to Harney County's private property, but I was also curious about the benefits the floods had provided wildlife, especially nesting waterfowl, at one of the largest and oldest wildlife refuges in North America.

In 1908, President Theodore Roosevelt established the Lake Malheur Reservation, an 81,786-acre preserve and breeding ground for native birds. This designation followed decades of neglect and misuse that included draining and diking historic marshes and heavy cattle grazing that denuded stream banks and eroded soils. Unrestricted bird hunting—not only by settlers for food but by market hunters who killed egrets, swans, and terns for feathers to adorn women's finery—decimated the local bird population. Protection for wildlife continued to expand, and by 1940 Malheur National Wildlife Refuge stretched thirty-nine miles in width and extended forty miles in length.

As Dave backed the boat away from a remote and primitive dirt ramp, he throttled up the powerful V-8 engine and it roared to life. But this was not a typical watercraft! Instead of an engine prop underneath the twenty-foot-long, flat-bottomed boat, an aircraft propeller sat on

41

SPRING ~ Malheur National Wildlife Refuge

top of it. A five-foot-long prop was reverse-mounted at the back of the boat to move the boat forward. This airboat seemed more at home in the Florida Everglades, yet it skimmed perfectly across the lake. It was well suited to newly expanded and shallow Malheur Lake, which was littered with floating woody debris of all shapes and sizes. But the howl from the top-mounted engine was deafening, so earplugs and headphones were a must. Little conversation could pass between us as we sped for miles past vacant, flooded homes and heaps of stranded farm machinery. Dave stopped occasionally and pointed to stands of towering cottonwood trees, planted years earlier to offer shade to farmhouses. Now that the human residents were gone, the trees offered nesting homes for hundreds of fish-eating birds like herons and egrets and cormorants.

Finally, we reached Dave's destination: a series of small islands that he'd been monitoring each spring since the floods began. They provided new nesting habitat and seclusion for hundreds of waterfowl. Dave was especially interested in the nesting success of Canada geese, which had been phenomenal. He showed us several

▶ **Malheur Wildlife Refuge offers countless wetlands, marshes, and ponds for wildlife.**

nests, each with a dozen or more downy goslings peeking over the feathered rims of their homes. "They do extremely well here," Dave offered. "I check this collection of six islands each week, and there's close to a hundred nests here. The birds have really responded to this human tragedy. We have hatching success here that reaches 60 percent or higher, and that's due to the high water. You see, the coyotes and other predators can't get to them. It's really one of those habitat stories that goes something like 'If you build it, they will come.'"

In a way, many years and many visits later, Dave's comment about the quality and quantity of wildlife habitat at Malheur seems more appropriate to me than ever. At 185,540 acres, today's Malheur National Wildlife Refuge is an oasis in the middle of Oregon's arid high-desert country. It consists of marshes, ponds, meadows, uplands, and alkali flats, diverse habitats that attract a wide variety of bird species that arrive at peak numbers each April through June. During the spring migration, more than 250,000 ducks—mallards, pintails, teals, redheads, canvasbacks, and ruddy ducks, among others—join more than 100,000 geese and 6,000 sandhill cranes. In the deeper marshes, gulls, terns, ibises, herons, egrets, and cormorants find ideal nesting habitat.

The refuge is primarily located in the lush Blitzen River valley, the surrounding sage uplands and basalt rimrocks, and the immense bodies of water that collect the Blitzen's outflow. I like to begin each visit at the refuge's visitor center, with its interpretive exhibits and bookshop. The visitor center overlooks Malheur Lake, and the trees and shrubs offer homey habitats to many migrating songbirds each spring. The adjacent Benson Memorial Museum contains nearly two hundred mounted specimens of local birds in one of the buildings constructed by the Civilian Conservation Corps (CCC) in the 1930s and 1940s. CCC workers constructed the buildings with volcanic rock that was mined from a quarry on the refuge.

Head south from the visitor center on the forty-one-mile-long automobile tour route. In about twenty miles, you'll come to the Buena Vista Overlook, where you'll find an outstanding view of the Blitzen River valley with towering Steens Mountain as the backdrop. You'll appreciate the short, easy hiking trail around the overlook, as well as the restroom. This viewing area also offers wheelchair accessibility.

Water is a magnet for wildlife, and along this route you'll need to slow down to savor the spring season that's bursting with birds. You'll be rewarded with views of migratory waterfowl. Sandhill cranes and shorebird species, as well as songbirds such as warblers, vireos, and tanagers, use the many wetland areas, including Krumbo Reservoir and Benson Point.

At the P Ranch, near the small burg of Frenchglen, you reach the terminus of the auto tour route at a site named for Pete French, who established a sprawling 150,000-acre spread—the French-Glenn Livestock Company—in 1872. Here you'll enjoy an opportunity to stretch your legs on the short Barnes Springs Trail.

This area is remote and rugged. Plan on traveling long distances on gravel roads, and make sure your transportation is reliable and your spare tire is in good shape. In fact, this area is so remote I suggest carrying two spare tires if you're planning to travel the back roads much. It's also a good idea to carry plenty of food and water (it can get pretty hot during summer months). That said, some areas are wheelchair accessible. The refuge is heavily signed and restrictions are plentiful, so heed where you're going and tread lightly. Remember that the refuge is full of marshy areas that are ideal breeding grounds for hungry mosquitoes. If you go between April and November, take plenty of insect repellent. And remember that hiking is restricted to designated and signed areas. In fact, a good rule of thumb is to hike only on roads that are open to automobiles.

■ Getting There
From Burns, drive south on Oregon 78, turn right onto Oregon 205, proceed approximately twenty-eight miles, and turn left at the refuge sign for another two miles.

■ For More Information
Malheur National Wildlife Refuge, HC-72, Box 245, Princeton, OR 97721, (541) 493-2612

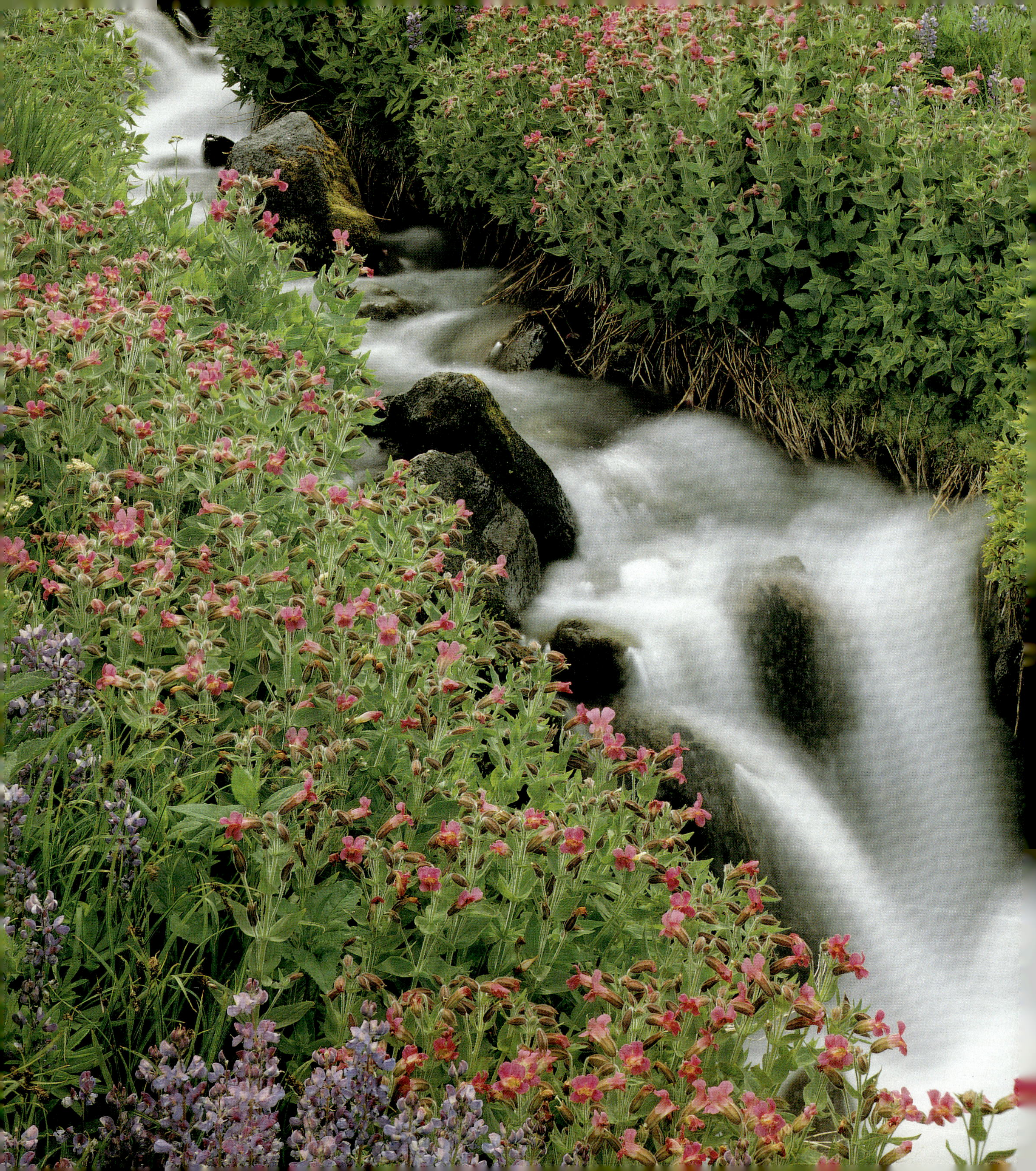

SUMMER

It is a great art

to saunter.

JOURNAL, HENRY DAVID THOREAU

◄ A pause that refreshes amid pink monkeyflowers and lupine along Elk Cove Creek in the Mount Hood National Forest.

COAST

Vanishing Wilderness

13

South Slough Estuary and Bastendorff County Park

The beauty of Oregon's coastal ports is that they shine like faceted jewels during an endless Northwest summer. I favor these quaint ports of call as I have a passion for traveling through them. I believe that's because at each turn there's a unique adventure waiting to be revealed.

A lonesome coastline swings southwest of Coos Bay and offers one of the most spectacular getaways in the Pacific Northwest. The Cape Arago Highway (Oregon 240) leads you along the south shore of the bay, through the suburban community of Barview, across South Slough, and along the southern arm of Coos Bay to Charleston. This village by the sea is a simple and friendly commercial and sportfishing port just inside the entrance to Coos Bay, and it is home to small shops, restaurants, charter sportfishing, a Coast Guard station, and the fascinating Oregon Institute of Marine Biology. Two miles west of Charleston, the roadway winds over a forested ridge, then approaches the Pacific Ocean at Bastendorff Beach, a great stretch of sand extending south from the bay's entrance.

Bastendorff Beach County Park offers a beach stop my family never misses for an extended visit. It is a spacious eighty-nine-acre park that sits on top of a hill overlooking the Pacific Ocean and has been a regular destination for McOmie family gatherings because of its fifty-five secluded and quiet campsites. You'll find a grass-covered play area for kids, fishing and fish-cleaning facilities, a basketball court, and horseshoe pits. This is a beautiful place to camp or spend the day because beach access is nearby. A clear view to Coos Bay's entrance is from atop the park bluff overlooking the beach. If you're lucky, you may observe a giant cargo ship navigating the channel entrance.

A short drive from Bastendorff Beach County Park is a pristine corner of the coast known as the South Slough Estuarine Research Reserve (ERR), a sanctuary that encompasses more than 4,400 acres of upland forest, 115 acres of riparian habitat, and 800 acres of tidelands that have been federally protected since 1974. The site includes an interpretive center that is open to the public each day and houses exhibits, a video-viewing area, a small bookstore, and facilities for formal lectures. An outdoor amphitheater located near the interpretive center serves as an area for presentations and also as a resting place for hikers.

In fact, hiking is the most popular way to explore the reserve. Recently my family was fortunate to join South Slough ERR's resident director, Tom Gaskill, for a half-day adventure on the Hidden Creek Trail and to learn more about this relatively untouched corner of the state. The trail is a 2.3-mile round-trip hike, and it follows Hidden Creek from the interpretive center to the estuary's edge. The trail descends three hundred feet to a boardwalk, which winds through freshwater and saltwater marshes, with the option of stopping at an observation platform or continuing to the water's edge. As we strolled, Tom showed us how estuaries form where freshwater flows from the land and mixes with the tidal flows of saltwater from the ocean. Tom pointed out that estuaries have a higher productivity than most other ecosystems on Earth. Hidden Creek flows through the ground to a narrow stream channel before expanding into a freshwater swamp of red alder and skunk cabbage. It is lush and inviting and abounds with wildlife species including deer, elk, soaring bald eagles, plentiful waterfowl, and myriad shorebirds.

"One of the reasons South Slough is particularly inviting is because it is fairly pristine," said Tom. "It has high-quality marsh and tide flat that are largely unaffected by human activity. As a result, we have been the center of scientific research since our inception over twenty-five years ago."

In fact, more than three thousand youngsters trek this trail each school year to gain a better understanding of natural

❯ Estuaries like South Slough are among the richest fish and wildlife habitats in the world.

science. As Tom explained all of this, I was reminded how rare clean, undeveloped estuaries have become in Oregon. In fact, up to 70 percent of the state's coastal wetlands and marshes have been diked, then drained, then filled—and as a result, lost forever. The Hidden Creek Trail fills your senses with an appreciation for something very special in Oregon.

Note: During the summer, guided tours on the water are available. While the South Slough ERR does not offer boats for rent, it will provide a trained interpretive guide to describe the natural and cultural history along the six-mile tour and a shuttle vehicle to transport drivers (participating paddlers) back to their vehicles at the put-in point. All participants are responsible for their own safety equipment, boats, and vehicles.

The park is open year-round for RV or tent camping, with dune, lake, and ocean access. Campsites are available on a first-come, first-served basis. The RV sites have electricity and water. There are handicap-accessible restrooms and warm, coin-operated showers.

■ Getting There

From the north: On coastal highway U.S. 101 south, cross the green, mile-long McCullough Bridge and enter North Bend. Take a right on Virginia Avenue (following signs to Charleston and Ocean/Beaches). Follow Virginia Avenue past the Pony Village Mall and Safeway. Take a left on Broadway (traffic signal intersection) and make your way into the right-hand lane. After eight blocks or so, your lane will veer right onto Newmark Avenue and continue past Southwestern Oregon Community College. Stay on Newmark as it merges with Ocean Boulevard at a traffic light. Shortly thereafter, the road turns ninety degrees left. You are now on Cape Arago Highway. Follow it for three to four miles, then cross the South Slough on a drawbridge and enter the small town of Charleston. After passing several small shops, a green highway sign on your right ("South Slough Sanctuary") will point left. Turn left here onto Seven Devils Road, and wind along it for four miles (the sign says five miles). The entrance to the South Slough Reserve Visitor's Center will be on your left.

From the east: From Interstate 5, take Oregon 42 through Coquille toward Coos Bay. Just west of Coquille, you will encounter a sign for Charleston. Make a left turn at this sign and follow North Bank Road for approximately four miles, at which point you will encounter another sign for Charleston at an intersection where the Coquille River will be visible on your left. Make this right turn and follow the road to the top of a steep hill where it intersects U.S. 101. Make a right turn onto U.S. 101 and follow the road north for a half mile. At this point, a green highway sign on your right will point left ("South Slough Reserve, Charleston, Ocean/Beaches"). Take this left. This road is called West Beaver Hill Road at U.S. 101, but it becomes Seven Devils Road in a few miles. From U.S. 101, follow this road for eight miles, past the south entrance to the ERR (signed) and to the main entrance. A large, wooden sign reads, "South Slough Reserve Visitor's Center" and the driveway is on the right. (Note: This route is paved for the entire length. Do not be confused by the gravel road that is "Old Seven Devils Road" as this will not lead you to South Slough!)

■ For More Information

Coos County Parks, (541) 396-3121, ext. 354

South Slough ERR, (541) 888-5558

Wavecrest Discovery Tours, (541) 267-4027

Adventure Kayak, (541) 347-3480

COAST

A Ride as Smooth as Silk

14

Kingfisher *and Supper from the Sea*

One of my earliest childhood memories—and I couldn't have been more than nine or ten—is an overnight visit to the central Oregon coast for a charter boat salmon fishing trip. It was thrilling to be in the company of men, mostly older cousins and a scattering of uncles who'd joined together to celebrate a family reunion of sorts. We had a date at dawn aboard a magnificent boat whose reputation was—even those many years ago—firmly established as legend. *Kingfisher*, a forty-six-foot-long boat crafted of Port Orford cedar, was owned and operated by Stan Allyn of Tradewind Charters at Depoe Bay. Even in the 1960s, Stan and *Kingfisher* were historic, larger-than-life figures, and *Kingfisher* had been trolling the ocean waters for nearly a quarter century by the time I stepped aboard. She was an eye-catcher, sheer beauty to behold, and notable for her glorious red, white, and blue exterior. Everyone knew her by the cut of her bow. Everyone knew Stan Allyn, too, wearing his well-worn skipper's cap and manning *Kingfisher's* wheel unless called upon to wield a salmon net. And Stan always wore an unmistakable mile-wide smile.

I recall that young and old alike also shared many smiles as they caught their limits of salmon from aboard *Kingfisher* on that distant summer's day. But my strongest memory was her incredibly smooth, exhilarating ride. You see, *Kingfisher* was distinguished from many other charter boats by a "harpoon spoon" platform at the farthest point of her bow. I coveted that two-foot-square space because it allowed me to stand, with fingers tightly laced around the cool steel rail, and feel the rush of ocean air across my cheeks, and listen to the whoosh of her bow slicing through azure water. It was a simple pleasure that provided a youngster with an absolutely moving experience. I am certain I am not the only boy ever introduced to the ocean aboard *Kingfisher*, but I will always think fondly of one short moment when (to borrow the well-worn phrase from a famous Hollywood movie) I was indeed the "king of the world." I would soar high atop the rising swells and then slide down their smooth backsides, the first of all aboard to feel the ocean's power and presence through *Kingfisher's* wooden deck. What a ride!

So there was no small amount of emotional longing when I learned that *Kingfisher* was to make her last official

➤ **Marked by her distinct "clipper bow," the Tradwind's *Kingfisher* is a floating museum on Yaquina Bay at Newport, Oregon.**

48

SUMMER ~ *Kingfisher* and Supper from the Sea

voyage in the summer of 2001. A pioneer of Oregon's seagoing tourism industry, she was to be retired after more than sixty years of service. I raced immediately to Depoe Bay with news photographer in tow to visit with owner Rich Allyn (Stan's son) at Tradewind Charters and to hitch a farewell ride while learning more about her place in Oregon maritime history.

"Riding the bow of *Kingfisher* has almost a cult status, Grant," Rich explained as we motored along the coast. "It's the heavy cedar hull and her clipper bow that allow the boat to slice through the water with just a slow up-and-down motion. It's really smooth as silk! So she holds a lot of good memories for many people—good vibrations, I guess."

How she was born is a remarkably memorable story, too. Stan Allyn started with a dream in the late 1930s of becoming the first sportfishing charter boat business along the central Oregon coast. He worked up a hand-drawn pencil sketch of his dream boat while dining in a local restaurant, then went to Westurland Boat Works in Portland, who birthed the cedar, oak, and mahogany vessel. *Kingfisher* began taking anglers to sea in order to catch limits of fish in 1941. World War II intervened, and after the bombing of Pearl Harbor, Stan Allyn volunteered the boat for Coast Guard duty. The Coast Guard painted the varnished mahogany a dull gray and mounted a machine gun on her foredeck. For five years, *Kingfisher* patrolled the coast, keeping Oregon safe from enemy ships.

After the war, Stan returned to Depoe Bay to pick up passengers where he had left off. He quickly repainted the dull gray boat the distinctive red, white, and blue colors that she still wears today. Although Stan passed away in 1992, when you step inside the cabin you can still feel his presence. Perhaps it's the wall of black-and-white photos—a veritable "wall of fishing fame" of friends and celebrities and politicians, each holding limits of salmon or bottom fish and wearing proud, toothy grins. Perhaps it is also the hand-carved

49

SUMMER — Kingfisher and Supper from the Sea

> ### Bob Waldron's Supper from the Sea
>
> ### Grilled Fish Fillets
>
> ½ cup plain yogurt
> 2 tablespoons mayonnaise
> 1 to 2 tablespoons dried chopped dill
> 2 to 3 pounds fish fillets (rockfish, lingcod, halibut, or snapper)
>
> Preheat an outdoor grill.
>
> Mix together yogurt, mayonnaise, and dill in a small bowl and slather across the fish. (The mayo helps to keep the fish moist. The dill adds a spark that complements the fish nicely.) Cook fish on grill with lid closed for about twenty minutes.
>
> ### Rockfish Tempura
>
> Rockfish fillets, cut into chunks
> Tempura batter mix (store-bought)
> Mango salsa (recipe follows)
>
> Follow instructions that come with the tempura batter mix and serve with mango salsa.
>
> ### Kay Waldron's Mango Salsa
>
> ¼ cup chopped mango
> ¼ cup chopped cucumber
> 8 ounces of Key lime yogurt
> 2 green onions, chopped
>
> Mix together all ingredients and allow flavors to blend. As Bob explains, "This salsa really gives a burst to the fish flavor. Altogether it's a lot of tasty fun."

detail of her cabinetry and the dark, rich patina on the well-worn oak trim. Whatever—it speaks of class and recalls an earlier time when perhaps pride mattered a bit more than today.

With no small amount of pride in his voice, Rich exclaimed that despite her retirement, *Kingfisher* was as seaworthy as ever! "*Kingfisher* is in excellent shape! We did a hull exam on her last spring and she's top of the Tradewind's small fleet of charter boats. That's because she was built with Port Orford cedar. You couldn't buy any better back in those days, and it will be around long after I'm gone, too."

Before Stan Allyn died, he asked Rich to donate the boat to a museum when the time was right. During the summer of 2001, Rich and his wife, Valerie, donated the $200,000 vessel to the Lincoln County Historical Society to pay homage to his father's wish. *Kingfisher*'s new home is on the Newport waterfront near the Embarcadero Hotel, where all can see her, and even go aboard, to come in contact with a chapter of Oregon history. The boat is moored at Bayfront Charters in Newport and is used for public education events, as well as private engagements.

Rich confided that saying good-bye to *Kingfisher* was like saying good-bye to an old friend. "She has so many good stories and so many good times wrapped inside her walls. Dad wanted to see that preserved for others to enjoy or witness or look at. And so it will be."

Recently, on a day that was far too glorious to stay indoors, longtime friend Bob Waldron called and suggested the time had come for us to head to his favorite fishing pond. "Pond" is quite an understatement, for actually Bob's favorite location to cast and catch fish is in the big blue Pacific just beyond the jetty rocks near Tillamook Bay.

This is where he likes to fish lures or bait into and among the near-shore rocks or shallow reefs to try and catch bottom-fish species like black rockfish or sea bass, kelp greenling, and lingcod. His favorite lure is called a "stinger," a jig-shaped metal alloy painted to resemble a small bait fish, like a herring or an anchovy, but with a large 5/0 treble hook on its end. Bob explained that the fishing technique is simple.

"I'm just taking this jig down and bouncing it off the bottom—you feel for the bottom and then when the fish hits, there's just two or three sudden jerks. They don't take it real deep—they don't swallow it or anything—rather, it's a grab that often finds them hooked in the lips."

It didn't take us long to find an eager school of black rockfish (we fished about forty to sixty feet of water just off the end of the south jetty). We'd launch our lures into the water and within seconds would feel the telltale "bump" of fish on the line.

"Bob," I offered, "do you know what I really like about this? When you're into them, you're really into them. Look around! There must be a dozen boats out here and everyone seems to be playing or landing a fish."

"Oh yeah," Bob replied. "It's amazing how productive these places can be, but we really don't need a limit to have a good time out here. I mean I also enjoy the

COAST

15 ~ Poor Man's Lobster
Trask County Park and Crawfishing

openness of it and the sunshine. I find it a very relaxing way to fish. Plus, the very best part is yet to come when we take them home and cook them."

Bob is a big believer that what he catches deserves respect and care, so when we arrived at his home we immediately set about cleaning and filleting the eight rockfish and two lings we'd caught. His favorite recipe includes cooking a thick fillet covered in dill sauce.

The recipe and cooking were a lot of fun and brought the day's adventure full circle from the ocean to the table. Give Bob's favorite (see sidebar) a try: It will leave you eager to head back to the ocean, or to your local grocery, to catch even more.

■ Getting There

To Tradewind Charters: Drive west on Oregon 18 to Lincoln City, then south on coastal highway U.S. 101 to Depoe Bay. The Tradewind Charters office is located on the north end of the Depoe Bay Bridge.

To *Kingfisher* moorage: Drive west on Oregon 18 to Lincoln City, then south on coastal highway U.S. 101 to Newport. Proceed into Newport to Oregon 20 and turn left (east). Proceed for one mile to Moore Road. Turn right and follow signs to the Embarcadero Hotel. *Kingfisher* will be moored at the Embarcadero docks.

■ For More Information

Tradewind Charters, P.O. Box 123, Highway 101, Depoe Bay, OR 97341, (800) 445-8830

Lincoln County Historical Society, 545 S.W. 9th Street, Newport, OR 97365, (503) 265-7509

The bedside phone jangled as dazzling morning light sliced between the window slats, dancing across my eyelids. The machine picked up the urgent voice of my good friend Birt Hansen, who seemed much too excited for the oh-so-early 6:15 A.M. that flashed across my alarm clock.

"It's getting too hot out there already, buddy, so let's get goin'. I told ya we needed to get an early start, so get the kids up and let's go now."

"Oh—that's right—uhh, I forgot," came my dazed and sleepy reply. "The heat must be doing things to my memory. Sorry. We'll be right there."

It had been a long, oppressively long, and unrelenting week of recordbreaking August heat. The century mark had been skirted several times, and on this Friday the local forecasters promised that a hundred degrees would be topped by late afternoon. On the day prior, Birt had promised me an escape to a little-known Oregon Coast Range river with a sheltered, sandy beach, flanked by towering alder trees, a cool retreat that had my twelve-year-old son, Kevin, primed and prepped for the day's adventure—especially after Birt mentioned we'd be "diving for our dinner."

Camping trips can be wonderful family adventures, and some of my favorite destinations are enjoyed on a single tank of gas not far from home. Such is the case high in the mountains above Tillamook, where

---

BIRT HANSEN'S BASIC CRAWFISH BOIL

This recipe relies on a handful of simple ingredients.

2 quarts water
1 cup vinegar
½ cup salt
½ cup pickling spice
4 bay leaves
2 to 3 pounds crawfish

Bring the water and seasonings to a boil, then add the crawfish. Cook no longer than three to four minutes. Overcooked, the crawfish become rubberlike and flavorless.

Spread out a sheet or two of newspaper on a picnic table, dump out the steaming crawdads, and dig in. Grab the tail section, pull it away, and simply peel off the tail shell—everything else will pull right out. Same with the claws—crack them open and pick out the meat.

This is hands-on eating at its finger-licking finest—and that's best with youngsters who really get into their meals. Enjoy with a twist of lemon!

the Trask River narrows and offers deep pockets of cool water for refreshing moments of swimming or wading and enjoying a picnic lunch. Trask River County Park, one of the easiest campgrounds to reach in Tillamook County, is a sprawling, forested affair with sixty campsites—and many of the sites are situated streamside. The park, open daily, is also a destination that's a bit of a secret, and except for holiday weekends crowds are seldom the rule. You're likely to find plenty of elbowroom at this Coast Range paradise.

Birt offered that during long stretches of intense summer heat, he has often made the park a starting point from which to explore the upper Trask River's hidden pools—in wading shoes and shorts and with a spirit of youthful adventure—in search of crawfish! As this sixty-something, gray-haired gentleman explained, when it comes to crawdads, you're never too old to be a kid again—especially during the dog days of summer.

"Crawfish and summertime go together—just a great thing you can do with your family because everyone can get involved with it. After all these years, I still get excited goin' after crawfish—just to see if you can get a bigger one than the last. They're a creepy-crawler kind of a critter and kids just love them—and they taste good, too."

Birt's been visiting the Trask River each summer for more than thirty years to explore the river's depths and catch those small crustaceans. He often dons mask and snorkel to dive and catch them by hand. But you can also use a small wire-mesh trap (readily available at any sporting goods store) baited with a can of cat food. Birt explained:

"The idea is that you place the bait inside the trap as an attractant. The crawfish walk inside through the narrow funnel-like openings at either end. Once inside they can't seem to find their way back out. We'll attach a rope to the trap, toss it into a likely looking pool that's ten feet or so deep, and then tie the rope off to a tree. We may leave it in the river for a few hours, or if we're camping at the park, we leave it in overnight. We'll retrieve it the next morning and it's usually full of crawdaddies."

With that, he tossed our trap into the drink and we spent the day lounging on the inviting beach. When the mood to move, or the heat of the sun, struck us—we would scamper into the river. My youngster and I had a ball—diving, exploring, searching the river bottom's nooks and crannies, and rolling over submerged rocks to see what secrets the river held. Whenever a sizable crawfish (we'd made a vow not to keep any under five inches in length) appeared, young Kevin would carefully maneuver his hand to capture the critter by its head, just behind its two impressive and sizable pincer claws. Catching crawdads by hand

◣ **Colorful crawfish are easy to spot and easy to catch in the Trask River. Try!**

is fun sport and a delightful way to beat the summer heat.

Before long, our crawfish stockpile was adding up, and when the trap was pulled in we had more than eighty crawdads among us—more than enough for supper. Later that evening, as we sat at the park's spacious wooden picnic table and prepared our streamside supper, Birt noted, "Crawfishing brings out the kid in us all, but dining on them is the best part." Crawfish or crawdads have been called "a poor man's lobster" for years. And to that end, Birt set a large pot of water on our camp stove and lit a flame to bring the pot to boil. He continued, "And when prepared correctly, they are a delicious, unique taste of the Northwest."

The taste of fresh-cooked crawfish is sublime—a very mild shrimplike taste that's somewhat delicate. The taste, the setting, and the adventure offer a stark contrast to the broiling sun during the heat of summer—a perfect cap to a day's adventure that your family will want to try soon.

■ Getting There
From Portland, drive Oregon 6 to Tillamook. Approximately two miles west of Tillamook, watch for the Trask River cutoff. Turn left and continue for approximately six miles to the Trask River. Turn left and follow Trask River Road to Trask River County Park.

■ For More Information
Oregon Department of Fish and Wildlife, 2501 S.W. First Avenue, P.O. Box 59, Portland, OR 97207, (503) 872-5268

INLAND

Lions and Tigers and Bears, Oh My!
16
Wildlife Safari

Summer vacations always put a little extra spring in my step! It's the anticipation of a new adventure with my sons and the chance to experience the outdoors through their eyes that motivate me to pack up a bit of our household and take our home on the road. That's especially true when I've a new destination in mind that will teach the youngsters about wildlife. For more than twenty-five years, Wildlife Safari in a unique southern Oregon setting has done just that for tens of thousands of families. The wildlife park spans more than six hundred acres of rolling, oak-studded hills and savannah-like grasslands near the small burg of Winston. As you travel through Winston, you cannot miss the centerpiece of the town: a life-size bronze sculpture of the rare cheetah, an endangered species that numbers but a few

Do You Know the Wildlife at Risk? Some Say It's Us!

The cheetah, like many other species you will see at Wildlife Safari, is an endangered species at risk of extinction. While extinction is a natural process—and for millions of years, plants and animals have become extinct—the current rate of extinction is far greater than at any other time in the past sixty-five million years. Today, the total number of species lost each year may be as high as forty thousand. Moreover, wildlife extinction is largely the result of human activities: Pollution, poaching, and habitat loss are often cited by biologists as the major reasons for such a rapid decline in the number and variety of species.

Many people may wonder why that is such a big deal. Cheetahs are only one among thirty-three million species of animals, plants, and other life forms, so does it really matter if they—or the elephant, or the rhino, or the gorilla, or the brown bear, or the salmon, or any of the thousands of species currently threatened with extinction—-survive? It is tempting to think that the loss of only one species here or another species there will not affect us, but as I like to tell students when I visit their classes, we need to think about the basic needs of fish, wildlife, and plants—that is, the clean air, food, water, and space that are so critical to survival. Who else needs these same resources? People! The diversity of life on Earth is amazing, and all species—plants, mammals, insects, and invertebrates—depend upon one another. We are all part of this amazing web of life. I believe a visit to Wildlife Safari may provide a new perspective on our roles protecting and preserving it.

► **Even the wildlife have fun at Wildlife Safari near Winston, Oregon.**

thousand in the wild. The statue serves as a symbol of the continuing efforts that Wildlife Safari established many years ago to help wildlife.

This parkland is very special, not only for the more than five hundred species that live there (some rarely seen outside their home ranges or even at city zoos), but because the visitors are in the cages—not the animals. Perhaps "cage" is a bit of a stretch, for you actually drive through this spread-out park in the comfort of your car. It's the kind of place made for family enjoyment, according to Dot Irvin, a member of the park staff, who joined us on a recent tour of the grounds. She told us that people get excited about seeing wildlife in this unusual setting "not only for the closeness you get to the animals, but the chance to learn more about them, too."

Three distinct wildlife communities (organized by continents: Asia, Africa, the Americas) are home to scores of species you rarely get to see so close. Flamingos, ring-tailed lemurs, Bengal tigers, Bactrian (two-humped) camels, hippos, brown bears, bison, and caribou are but a small sampling of the mix of wildlife. As we slowly motored along the paved roadway, I was struck by how often we'd be at arm's length from many exotic critters I'd seen behind bars in zoos or on television. In fact, in the Africa area, we were suddenly stopped by a pair of stubborn ostriches, who, like dutiful traffic cops, had taken up position smack in the middle of the road and wouldn't budge an inch. Then they moved toward our car and began to peck away at the windshield. This brought on a raucous, rowdy chorus of laughter from my sons, who'd never seen such a sight. We were baffled and couldn't understand their behavior. Dot then pointed out that the giant birds were actually eating the bugs that had taken up permanent, fatal residence on the car's front window.

"Oh, it happens all the time," she laughed. "This pair's a real hit with the visitors—quite an act, huh?"

"I'll say," my young Kevin noted. And with a giggle he added, "They must think we're the blue plate special."

After an hour or so, we arrived back at the Safari Village, near the park's entrance, where you may stroll around the manicured lawns, neatly trimmed hedges, masses of blooming daylilies, and carefully trimmed shade trees of Safari Village Gardens. The gardens play the major role in setting the atmosphere and help provide a tolerable microclimate in southern Oregon's often sweltering summer heat, especially after a drive through the park in a car without air conditioning. The Safari Village offers an air-conditioned restaurant where you can get a fine meal, a snack bar for your favorite soft drink and light lunch, a gift shop for memorabilia, and regular educational animal shows. It's so comfortable and so inviting, you may not wish to leave, but you'll miss more interesting parts of the parkland.

If the village is not to your liking, a number of benches are strategically located beneath ample shade trees next to ponds of water where you can watch the pink flamingos. Ah yes, the pink flamingo, practically an icon in America's landscape, except that these are not plastic; they are very real and happy to pose for you in front of bright yellow daylilies and a shimmering pool.

As my family took advantage of the colorful photo opportunity, I sat and chatted with Dot to learn more about Wildlife Safari's cheetah icon. She explained that the cheetah has been the park's symbol from the beginning because the graceful cats face such terrible odds against their survival in the wild. Only 12,400 cheetahs remain in twenty-five African countries. Namibia has the world's largest population of cheetahs, yet only 2,400 remain in the wild there. The plight of cheetahs symbolizes the problems that many predators face throughout the world. As Dot explained, "Many people fear predators, especially big cats such as the lion, cheetah, and leopard. We are often taught to fear carnivores without understanding their unique behaviors and essential roles in healthy ecosystems. Our attitudes and misconceptions have led to their endangerment because what people fear they often choose to destroy." Wildlife Safari tries to change that attitude by helping you to understand and care about wildlife. Perhaps that will improve their chance of survival in the wild.

■ **Getting There**
Travel south on Interstate 5 to exit 119 and then drive west three miles.

■ **For More Information**
Wildlife Safari (and campground),
P.O. Box 1600, Winston, OR 97496-0231,
(800) 355-4848

INLAND

17
Another Time, Another Place
~
Erratic Rocks State Park

"Summertime . . . and the living is easy." Or so the lyrics of a popular song from a musical stage show would have you believe! For the most part, that is true enough for the folks who make their homes in the Pacific Northwest. But it wasn't always so! In the vast Willamette Valley—with a little imagination—you can travel into a turbulent and tumultuous chapter of geologic history, when gigantic icebergs carried by floodwater that was more than four hundred feet deep floated across the broad-shouldered valley.

It may be hard to believe, but it's true! In the blink of a geologic eye, a series of tremendous floods occurred, perhaps twenty times every fifty years for two thousand years—beginning nearly fourteen thousand years ago near the end of the Ice Age. Gigantic, glacial Missoula Lake (in what is now Montana), backed up by an ice dam several miles wide and half a mile high, burst through its western wall and raced across the plains and valleys between Montana and the Pacific Ocean.

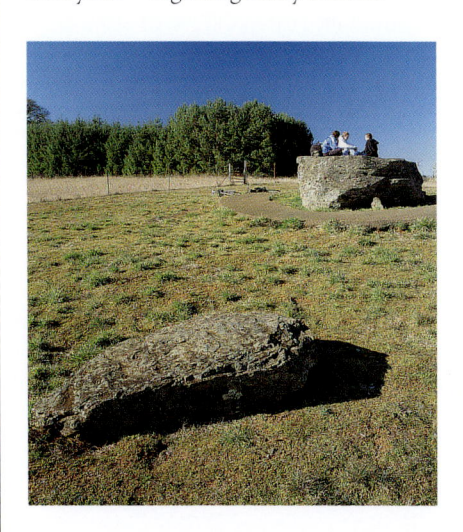

Geologists say some five hundred cubic miles of floodwater and icebergs roared across the Northwest, carrying away anything and everything in its path. As the ice flowed, it broke into thousands of pieces, and many of the pieces ended up stranded along the flood route. Like ticker tape from a spent parade, the icebergs scattered, then melted and deposited what was trapped inside: granite rocks! These "erratics"—a geological term that describes a rock found a considerable distance from its place of origin—range from pebble- to baseball- to car-size boulders that still dot the Willamette Valley.

Near present-day Sheridan, off Oregon 18, one giant berg melted and tipped its load, a massive rock that is called the Belleview Boulder. It is the centerpiece of Erratic Rocks State Park and rests on the shoulder of a hillside overlooking the

◣ **The rare and unusual erratic rocks offer you a new perspective on the passage of time near Sheridan, Oregon.**

55

highway. As you stroll the short but steep paved trail, consider that more than sixty years ago, Oregon State University geologist Ira Allison mapped 249 locations in the Willamette Valley where erratics could be identified, but over time many of the long-distance travelers have been moved, or buried, or used as farmstead foundations—or blown to bits. As you hike, notice the gently rolling landscape of the surrounding vineyard-laden hillsides. This landscape is a stark contrast to the Belleview Boulder! Notice the smoothed edges and scratches across the boulder's surface and its sharp angles compared with the rest of the valley. Consider also that the Belleview Boulder is getting smaller—not from time or weather—but from people! When the rock was first measured in 1950, the five-foot-tall, iron-shaped erratic was found to weigh about 160 tons. Today, as more folks have taken rock chips and bits home as souvenirs, the boulder is less than half its original size. That's a good reason to take only photos and memories at this remarkable example of a moment frozen in time.

■ Getting There

Drive south from Portland to U.S. 99W and proceed west to Oregon 18. Take Oregon 18, six miles east of Sheridan. Park along Oldsville Road (signed). From Oldsville Road, walk up a short paved path to the Belleview Boulder. The trail becomes steep as you near the rock.

■ For More Information

Oregon Parks and Recreation,
(800) 551-6949

INLAND

Fickle Mother Nature

18

Fern Ridge Reservoir

One of the most fascinating aspects of my news job has been covering the Northwest's dramatic environmental events and issues, particularly when severe weather affects us. The powerful periods of drought or deluge or blizzard or windstorm can have extreme effects upon our landscape and our lives, sometimes in heart-wrenching ways. For example, the infamous "Flood of '96" hit western Oregon with a sudden one-two punch of rapid snowmelt and endless days of rain. The February rain was not the typical gray-shaded drizzle either, but steady buckets of the stuff. Scores of forested canyons blew out a torrent of mud and debris into swollen, log-choked streams that washed out countless roads. Such was my beat in Oregon's Tillamook County for nearly two very long winter months. I can still vividly recall the devastation and the damage—millions of dollars' worth—not only to the land but also to the lives and livelihoods of small-town businesspeople who lost their shops and stores. Farmers lost their homes and barns, plus entire herds of milk-producing cows and other livestock that couldn't escape the fast-rising floodwater.

Five years later, the "Drought of '01" was just as ruinous for people who depended upon water for their farms and businesses. Hardest hit were the recreation-related businesses at Detroit Lake in the Willamette National Forest. This water-sports mecca in the Santiam River basin became a puddle compared to its normal gargantuan size. It left marina operators, restaurateurs, and hotel owners in the red, while disappointed summer campers and boaters were left stranded high, dry, and seeing red, too.

The drought also prompted unusual wildlife behavior. In fact, in the parched Willamette Valley at the normally wet world of Fern Ridge Reservoir in Lane County, a bird species arrived that hadn't been seen there in more than half a century: white pelicans! Stumps, mud flats, and low, low water created a scene largely devoid of people on Fern Ridge Lake that summer. In fact, the lake shrunk to about half its normal nine thousand acres, so the contrast to previous summers was startling. Usually Fern Ridge Lake is a boater's playground, but the drought meant no more fill-ups at the county boat marina, where dozens of wooden boat docks were stacked atop each other like cord wood, and popular swimming holes were transformed into lonely beachfronts.

Yet the wildlife adapted just fine. Shorebirds still probed the muck of the shoreline for food while ospreys soared

SUMMER ~ Fern Ridge Reservoir

Lupine offer a blush of summer color along the Fisher Butte Trail in the Fern Ridge Wildlife Area near Eugene, Oregon.

Department of Fish and Wildlife, just a short distance from the rare presence of about three dozen white pelicans preening and resting on a treeless sand island.

"My gosh, Wayne," I whispered, "pelicans are really huge."

He smiled, nodded, and in a hushed tone offered, "Oh yeah—they are unmistakable! You know, it's so neat to see them here, too. Last time was just after World War II. There are so few people around this summer that the birds may find the lake much more appealing. Plus, there's more exposed sandbar, which is ideal for the birds to rest on."

Pelicans weigh up to twenty pounds with wingspans reaching seven or eight feet. They are a brilliant bright white, so they stand out from quite a distance. White pelicans are usually found only in the Malheur or Klamath regions, but the drought brought them much farther north and west than normal. As many as forty were spotted on the lake where shallow water, mudflats, and a steady diet of freshwater clams created their ideal habitat. Wayne suggested that the pelicans may have rediscovered historic habitat and he wouldn't be surprised if they return for many summers to come. And in fact, they have. If you travel the Fisher Butte Trail, you may see them, too.

This seasonal nine-thousand-acre lake is one of Oregon's most popular, with over a million visitors per year. Built by the

high overhead. Even though the lake dropped to ten feet below its normal height, many hiking trails, usually swampy adventures at best, were actually bone dry and easier to follow. Such were the conditions I found when I traveled down the Fisher Butte Trail at the southeast corner of the lake, where a short trek to the shoreline put me and my partner, Wayne Morrow, a biologist with the Oregon

COLUMBIA

19
A Byway Restored
~
Eagle Creek and Cascade Locks

Corps of Engineers in 1941, the Fern Ridge project includes about twelve thousand acres (more than nineteen square miles) and was built for flood control and irrigation. Popular for sailing, powerboating, water skiing, and swimming, Fern Ridge Lake offers several park sites for day use and for overnight camping. Two public marinas and the Eugene Yacht Club host several sailing regattas each summer. Wildlife-viewing opportunities are abundant, and refuges comprise a large part of extensive adjoining wetlands.

Approximately five thousand acres on the east and south sides of the reservoir are leased by the Corps to the Oregon Department of Fish and Wildlife as the Fern Ridge Wildlife Area. Throughout the seasons you can depend upon seeing a wide variety of waterfowl and shorebirds—raptors, too—that live or travel across its marshes and open areas.

■ Getting There
Fern Ridge Wildlife Area surrounds Fern Ridge Reservoir. From Eugene, travel approximately five miles west on Oregon 126, with parking areas, canoe access sites, and parks providing lake and wildlife area access. Parking and trailhead for Fisher Butte Management Unit are on the southeast corner of the lake.

■ For More Information
Fern Ridge Wildlife Area, 26969 Cantrell Road, Eugene, OR 97402, (541) 935-2591

It is a lingering, sweltering summer afternoon, and the only coolness for miles is found under the soaring branches of the big-leaf maple trees that rise above cozy Eagle Creek in the Columbia River Gorge. The narrow stream, flanked by steep canyon walls, is low and clear at this time of year, and as I pause along its shore I find it a soul-refreshing moment. But wait! What's that—just under the historic stone and mortar Eagle Creek Bridge? A flash of silver and then a swirl of a tail fin signals I am not alone. The chinook salmon have come home to Eagle Creek. You can see them in the shadows of this historic bridge, which connects remnant segments of the Historic Columbia River Highway. Down in the depths are hundreds of the broad-shouldered fish, and like a slippery wad of fins and tails, they weave around and across and past each other. The big fish are mottled with scars and sores from their upriver journey and provide a certainty that the end of the line is at hand. They swim and wait and mark time at this deep point until a freshet arrives to raise the creek high enough for them to move farther upstream.

The stone bridge wears its engraved birth date of 1935 on its upstream side and marks the start of a new hiking trail you may wish to explore. I recently joined Mike Ferris, of the U.S. Forest Service, who's pleased and downright proud of the recently completed two-year-long restoration project that's given new life to an otherwise forgotten stretch of the historic highway. We strolled the newly paved hiking and biking trail that was once a highway for autos, and although it parallels nearby Interstate 84, it is a far cry from that road's shattering pace of traffic and noise. As we walked the 2.3-mile stretch, Mike explained, "What we have along here is something you won't see from the interstate, Grant. For example, just off to the left is an old-growth forest—hundreds of trees here, and some are two hundred fifty years old! It's just wonderful to pause a bit, look around, and appreciate the natural aesthetics of the Columbia River Gorge—plus it's so quiet and cool!"

The new trail winds and wends among Douglas fir, maple, and alder stands until you reach another historic destination at the community of Cascade Locks. This small town is where the gigantic Bridge of the Gods spans the Columbia River,

➤ Your spirit will soar in the splendor of the Columbia River Gorge on the Eagle Creek–Cascade Locks Trail.

and where history runs as deep as the nearby waterway. According to ancient legend, the Great Spirit built a bridge of stone across the river, but today scientists say that about thirty thousand years ago, a mountain on the Oregon side of the river (near the town site of Cascade Locks) caved off and blocked the river. The water behind the dam backed up as far as Idaho before it eventually eroded and washed away the land.

The first steel structure was completed in 1926 and was raised higher in 1938 to provide clearance over the waters rising behind nearby Bonneville Dam. Below the bridge and a bit upstream at Cascade Locks, watch for anglers, cued up in line with their rods and reels at attention along the old stone locks. Like sentinels on duty, the anglers wait for a passing salmon or steelhead to bite their bait. Meanwhile, a smooth yet constant current pulls through the stone locks. Dismantled in the 1950s, the locks only hint of the boom times that occurred here little more than a hundred years ago.

When you step inside the nearby Cascade Locks Museum, you'll learn the story of the massive project that moved the earth to create the locks, an engineering feat that resulted in gravity-fed chambers with steel gates that were the largest in the world. The story goes that the huge rocks of the legendary natural bridge came to rest on the bottom of the Columbia River.

The resulting rapids or "cascades" presented a serious navigation hazard to pioneers because they were so dangerous to travel through by boat or raft, so for many years it was necessary for river traffic to portage around the Columbia Cascades rapids. Finally, the government decided to construct a canal and locks at this site to bypass the rapids. Construction began in 1878.

Delays from winter storms, uncertain funding, and difficulties in receiving materials meant eighteen years would pass before the project was completed. Once finished, the locks allowed stern-wheelers

CASCADES

Birth of a River
20
Metolius River and Camp Sherman

to skip the powerful rapids and make quick time east to The Dalles. During this time, the community grew from a small settlement to a booming construction town. In fact, late in the nineteenth century, more than a thousand people lived at Cascade Locks.

The museum also contains exhibits about the western Columbia Gorge, with a special focus on historic paddleboats. The museum is a fun way to pass the time, but when you step outside here, be sure to stroll across the stone walkway that straddles the old locks to enjoy the rambling and tree-shaded parklands. Scattered picnic tables under maple canopies offer quiet respite and time to contemplate all the history you've explored. It's a magnificent experience in the heart of the Columbia River Gorge that you won't soon forget.

■ Getting There
Eagle Creek Fish Hatchery and Eagle Creek Trail: From Portland, drive east on Interstate 84 to Eagle Creek, exit 41. Park at the Eagle Creek–Cascade Locks trailhead, which is near the Cascade Fish Hatchery.

Cascade Locks Museum: From Portland, drive east on Interstate 84 to Cascade Locks, exit 43, and follow signs to the Cascade Locks Museum.

■ For More Information
Eagle Creek–Cascade Locks Trail, Columbia Gorge National Scenic Area, 902 Wasco Avenue, Suite 200, Hood River, OR 97031, (541) 386-2333

Cascade Locks Museum, (541) 374-8535

Port Marina Park, (541) 374-8535

In early morning light, when the summer air is clear and cool, peaks in the Oregon Cascades like the Three Sisters and Mount Jefferson are marvels. That is especially true from the central Oregon point of view at a place where the Metolius River is born near the north base of Black Butte, a once-active volcano that rises more than 3,400 feet above the river.

At the head of the Metolius (just off U.S. 20 near Camp Sherman), you can watch as a river comes to life. It bubbles up through an ancient lava flow and forms a shallow creek, then weaves through grassy meadows. The clarity and color and coldness of the water are amazing, ranging from deep blue and turquoise to frothy whitewater as the flow gains volume from snow-fed tributaries. Bordered by ponderosa pines whose cinnamon-colored bark seems to glow under dazzling sunshine, the river splashes and speeds up as the Metolius reaches its full size on a sixteen-mile journey toward Lake Billy Chinook. Little wonder the Metolius and its 8,560-acre river corridor were designated one of America's Wild and Scenic Rivers in 1988.

Clear water, green meadows, and majestic pines draw thousands of visitors and anglers to the Metolius each year. Near Camp Sherman—a small burg that holds on to its heritage as a fly caster's mecca—you can visit Wizard Falls Fish Hatchery, named for a nearby river falls. According to hatchery manager Steve Hamburger, it's one of Oregon's few hatcheries that's more akin to a park, and people love to stroll here.

"That's easy to explain, Grant. Just glance around. These old ponderosas and Douglas firs are hundreds of feet tall and hundreds of years old. Plus the cool, inviting grass lawns—hey, you'd feel comfortable pitching a tent and laying out a sleeping bag right here." He chuckled and with no small amount of pride continued. "We've been told many, many times by visitors that this is one of the prettiest—maybe the prettiest—fish-rearing facilities in Oregon."

This is a "must visit," for adults and children alike will enjoy feeding some of the big fish held in dozens of rearing ponds. Ironically, the Metolius River has been managed entirely for its wild or native fish populations since 1996 when the state discontinued its stocking program, so all of the fish raised in this hatchery are actually distributed to nearby lakes.

While you cannot camp on the hatchery grounds, you won't lose sleep at any of the ten nearby U.S. Forest Service campgrounds. There are no hookups, no phones, no TVs, and your RV must be self-contained or you must be ready to pitch a tent and live without fancy conveniences for awhile. This is a place where families gather streamside for a game of cards—or float in small rafts down the river—while still others come to the river shore with another game in mind.

"Gotta find some fish. I heard a rumor there was some in here." Glenn Young, with tongue firmly planted in cheek, was enjoying his day of hiking and casting into the Metolius River's secret spots of

◣ **The Metolius River is quietly born amid wildflowers and ponderosa pine trees near Camp Sherman, Oregon.**

native rainbow trout. He and I had met early in the day to don our neoprene waders along the river not far from the Allingham Bridge Campground. Glenn had grown up fishing these waters, and I heartily agreed with his assessment that the water is a fly caster's heaven.

"The water quality and the river's constancy are the big reasons. It never gets too high and it never gets too low, too hot, or too cold, regardless of the outside environment, like rain or snow. It's the spring-fed nature of the Metolius that maintains this gin-clear water quality." We waded and we cast woolly buggers, muddler minnows, and caddis flies into the seams just off the main current edge and limited our false casts and mended our lines constantly to maintain a natural drift and fly presentation.

"Come on, Grant, let's wade out across this shallow bar to midstream. See where the main feeding channel is over there? That's where we want to line up our casts and cover as much water as we can with our flies. Let it out and let it go deep, then strip your line back through."

Glenn had guided our casting around bridges, the grassy banks and clusters of grass, and logs in the river. He pointed out to me that the deeper runs hold larger trout but are more difficult to fish. Overhanging trees alongside the river are also good places to locate trout.

Within moments a muscular trout struck and tore off downriver. I set my hook, then held on for dear luck. The fish was big—really big—and had not slowed a bit. I knew the Metolius offered wild rainbow trout ranging from eight to thirteen inches and can reach up to five pounds. This trout was in the upper end of that magical range. In a heartbeat, as quickly as it began, it was over. The giant fish was off. I rapidly retrieved my line only to discover I'd broken a cardinal rule: The telltale pigtail at the end of my leader showed for all the world that my knot had come undone. Yikes!

"I goofed up on that one," I offered meekly.

"Welcome to the land of big fish, Grant. Sorry to see that happen, but so you don't feel too bad, I had the exact same thing happen last week, and I think mine was even larger."

I was silent. Glenn smiled. The river rolled on its magical way.

In addition to rainbow, the Metolius serves up a varied menu of other fish as well. Brown trout found mostly in the tributaries and the upper stretches run under twelve inches. A few brook trout are offered with an average size of eight inches; they are found mainly in the upper five-mile stretch of the river. Bull trout up to fifteen pounds are present with an average size of five to six pounds. Kokanee swim up from Lake Billy Chinook in the fall and can provide some good angling before they spawn. And white fish are found throughout the river and can provide some solid angling.

The Camp Sherman community comprises many homes, a post office, a restaurant, and a general store with a fly shop. It is an extremely popular area, so expect crowds during the peak summer

CASCADES

21 ~ Watching the Clouds Roll By
Cloud Cap Inn

season. If you hope to camp during late summer, your best chance is midweek because the campgrounds often fill up on weekends.

"Just a super destination!" Young told me later at our camp as we reveled in the evening quiet. "The Metolius is a difficult river to fish for the beginner. In fact, each year thousands of anglers come and get skunked; yet they still manage to enjoy themselves soaking in the peace and scenery. The campgrounds are clean and the scenery is unbeatable and the weather—well, with more than two hundred rain-free days a year, you can depend upon the Metolius for comfortable conditions."

■ Getting There

From Portland: Take U.S. 26 east to Redmond and the junction with Oregon 126. Take Oregon 126 west to Sisters, then proceed north to the junction with Forest Service Road 14, which will take you to Camp Sherman.

From Salem: Take Oregon 22 east over Santiam Pass. After you pass the Suttle Lake turnoff, head north on Forest Service Road 14, which will take you to Camp Sherman.

From Bend: Take U.S. 20 west, past the town of Sisters. Just beyond the Black Butte Ranch turnoff, head north on Forest Service Road 14, which will take you to Camp Sherman.

■ For More Information

Oregon Department of Fish and Wildlife, (503) 872-5268

Deschutes National Forest, (541) 549-7700

A much-loved part of my Sunday afternoons as a child was when my parents would bundle us youngsters up and "shoo" us out the door and into the family station wagon for a "weekend country drive." It was natural for me to establish the same tradition when I became a father, and together my kids and I have had many wonderful times on the road from here to there, bound for no particular place and unburdened by cares.

A favored excursion runs the little-traveled northern route toward Mount Hood via Cloud Cap Road near Parkdale. This trail puts you face-to-face with a more dramatic side of Mount Hood, and to coin the phrase of a free U.S. Forest Service brochure (available at an information kiosk along the route), "The mountains seem closer and the valleys deeper."

It's a drive offering exceptional views—especially at Inspiration Point, where on a cloudless day you can gaze from the small parking area across to Wallalute Falls and Mount Hood. The high elevation (five thousand feet) is noteworthy, too, for the air seems cleaner and the views sharper as you round each bend on this rough roadway. The fir and hemlock part every now and then to reveal spectacular forest scenery. Take note of the trees throughout these sites. Forest rangers have told me that tree-ring samples taken from this part of the forest indicate volcanic ash is present here and dates to approximately 1800—a clear indication of Mount Hood's eruptive past. Note, too, that the road changes from pavement to rock and gravel and includes nine miles of rutted and steep dirt road with many potholes. It is not for the faint of heart, so be prepared for some bumps along the way unless you drive a vehicle with two feet of ground clearance.

Two primitive campgrounds are located along this route, one at Cloud Cap and the other at Tilly Jane. Cloud Cap Inn is a rustic log and stone cabin—anchored to the mountain by cables to protect the structure from the powerful winds that blast across the mountain in winter. It was built in 1889 as a six-room hotel, and it was accessed via railroad from Portland and from Hood River, followed by a rough-and-tumble ride in a stagecoach. According to Kevin Slagle, a U.S. Forest Service Ranger, there is much controversy about whether this log-and-stone structure represents a truly American type of mountain architecture as compared to European styling like a Swiss alpine chalet. "Regardless, Cloud Cap is actually the very first hotel ever built on Mount Hood," Kevin said. "In fact, folks came from all over the world to make the

SUMMER ~ Cloud Cap Inn

two-day trip to get up this side of the mountain for the rugged, alpine scenery."

But distance and transportation, plus tough economic times, made the Cloud Cap Inn a dicey business operation. Its run ended thirty-five years before World War II rang a death knell for the inn as a mountain hostelry. In fact, people's interest in alpine vacations disappeared entirely with the start of World War II, as interest in the home-front defense effort rose. By 1950, the Forest Service was talking of demolishing Cloud Cap because of vandalism and the effects of the weather.

That's when the Crag Rats took over. The Crag Rats had formed in 1927 as the country's first mountain rescue team, and in 1954 the Hood River–based search-and-rescue team took responsibility for Cloud Cap Inn and saved it from demolition. Kevin told me that the early rescue pioneers also came together as the result of collective action, because, according to

🌲 **You'll be spellbound by the rugged scenery at Ghost Ridge along the Tilly Jane Road in the Mount Hood National Forest.**

Slagle (also a Crag Rat), "They knew they might need assistance themselves someday." The highly experienced mountaineers banded together to form a rescue group with professional skills and "volunteer" pay. The Crag Rats now use Cloud Cap Inn as their base camp.

"This is the most dramatic side of the mountain," noted Kevin. "There's the Cooper Spur Trail and climbing route, there's massive Elliot Glacier with incredible geologic formations, plus the quiet alpine setting of trees and wildflowers. Such a different world from the Timberline [southern] point of view, and it just gets into your heart."

If luck is on your side, the Crag Rats may be at Cloud Cap when you visit. If so, take time to talk with them and learn more about their interesting search-and-rescue history and their appreciation for this beautiful setting.

■ Getting There
Follow Interstate 84 to Hood River. Then drive south on Oregon 35 about 25 miles to a sign for Cooper Spur Ski Area. Drive west on Cooper Spur Road for 3.3 miles to Tilly Jane Junction. Turn left onto Forest Service Road 3512 (Cloud Cap Road) and for approximately ten miles follow the signs to the Cloud Cap Campground and parking area.

■ For More Information
Mount Hood National Forest, Hood River Ranger District, 6780 Highway 35, Parkdale, OR 97041, (541) 352-6002.

CASCADES

Volcano Views
22
Windy Ridge and Ape Cave

In the spring of 1980, when a major eruptive cycle blew the top off Mount St. Helens, resculptured Spirit Lake, and spread ash across the countryside, it also created a new barren wilderness that was named the Mount St. Helens National Volcanic Monument. Twenty-three years later, most visitors travel the steep and winding approach from the west on the impressive Spirit Lake Memorial Highway. It whisks you past three highly educational visitor centers to complete the journey at Johnston Ridge. Although these three centers can provide an idea of the power of the explosion that blew off St. Helens's top, I think a more adventurous route into the volcanic devastation takes you little more than a hundred miles from the Portland metro area on an approach from the east.

The monument's east side offers a close-up view of how the eruption affected the surrounding lands. Here you will see the forest that was blown down by the eruption. Forest Service Road 26 travels through mile after mile of awesome blowdown, where huge timber stands lie toppled, jumbled, and tossed about, hillside after hillside resting as quiet testimony to that explosive time in 1980. Windy Ridge is at the end of the road, but a short, easy quarter-mile hike to the top of Windy Ridge Viewpoint offers the best views and a firsthand look at what was once a complete mountain.

Biologists have called this place a living laboratory of nature, but you won't need a science degree to see that life is returning across the landscape on the smallest to the largest of scales. From wildflowers to wild elk, there's a rebirth of new life with bursts of color against an otherwise bleak background. Below Windy Ridge lies Spirit Lake, which was once one of the most popular summer vacation spots in the Washington Cascades. I am among the fortunate news reporters who have visited the interior of the crater several times over the years, and I must admit that the view from Windy Ridge feels the most spectacular to me. I think I prefer and appreciate the enormous scale and vastness visible from this vantage. Geologists have told me that this devastation will eventually become an area of lush forest and meadows again—and that someday Mount St. Helens will erupt again. Now that is a cycle of life and death that's worth pausing to consider.

▶ **Mount St. Helens will steal your heart near Yale Reservoir in the Gifford Pinchot National Forest.**

SUMMER ~ Windy Ridge and Ape Cave

Another often-overlooked perspective on the Mount St. Helens National Volcanic Monument is one that leaves you in the dark, yet lights up a little-appreciated chapter of geologic history. Really! Try the short drive to the southern flanks of Mount St. Helens. It will bring you face-to-face with a unique geology lesson below the Cascade Mountains, if you bring a flashlight or a lantern. On the south side of the monument, you can explore Ape Cave, a lava tube that was formed centuries ago when lava poured from the volcano. When the lava finally stopped flowing, it left a two-mile-long cave that is the longest continuous lava tube in North America. At the U.S. Forest Service Ape Cave Headquarters (open from late May through early September), you can join a ranger-led exploration of the cave or rent a lantern for exploring the cave on your own.

I recently met an energetic and fascinating U.S. Forest Service ranger (a recent transplant from East Asia) by the name of Neemedass (pronunced "NEEM-ah-dazz") Chandool (pronounced "shan-DOOL"). The young man was so well versed on the geology of caves and was so enthusiastic about sharing his knowledge that I learned more in two hours from his guided tour than from a semester in a college classroom.

65

"I want to invite you to come with me on this walk back through time," said Neemedass, as our small group gathered near the entrance. "And for those who've never been here, remember that it's always about forty-two degrees, so you want to bring something warm to put on down below. Follow me!"

And we were off—down deep into the ground. The main entrance to Ape Cave is a sinkhole with two sets of stairs. The first leads into the sinkhole, where a passage leads you several yards to the second stairway. You feel the change as you descend into the cave: the warm comfort of July and the accompanying sounds of many visitors replaced by an abrupt stillness that takes a few moments to get used to. Neemedass noticed our silence and said that it's not unusual for some people to be a bit uncomfortable as they warm up to the quiet coolness.

"This tube was formed by an eruption that occurred almost two thousand years ago as the lava oozed and flowed from St. Helens. In some places the overhead roof is as much as sixty feet thick," he told us as we huddled around him in the dark. In fact, the inky darkness was so eerie that my flashlight left something to be desired in the oppressive blackness. Like many in my group, I was eager to move forward and learn more.

I learned that there are actually two caves in Ape Cave and that both begin in the middle of the lava tube near the interpretive center. The upper cave is 1.5 miles long and requires some scrambling skills, but there is an exit from the upper level with a 1.5-mile trail back to the parking lot. The lower cave is a much easier three-quarter-mile walk to the end of the cave, which shrinks down to a crawlway filled with sand. You hike out by the same route. While our group stayed in the lower cave, more experienced spelunkers can hike either cave.

"The evidence of long-ago molten activity cannot be missed," he continued as we journeyed deeper into the dark. "Look around you! We are now in what's called 'Big Room,' the largest open area of Ape Cave. Big Room has distinct flow markings on the walls that seem to have dripped and were then glazed over—almost like they were frozen in time."

There is a lot of moisture in the cave. At times, there are pools of water and mud on the floor, and the ceiling drips with cold water. I quickly realized my heavy hiking boots, long wool pants, and warm jacket were exactly what's needed for this kind of adventure. I also realized a willing spirit is needed to fully enjoy hiking in Ape Cave, so some may choose to stay above ground. Yet I discovered a certain comfort and enjoyment in so much darkness and quiet. In fact, at times Ape Cave was so still the quiet seemed to shout at me. It was a thrilling experience, and I will return.

Be advised: Each person will need warm clothing and a good flashlight. During the summer you can rent lanterns at the interpretive center for a small fee. No food, pets, or firearms are allowed in the caves. Running or hiking shoes are adequate for the lower cave, but some of the lava formations are sharp enough to shred them; open-toed sandals are definitely not a good idea. You'll need to purchase a Northwest Forest Pass at any of the monument visitor centers or at Pine Creek on the south side of the mountain; it will be good for three days at all areas of the monument.

■ Getting There

Windy Ridge Viewpoint: Take Interstate 5 to exit 68 and U.S. 12. Drive east on U.S. 12 to Randle. Head south on Washington 25 and then take Washington 26. (The Woods Creek Information Station, on Washington 25 just before the junction with Washington 26, has information on this part of the monument.) At Meta Lake, Washington 26 joins Washington 99, which continues to the Windy Ridge Viewpoint.

Ape Cave: Take Interstate 5 to Woodland (exit 21) and head east on Washington 503 to Yale. At Yale, turn left on Forest Service Road 90 to Cougar. At 7.5 miles east of Cougar, turn left (north) on Forest Service Road 83. In less than two miles, turn left (west) on Forest Service Road 8303 to the parking lot at Ape Cave Headquarters.

■ For More Information

Mount St. Helens National Volcanic Monument Headquarters, 42218 N.E. Yale Bridge Road, Amboy, WA 98601, (360) 449-7800

Ape Cave Headquarters, (360) 247-3900

CENTRAL/EASTERN

Golden Nugget
23
Sumpter Valley Dredge State Park and Railway

Reporters are like stones skipping across a pond of water, zipping from story to story each day of the week, but I've been very lucky: My assignments always seem to get me thoroughly immersed in some timely issue or topic. In fact, four or five times each year I have produced lengthier special programs or documentaries on the outdoors, and I've spent days traveling across the region for each one. I've loved every minute of it!

One summer I got to dig into a real nugget of an environmental issue about a modern-day gold rush in the Oregon high desert. The mining industry was busily staking out silver and gold claims with the hopes of striking it rich through the business of massive open-pit gold mining. The open-pit method was controversial because it left behind gargantuan holes—perhaps a mile wide and a half mile deep—and because it used a complex chemical process to release minute flakes of gold from the crushed rock. One of the chemicals was cyanide, and since some companies in the mining industry had a rather checkered environmental past, there was much distrust and significant opposition to the idea. Many Oregonians were worried about how the new gold mining industry might operate. Eventually, state mining regulations were toughened and the industry backed away. As a result of travel for this program, I was in touch with folks who were—at one time or another—interested in and savvy about mining. That's how I met a fascinating group of volunteers who continue to bring the history of the once-booming gold mining era to life for summer visitors aboard the Sumpter Valley Railway.

The narrow-gauge (36 inches wide versus the standard 56.5-inch track) SVR, affectionately known to its friends and followers as the "Stump Dodger,"

◤ Hop aboard the Sumpter Valley Railway's "Stump Dodger" for a unique journey through local history.

first whistled into Sumpter on October 31, 1896. When it arrived, the town's population was but two hundred people, yet a year later the residents had swelled to nine thousand. According to Mark Ferns, a state geologist by profession and a local historian by avocation, the gold boom and the railroad that followed it carried passengers, logs, lumber, livestock, mining equipment, gold, and mail from Baker to Prairie City in eastern Oregon (a distance of more than eighty miles). As Mark put it, gold and silver mining was the lifeblood of the local economy.

"It was just after the Civil War and still the time of the Indian Wars. Americans were trying to settle the West and the belief at that time was—and this was true for all of the natural resources—we had to do something with all this wealth—be it timber, gold, silver, or even salmon. If someone found something—like gold or silver—they had a right to it."

As with most boom-bust cycles, by 1905 the gold mines began to lose their luster and their yield and many closed down. As the population declined, the town's glitter faded, too. The railway continued to haul logs and lumber until 1947, when the line was eventually removed and never expected to run again. However, people throughout the area never could forget the "Stump Dodger," so plans were developed to restore the railroad. On January 4, 1971, the Sumpter Valley Railway Restoration was incorporated as a nonprofit and operational tourist railroad. Today, the roadbed and track are mostly on the original SVR right-of-way, thanks to an all-volunteer workforce rebuilding more than seven miles of track.

When you travel to the train depot near Sumpter and climb aboard, you travel back to the days of steam railroading. You'll see the crew fill the steam locomotive with water and then couple onto antique narrow-gauge passenger cars and a caboose. Sit back and relax as the SVR chugs and rolls and hisses over miles of track, for it also gives you perspective on another monumental chapter of this gold mining era that scarred the Powder River Valley.

During a brief rebound in the gold mining industry in the 1930s (and continuing until 1954), monstrous gold-dredging machines ravaged the river valley floor. Square-bowed and built of steel and wood and iron, the Sumpter dredge (one of three dredges that worked in the valley) lifted and sifted the terrain, reaping a golden harvest worth an estimated $12 million.

My guide, Mark Ferns, noted, "It was a time when some other nearby mines, like Cornucopia, were still pretty productive, and so dredge mining got started with a simple but dramatic and very effective method: scoop it up, sift out the gold, and leave the tailings behind."

I hope you will be as awestruck as I when you come face-to-face with the Sumpter dredge, whose massive boom bears seventy-two one-ton buckets. The buckets moved like the chain links of a chainsaw, bored into the riverbank, and carried loose rock back into the dredge's hulking interior. Once inside, the rock passed through a series of steel cylinders that separated the rocks and dirt by size.

Water and sluices separated the gold from the sediment and the spoils from this process were discharged behind the behemoth as it moved across the valley. Whether you wander across the surrounding grounds near the dredge or travel across the valley by rail, the endless, undulating heaps of rocks that were discharged from the dredge are impossible to miss. Even decades later, the tailings from the mining process hint at the devastating effects wrought by the era of the gold dredges. Time has a way of healing the land's wounds, though, and you can see trees, other vegetation, and even wildlife returning amid the extensive destruction of a bygone era.

The Sumpter Valley Railway operates each weekend from Memorial Day to the end of September and includes several special night and photography runs.

■ Getting There
Take Interstate 84 to Baker City and continue west on Oregon 7 for twenty-two miles.

■ For More Information
Sumpter Valley Railway, (541) 894-2486, (800) 551-6949

CENTRAL/EASTERN

Oregon's Swiss Alps
~ The Wallowas

24

I am a big believer in the adage "Our lives are but houses built of memories." It certainly holds true for me! Yet, strangely, I have the strongest, most lasting memories of meeting people and visiting places and experiencing adventures that unfortunately just didn't last long enough. Often, my fondness for a particular time and place has been the result of an escapade into a very distant, very wild place that demanded a great deal of planning and preparation. The Wallowa Mountains in far northeastern Oregon is such a place. Not so long ago, on assignment with news photographer Don Stapleton, I traveled into the Eagle Cap Wilderness of the Wallowas, a wild place often referred to as the "Swiss Alps of Oregon."

We journeyed there to chronicle a horse-packing expedition for a special KATU program. Our hosts and guides on the four-day trek were a couple of fellows who had horsemanship in their blood and seemed more comfortable in the saddle than the suburbs. For close to twenty years, Howard Cornutt and his brother Phil (both native Portlanders) have made the Eagle Cap Wilderness a featured part of their summer vacation plans. Born of childhood interests in horses and wilderness areas, the duo slowly accumulated stock and gear that developed into a thriving hobby. Following even more time and more travel, the hobby soared into a passion to see the great outdoors from a different point of view: sitting tall in their saddles. These days, the two are on the trail eight to ten weeks each year, stringing together horses and mules to travel into otherwise hidden and hard-to-reach locations.

On a brilliant mid-July morning, Don and I linked up with Howard and Phil for the start of our Eagle Cap trek at the Two Pan trailhead near Lostine. Howard had been hard at work a couple hours before sunrise, assembling and packing everything we'd need for the fifty-mile journey. I noticed the great care and concentration he used in loading and preparing the panniers (boxy storage containers that held our food, gear, and equipment). Each slid into pack frames that were harnessed on both sides of each animal. Howard explained there was good reason to be cautious at this early stage of our trip: "It's real critical how these ride on the mules and horses, Grant. You have to make sure the panniers are of equal weight, and that they are tightly secured to the frame. You don't want them to slip to one side or the other. If you don't get it right, you could have a wreck."

A wreck? Now that was certainly the last thought on my mind. How might a four-legged, surefooted master of the outback trails possibly have a wreck? And with me on board? Howard assured me not to worry, that each of his six animals had done all of this many, many times, although on this trip he'd also included two youngsters in the pack train: a young mare—following her mother's footsteps, so to speak—and a young mule, both new to the wilderness trail game. Each would carry a small amount of equipment on the trip, for as Howard explained, trail packing is a game of "one step at a time."

"These two are at a critical stage of their learning right now—both good habits and bad habits—who to follow, how fast to go, when to stop. On top of that, just like children, they each have their own personalities. So this trip is

◣ **The Eagle Cap Wilderness is rugged, remote, relentless, and an oh-so-inviting adventure in distant northeast Oregon.**

as much a time to teach them as it is recreation for us. It's a lot of work and challenge! But fun challenges!"

And with that we were off, each of us humming bars to the western ditty about being back in the saddle again. We quickly rose in elevation along the well-traveled Lostine Trail, bound for Glacier Lake in a distant corner of the Eagle Cap Wilderness. Before long we penetrated an area of magnificent woods and mountains, and each bend of the trail revealed another breathtaking view of a high alpine lake and spruce-fringed meadow. Don was giddy with excitement. The fifty-something professional, with more than thirty years of worldwide travel and camera work to his credit, seemed like a youngster fresh out of school on his first day of summer vacation.

"Look at that over there. My gosh! The white granite against that sapphire sky is spectacular! The air's so clean, you can see forever." I listened to him exclaim at one dazzling overlook after another. "Remarkable! And I thought I knew Oregon. Oh my, great shots, great shots!"

The Eagle Cap Wilderness was established in 1940, and at nearly four hundred thousand acres today, it is Oregon's largest wilderness area. It includes 37 miles of rivers and streams, plus seventy-five lakes, all of them connected by 534 miles of trails. Bare granite peaks and ridges and U-shaped glaciated valleys characterize this enormous wilderness area, where elevations range from five thousand feet in lower valleys to near ten thousand feet on Matterhorn and Sacajawea Peak, the highest of the majestic crests. At any time you could cross paths with a peregrine falcon, a bald or golden eagle, a mule deer or Rocky Mountain elk, or a bighorn sheep (the latter were reintroduced in the 1950s, along with mountain goats).

Twenty-five miles from the Lostine trailhead, we arrived at Glacier Lake, at about 8,200 feet in elevation, which would serve as our base camp for the week. The lake, about 125 feet deep, is nestled at the foot of imposing Eagle Cap Peak. Like many of the high lakes, it's been stocked with rainbow, eastern brook, and golden trout, so I wasted little time unpacking my fly rod, neoprene waders, and a float tube so I could cast about for an evening meal. The speckled brook trout wasted little

▶ **Eagle Cap Mountain soars above Moccasin Lake in the Wallowa Mountains.**

time gobbling my offerings of assorted dry flies, and soon our dinner table was set. Our camp was set back from the lake a couple hundred yards on a small rise with a stunning view of the lake and the mountain towering above us. As we dined on cooked fresh trout, the warmth of a fading sun warmed us and Howard confided that, for his money, the Eagle Cap Wilderness is unmatched. It's a place where you will experience solitude, risk, and some soul-refreshing moments amid humbling beauty.

"We like getting away from it all, and you can certainly do that up here! Plus, there are so many trailheads that come into this fine-looking country, so the views are never the same twice. It does take a lot of planning to get in here because it is so remote, but whether on foot or on horseback—or even with the help of llamas as pack animals—this place will give you a peace of mind you cannot find anywhere else."

A week of horse packing is certainly a rare and cherished event for me. More often, like thousands of other visitors, I have enjoyed a nearby campground surrounded on three sides by nine-thousand-foot snowcapped mountains and a large, clear lake at Wallowa Lake State Park. Just eight miles from Joseph, this spacious park is the second-most-visited state park in Oregon, and according to ranger Gary McDaniel, families make it a vacation destination for good reason.

"First, it's the natural beauty! We have Wallowa Lake, which is more than three hundred feet deep and crystal clear, so it's a popular fishing and boating site. Then there are the two glacial moraines that descend from on high all the way down to the lakeshore to frame the lake. They are quite unique for this part of the country and really capture people's appreciation."

This state park is adjacent to Wallowa Lake Village, home to several commercial lodges, restaurants, cafes, and other amenities, such as bumper boats, canoeing, bike rentals, and miniature golf. The nearby Wallowa Pack Station is the oldest continuous packing business in northeast Oregon, offering a variety of guided rides from hourly to ten-day vacation pack trips for those who seek adventure on horseback.

With the opening in 1970 of the Mount Hood Tramway—the steepest in America—Wallowa County added one of its most popular attractions. Rising 690 feet a minute to an elevation of 3,700 feet, the tramway will take your breath away. The exciting trip to the top of the mountain allows you to enjoy the view as the four-passenger gondola rises above Wallowa Lake Village and the azure blue waters of Wallowa Lake. During this spectacular ride, you get a view of the Eagle Cap Wilderness and its rugged peaks. Upon arriving at the upper terminal, you can explore the summit area and enjoy the extensive variety of alpine plants and vegetation along any of the many trails. Interpretive signs and information help you make the most of your walk. The tramway manager, Kevin Almas, told me, "It's your chance to look down at a real pristine area. From below, you just cannot see the entire valley, but way up here you can see everything for miles around."

The walk to the Wallowa Valley overlook is about a quarter mile and takes most people between fifteen and twenty minutes one way. It serves up a breathtaking view of the valley where Chief Joseph and his people spent their summers. The communities of Joseph, Enterprise, Lostine, and Wallowa are visible. The summer and fall season typically begins at the end of June on the lower elevation trails and runs to the end of November.

All wilderness visitors to the Eagle Cap Wilderness must obtain a required Wilderness Visitor Permit before entering the area. Only one permit per group is necessary, and there is no fee for the permits. Under permit from the Forest Service, a number of outfitters and guides offer wilderness trips ranging from drop camps to deluxe services and using backpacks, horses, llamas, mules, and skis. Call the Wallowa Mountains Visitor Center for a complete list of permittees.

■ Getting There
From Portland, drive east on Interstate 84 to La Grande. Proceed to the town of Joseph, via Oregon 82. Wallowa Lake State Park is located approximately six miles south of Joseph.

■ For More Information
Wallowa Lake State Park (information), (541) 432-4185, (800) 551-6949; reservations, (800) 452-5687

Wallowa Mountains Visitor Center, (541) 426-4978, (541) 426-5546

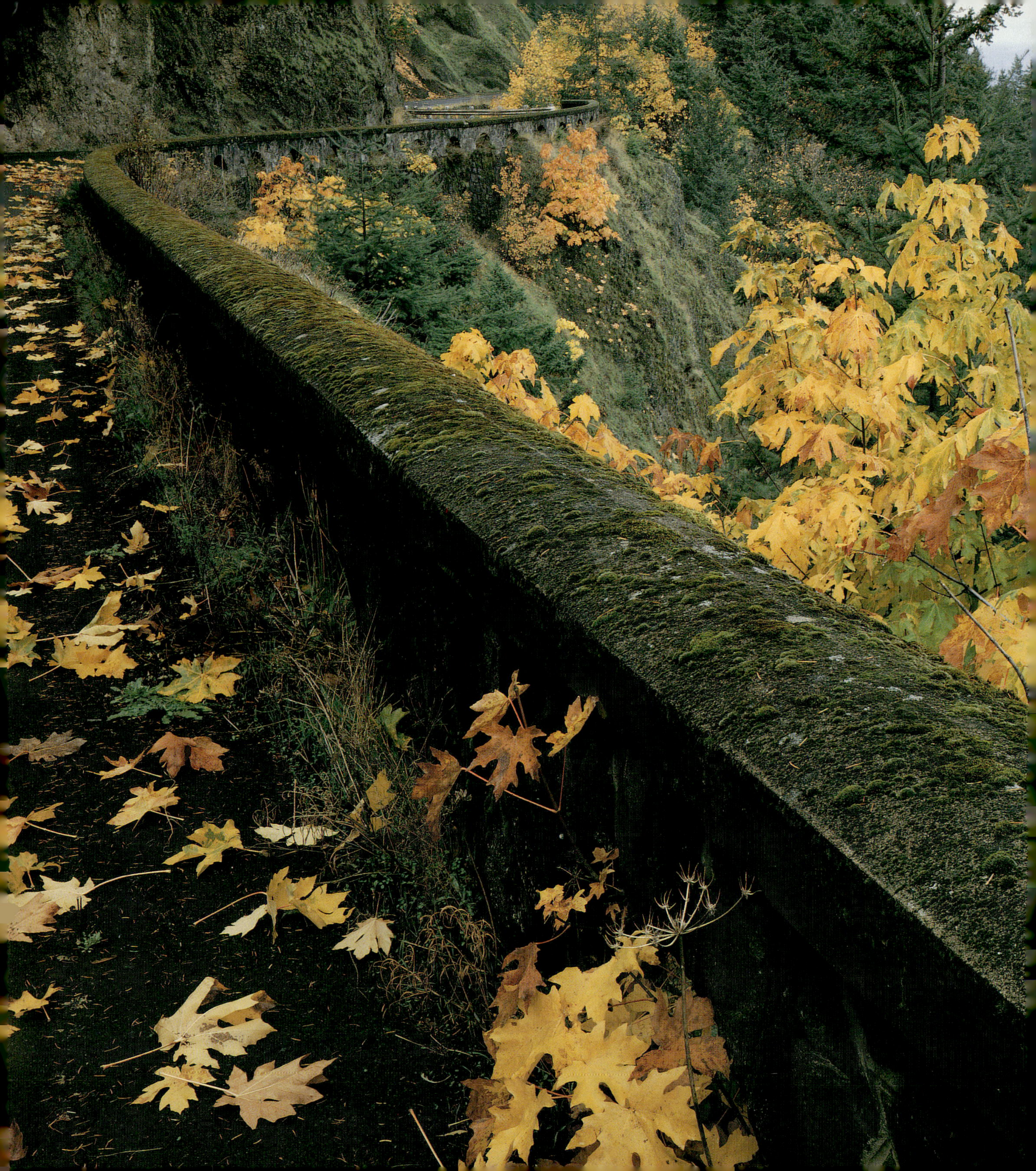

FALL

The use of traveling is to

regulate imagination with reality,

and instead of thinking how things may be,

to see them as they truly are.

SAMUEL JOHNSON

◄ Sun-burnished big-leaf maple leaves mark the changing seasons along the Historic Columbia River Highway.

COAST

Whitewashed Wonder
Yaquina Head
25

As the seasons change, surf and sand often seem to merge into a golden, sun-burnished moment along the coast. The rocky headland called "Yaquina" (pronounced "Yuh-quinn-uh"), marked for miles by a towering white sentinel on the central Oregon coastline, is a wonder. Once a lonely outpost above rocky cliffs, Yaquina Headland and Lighthouse are anything but lonely on crisp, clear fall days as schoolchildren scamper and tourists wander across some of the most accessible tidepools of the area. Managed by the Bureau of Land Management, the Yaquina Head Outstanding Natural Area is home to many seabirds and other sea life. Harbor seals lounge on a nearby series of low rock islands, the mass migration of gray whales can easily be observed, and low tide reveals seaweeds, sea stars, hermit crabs, purple urchins, and anemones in the nearby "marine gardens."

Yaquina Headland has endured for eons, and according to my friend Michael Noack, the BLM's Yaquina naturalist, with whom I've spent time on countless visits to the site, geology is the reason the site was chosen for a lighthouse station in 1872. Yaquina Headland is really an ancient lava flow that originated fourteen million years ago in eastern Washington and then spread three hundred miles to the west before reaching the ocean. Despite a battering by ocean waves, relentless winds, and seasonal rains, the basalt rock refuses to be worn away as quickly as surrounding beaches.

The headland's enduring prominent face made it a natural choice for the lighthouse. During a recent tour, Michael pointed out some of the finer details of the massive white, conical-shaped light tower—starting with the 114 steps in the circular stairway to the top: "The Yaquina Lighthouse is the tallest and second-oldest lighthouse still in operation and provides the headland its most distinguishing feature. But it's what you can't see that's also amazing, for it's actually built of double-walled brick, more than 370,000 of them, for insulation and dampness protection."

The light was equipped then as it is today with a Fresnel lens that was manufactured in Paris in 1868. It was shipped from France to Panama, transported across the isthmus, and then shipped to Oregon. What a journey! With a laugh, Michael added that Yaquina Head was always a popular tourist attraction. "When it was built in 1873, the ninety-two-foot tower was a skyscraper, and so many tourists came to see it that the keepers had to ask the local officials to declare visiting hours. It was the only way they could get their work done and get some sleep."

What a magnificent feat the light's builders accomplished! Think about it.

Year after year after year, the winds whistle across the headland at seventy to eighty miles per hour, especially hard during Oregon's long, wet winter months. Yet the Yaquina Lighthouse stands to this day as a constant, reassuring thousand-watt beacon of safety for sailors at sea.

Several miles of trail connect visitors to various interpretive sites throughout the headland, as do abundant information kiosks, waysides, and observation decks. You'll likely want to spend time in the recently completed Yaquina Head Interpretive Center to learn more fascinating natural and cultural history. Displays teach about the plentiful wildlife of the area and introduce the people who endured hardship to provide service. Gary Meyer, the BLM's Yaquina Head historian, explained to me that a hundred years ago this central coast region was so isolated, especially in winter, that the light keepers and their families had to be a very dedicated lot: "The men had a variety of responsibilities, but the main thing was always making sure the light was working. That service was critical above all because there were so many shipwrecks along our rugged coast in those days. The light had to stay on at all costs. It was more important than anything else out here."

◤ Yaquina Head Lighthouse has shone a beacon of safety for sailors at sea since 1873.

◥ Sea stars and sea urchins are yours to admire in the Quarry Cove Tidepools at Yaquina Head.

TIDEPOOL TIPS

Yaquina Head is a protected natural area. Please tread lightly and take only pictures. If the tide is low, and you plan to explore some tidepools, following are some ideas to make your adventure safe and gentle on the creatures that live there.

- Go slowly.
- Do not walk in the pools.
- Step only on bare spots, not on plants or animals.
- Don't touch any of the plants or animals

A trail leads from the interpretive center to an observation deck, passing under the main entrance road via a tunnel to a dramatic vista of the ocean and Newport—just three miles away. From this location, you also have a unique perspective on the headland's more recent history.

For decades prior to federal protection, the headland was a rock quarry that provided crushed rock and gravel for building local roads and driveways. But in the early 1990s, an ambitious plan was begun to transform the three-acre rock quarry into "Quarry Cove Tidepools," a dozen sculpted tidepools on the old quarry floor, and the first human-made intertidal system. The elderly, young and old in wheelchairs, and children can easily reach these pools and peer into a colorful and mysterious world full of sea life. The BLM's Yaquina Headland manager, Steve Gobat, explained that you will see some very unusual critters in the new Quarry Cove Tidepools, from hermit crabs to sea anemones, plus scores of fish species and seabirds. "I look at Quarry Cove as a zoo in reverse!" he said. "People are in the zoo and these animals get to do what they want to do. It's developed into a pretty interesting and educational place for folks who ordinarily couldn't get close to the ocean. Well, now they sure can."

The surging tide brings marine newcomers each day, from microscopic plankton to pencil-size tubeworms—and almost two hundred species of marine animals have made these tidepools home since completion of the project. It's an amazing place where Mother Nature is creating something beautiful from an open and barren wound on the landscape—a natural place where marine creatures can live and humans can easily observe them.

■ Getting There
Take Oregon 18 to coastal highway U.S. 101. Approximately three miles north of Newport, turn west (toward the ocean) onto Lighthouse Drive.

■ For More Information
Yaquina Head Outstanding Natural Area, (541) 475-3100

COAST

Gone, Never Forgotten
Tillamook Air Museum

26

From many miles away, the gargantuan size draws visitors near. Is it the eleven acres of arched roof? Perhaps the hundred-foot-tall letters boldly printed on its side? Or maybe it's the A-4 jet perched on a pole to signal that they've arrived? Regardless of how they find it, size—"Massive!" "Enormous!" "Colossal!"—is on everyone's lips when they are face-to-face with the Tillamook Air Museum just off U.S. 101.

The museum is housed in the largest freestanding wooden structure in the world, a former blimp hangar. Built in only twenty-nine working days during the winter of 1942–43, the hangar continues to inspire visitors by its sheer scale. Imagine: Three *Titanics* (yes, the famous cruise liner) or six football fields lined up sideline to sideline could fit inside this mammoth building. Also amazing is the fact that nine other structures like this were built along the coastal perimeter of the United States in the early days of World War II.

The time was just after the Japanese attack on Pearl Harbor on December 7, 1941. Stunned, but not entirely unprepared, the United States was immediately caught up in the throes of World War II. Faced with the startling realization that the West Coast was vulnerable to enemy attack, especially from submarines, a series of defense plans was quickly drafted as the nation mobilized. In the sleepy coastal town of Tillamook, Oregon, located just six miles from the Pacific Ocean, the flat landscape surrounded by a semicircle of gently rolling hills offered the perfect terrain for the U.S. Navy's vision of "Blimp Squadron ZP-33," a home at the Tillamook Naval Station for lighter-than-air blimps.

Eight 252-foot-long, helium-filled K-class airships were based inside the hangar (a total of 138 airships was built during the war). The crew of ten shared a forty-two-foot-long gondola mounted to the underside of the blimp's envelope. This cabin was roughly the size of a Greyhound bus, and it was manned by a pilot, two copilots, and a crew of seven. Each ship was armed with a .50-caliber machine gun and four 325-pound depth charges. The K-class blimp was powered by two 425-horsepower Pratt & Whitney Wasp engines and cruised at a speed of fifty-seven miles per hour—plenty of speed for their missions. Patrol duty took crews on the lookout for enemy submarines from northern California across the Strait of Juan de Fuca to Vancouver Island.

As Bob Favret, the Tillamook Air Museum's curator, described, "The blimps could outpace all other ships and submarines with ease and stay aloft for three days without refueling. When you consider her impressive range, duration, and limited servicing needs, no other vehicle of the period could come close to touching the blimp's effectiveness for antisubmarine patrol."

As you stand inside this hulk of a hangar (more than seven acres of land enclosed within), gaze up nearly two hundred feet to the arched roof and six-inch-by-fourteen-inch beam support system and realize that about three million board feet of lumber (enough to build 350 three-bedroom homes) were required for this construction. Fortunately, Douglas fir forests thriving nearby provided an abundant source of local lumber.

Though they have passed, the days of Blimp Squadron ZP-33 were certainly significant: ninety thousand U.S. or Allied ships were escorted during World War II, and not a single K-class blimp was lost. This level of service to country is recalled in the impressive exhibits of old photos, written accounts, and other artifacts of the officers and crew who served here. They provide a well-researched, detailed account of a unique chapter in U.S. history.

Another patriotic salute to military service inhabits the giant museum, for the

▶ **You'll enter the "Age of Aces" when you step inside the Tillamook Air Museum in Tillamook County.**

Tillamook Air Museum also whisks visitors back to an era when air battles were waged over the skies of Europe and the Pacific, the time of Spitfires, Messerschmitts, Mustangs, Zeros, Corsairs, and the like—powerful prop-driven aircraft. This "Age of Aces" pitted World War II fighter pilots against one another for control of the air and, ultimately, the outcome of the war. Inside the museum, that era lives on, more than fifty years later, as the museum staff strives to teach visitors the history of military aviation.

Larry Schaible, the museum's manager, recently confided that the museum draws two types of people. "Curiosity drives many to learn more about the hangar building and the blimp stories, but they also come to learn more about our warbirds."

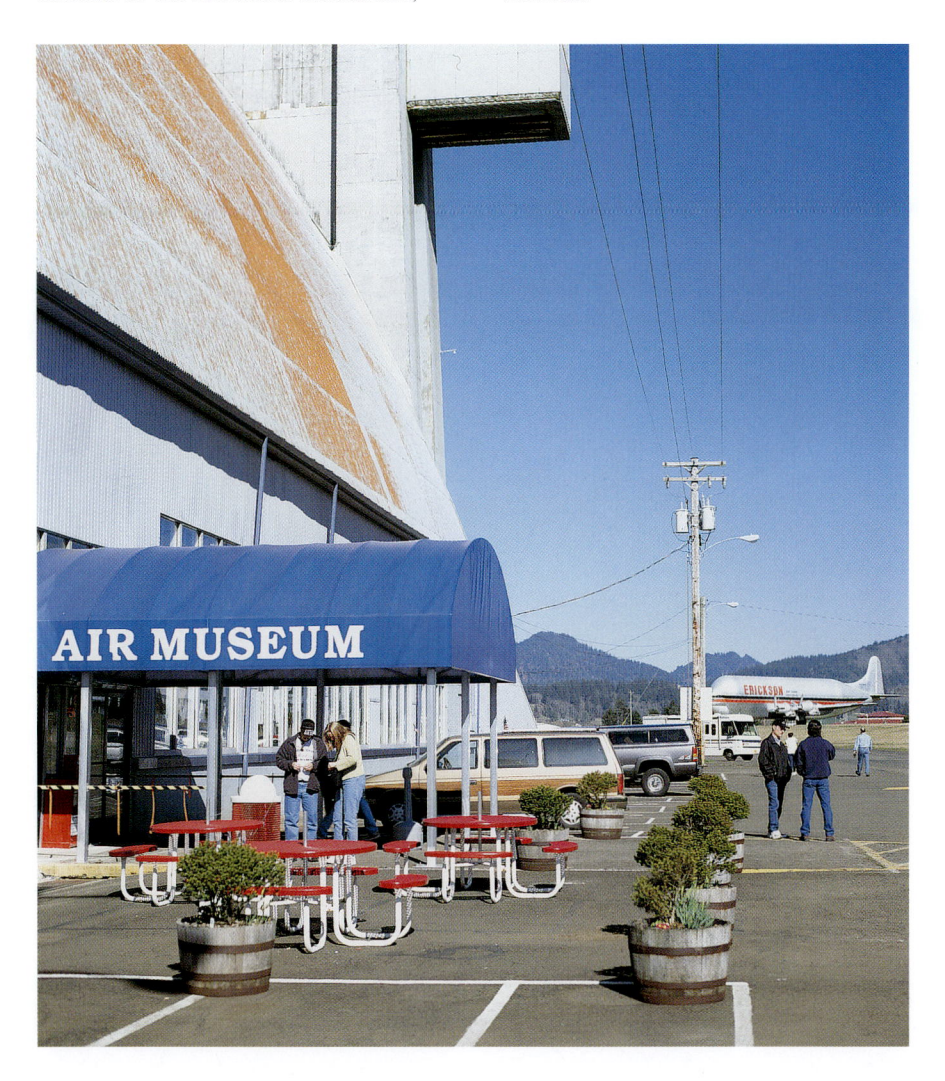

More than fifty vintage aircraft include a PBY-5A Catalina, P-38 Lightning, BF-109 Messerschmitt, P-51 Mustang, and an F4U-7 Corsair that was nicknamed "Old Hognose." According to Larry, "The Corsair was the most famous plane in the Pacific theater during the war. You've seen the pictures of Iwo Jima and Okinawa. Well, the Corsairs would scream by to drop ordnance, often with their landing gear down." He laughed and added, "That was to slow the plane down enough to hit the target accurately. Corsairs flew better than any of the other fighter planes."

While the museum honors aircraft warbird aircraft—its greater dedication is to the people who gave so much for our freedom. "It was a time when everyone—I mean everyone—was working for a common goal and accomplishment," Larry said. "For example, just look at this massive hangar—all of this—the hangar, the runways, the base itself—built in just nine months." He chuckled and concluded wryly, "Today, it would take you longer than that to get a permit."

■ Getting There
Take U.S. 26 west to the junction with Oregon 6. Continue on Oregon 6 for fifty-five miles to U.S. 101 in Tillamook. Continue two miles south on U.S. 101. Turn left at the flashing light, and watch for the A-4 jet trainer displayed on a pole. The museum is wheelchair accessible throughout.

■ For More Information
Tillamook Air Museum, (503) 842-1130

COAST

Secrets in the Sand

Float Fairies

27

In November, except for the surf and wind, the pace of life along the Oregon coastline slows down. Long gone are the jam-packed summer vacation days when the tourist traffic on U.S. 101 speeds by with a deafening roar. Nor are the campgrounds filled with youngsters' raucous, rowdy chorus under a shimmering sun. Those days are on hold—at least for another six months—and there's a very powerful and practical reason for this fact: Fall and winter storms can be downright nasty, scary affairs! They tease you, dare you, and then lash at you in the secluded warmth of your vehicle as you prepare for a beach stroll. Then they descend upon you with a blast that jostles and rattles and shakes your car from side to side. That's before the pelting rain begins—the stuff that pops and explodes across the hood and windshield and then wraps its watery arms completely around you.

No doubt about it, storm watching on the coast is a chilling proposition, but let's also be clear that it can be addicting fun! In fact, there's a growing crowd of storm watchers who thrive in this seasonal mayhem, folks who love to visit the coast when the weather's at its worst. They know there's a breathtaking reward between the storms, especially during a stroll along the seven miles of sandy shoreline at Lincoln City.

As I discovered, fall can be the best time to chance upon unique and artistic "treasures" in the form of beautiful glass floats that have been "seeded" on the beach for you to find. On one chilly, damp, gray November morning, with a promise of glistening sun breaks to entice me, I joined Jennifer Sears and Tony Barnett, Lincoln City's self-proclaimed "float fairies." The duo are part of a small, secret army of volunteers who head out to the Lincoln City beaches each week between October and Memorial Day to hide up to sixty-five stunning glass floats on the beach.

Jennifer explained to me that decades ago the storms would often deposit Japanese glass fishing floats, softball-size greenish globes that had floated for thousands of miles over many years across the Pacific Ocean, where they would finally go ashore on Oregon's beaches. As fishermen converted to plastic floats, the flow of glass floats virtually ended—until three years ago, when the first "Glass Float Odyssey" was born. Originally designed by local artist Bryan Duncan, Lincoln City's inaugural glass float event took place in 2000. The idea was a hit and is now an annual winter event. Along the windswept shoreline near the mouth of the Siletz River, Tony explained, it's the anticipation of finding a special treasure that intrigues so many visitors.

"It is really fun to come down here and actually find something that you can take home with you, say driftwood or agates or shells. I look for places among the logs or little clumps of grass. Sometimes, if there's an open sandy area, I'll just drop one down." He sheepishly grinned and added, "Walk, walk, and walk—it's the only way you're going to find them."

Well, that's not entirely true, for each of the exquisitely colored eight-inch globes is autographed and numbered by one of the area's local glass artists. So if you'd rather not search for treasure on the beach itself, visit one of the artists, like Andrea Schmitz of Pyromania Glass in Newport. Stop in anytime at her family's small store and watch how she and her partner, David Guantlept, create the remarkable glass floats.

First, using a special hollow steel rod, Andrea reaches deep into a two-thousand-degree furnace to pick up a molten glob of silica sand on the end of the rod. She'll then spin and whirl this material, as David blows through the six-foot-long rod, and together the two expand and shape the glass. Soon the glob becomes a gloriously brilliant red glass orb to which colored glass is added.

Like fiery, miniature suns, the glass floats reflect a million moments of colorful light, magical moments that will leave you spellbound. As Andrea offered, her work is a very personal affair. "The whole

FALL ~ Float Fairies

◤ Jewels of glass are waiting for you in the sand of the Lincoln County beaches. Seek and you will find!

digging in the sand, it's a treasure they're going to remember all their lives, so it's well worth it."

Which brings us back to the Lincoln City beaches you can visit anytime—and where those floats are planted. Jennifer noted that every float bears the "Lincoln City" mark and is individually numbered. Once you find a float, you can register it and receive a certificate of authenticity from the Lincoln City Visitor and Convention Bureau. As I hiked alongside Jennifer and Tony and watched them hide a half dozen floats, Jennifer offered a useful tip for visitors: "We'll be out on the beach hiding these floats during the day, between the high-tide line and the base of the cliff. We're not putting them anywhere you'd have to climb up, so look in dips in the sand or around logs, even in small piles of seaweed that have washed ashore." Such helpful advice will help you turn a treasure hunt into a getaway memory of discovery along the coast.

■ Getting There
Lincoln City is about forty-five miles west of Salem via Oregon 22 west to Oregon 18 west to U.S. 101 south.

■ For More Information
Lincoln City Visitor and Convention Bureau, (541) 994-8378, (800) 452-2151

Pyromania Glass, (888) 743-4116

process is a creative experience for me. It's my passion! If I didn't do it, it would be like holding my breath for a really long time. It's like breathing—I have to do this."

Andrea's father, Dennis Schmitz, who owns and operates the small family business based in Newport, added that the reward for their efforts is knowing the pleasure they unlock. "Everybody's fascinated with fire! There's something about that enormous heat and being able to create from something so hot. And then when you talk to an eight- or twelve-year-old child who's found a float while

INLAND

Gaggles of Geese

28

National Wildlife Refuges (Willamette Valley)

They come by the thousands and fill the sky with urgent cries that seem to celebrate their arrival. The endless skeins of Canada geese, like dark silky threads, intersect with one another to weave a multitude of fine, feathery mosaic patterns that mesmerize, transfix, and confound you. Your eyes will be opened wide when you cross paths with such scenes at Baskett Slough, Ankeny, and William Finley National Wildlife Refuges (NWR), the largest collection of refuges in the Willamette Valley. Flock after flock of geese glide to ground to rest and restore themselves on blades of grass following their thousand-mile journey from the distant subarctic reaches of North America. This remarkable wildlife show begins each October as an estimated quarter million geese arrive at the refuges and continues through winter.

For nearly forty years, each refuge has been home to the wintering waterfowl. In fact, a winter sanctuary was one of the main reasons the refuges were established, because each site provides protection for a declining subspecies of Canada goose, the "dusky." For much of the past four decades, the dusky Canada geese (so named for their distinctive chocolate brown breast feathers) have been near the brink of extinction and struggling for survival. The duskies' tale of trouble began in 1964, following a major, magnitude 9.2 earthquake that shook, rattled, and rolled much of Alaska. When the great earthquake hit the southeast corner of the state along the Copper River Delta near the small fishing town of Cordova, the landscape rose as much as eight feet above its historic level. The event transformed the duskies' historic nesting grounds of wetlands and marshes into uplands and deciduous forest. Since the duskies had relied upon the wetlands for relative isolation from predator animals like bears, foxes, and wolves, they became more vulnerable. The drier, easier-to-travel ground with brushy cover was perfect for predators. They soon took a heavy toll on either incubating dusky eggs or newborn goslings. In fact, since the event, some breeding years have produced few, if any, young geese. Over time, as the mature geese grew older, their reproductive abilities declined. Thus began an overall decline in the dusky goose population that continues today.

The Willamette Valley wildlife refuges were created to offer protection to the wintering dusky population, but the duskies are not the only birds in town, so to speak. There are also healthy and abundant populations of six other Canada goose subspecies that thrive in the Pacific Northwest. That's why on any given fall day you will see tens of thousands of geese, ducks, shorebirds, and other waterfowl throughout the refuges.

These days, more people are visiting, too, according to federal wildlife biologist Chris Seal, whom I spoke with recently about wildlife viewing opportunities on the refuges. He said folks are learning of the many new hiking trails that lead to wildlife viewing platforms and offer superb views of a variety of birds. As Chris explained, each refuge is a place whose primary mission "caters to the critters" because the wildlife have lost so much of their historic habitat. We strolled and chatted near the Finley refuge headquarters, which overlook an expansive lake jammed with ducks and geese.

Chris explained, "Ever since European settlement in the valley, waterfowl habitats like ponds, marshes, and sloughs have been severely reduced or eliminated. Conversion to agriculture and more people developing homes or shopping areas have also played significant roles. In fact, today we have less than 10 percent of historic wetland habitat left across the entire Willamette Valley. That makes it tough for waterfowl." Chris added that each refuge is restoring wetlands wherever possible, plus increasing the sizes of roosting and feeding areas for the birds. In addition, since hunting is prohibited on

▶ **Thousands of Canada geese arrive at the wetlands and fields of Ankeny Wildlife Refuge each winter.**

the refuges, the birds are afforded protection from disturbance.

The Finley NWR is the largest of these three refuges and covers more than five thousand acres. It encompasses about a half dozen types of habitats, from Douglas fir forest to oak woodland to oak savannah and rare wetland-prairie country. As you drive along the Finley refuge roads, notice the many colorful, informative kiosks that illustrate the varied wildlife species you will encounter here. Each kiosk also exhibits a brief description of the animals and their biology. Access to this refuge is limited from November 1 through April 15.

Finley NWR was named for renowned wildlife conservationist William L. Finley, who helped found the Oregon Audubon Society in 1902, assisted in setting up Oregon's first Fish and Game Commission in 1911, and served as state game warden from 1910 to 1912. Finley was an avid filmmaker. He and his partner, Herman Bohlman, made their first motion picture in 1910, and in the 1920s and 1930s made several wildlife films of expeditions to Alaska, the Rocky Mountains, British Columbia, and other places. Together, the duo used the films in nationwide lecture tours sponsored by the American Nature Association.

The next-largest Willamette Valley refuge is Ankeny and it's located just south of Salem. Ankeny covers just about 2,800 acres, mostly of level bottomland. Open fields dominate the landscape, and there are shallow ponds favored by migrating waterfowl. Scattered woody patches contain short hiking trails. One of the newest is a quarter-mile-long trail that leads to a wheelchair-accessible boardwalk stretching through a towering oak stand. This novel boardwalk was built several feet above ground level to keep your feet dry during the region's dripping-wet fall and winter months. The trail ends at a large covered photo blind that overlooks a pond brimming with birds, so be sure to bring a camera and a telephoto lens.

At just under twenty-five hundred acres, Baskett Slough NWR sprawls across an ancient lake bed surrounded by oak-studded, rolling hills. It contains grasslands, farmland, three hundred acres of forest, and three hundred acres of shallow wetlands. An information kiosk/visitor center just off Oregon 22 offers a good overall perspective on Baskett Slough.

Take a little time to drive down nearby Colville Road, which bisects Baskett Slough. Your reward will be a closer look at the wildlife, and you'll discover there are more than ducks and geese here. Keep an eye out for raptor species like red-tailed hawks and bald eagles, which are often seen hunting for food or roosting in nearby trees. Colville Road also gives access to Baskett Butte Trail, which winds uphill through open meadow and oak-fir forest and is the only year-round trail on the refuge.

■ Getting There

William Finley NWR: Drive ten miles south of Corvallis along U.S. 99W. Entrance sign is on the west side of the road. Turn west and follow signs about four miles to the refuge office.

Ankeny NWR: Exit Interstate 5 about ten miles south of Salem at Ankeny Hill, exit 243. Follow Wintel Road west (toward Sidney) about two miles to the refuge boundary. (Currently, two viewing kiosks are open and there are numerous turnouts along county roads that provide year-round viewing areas. The first one is located on Buena Vista Road, one mile southwest of the junction of Ankeny Hill and Buena Vista Road, and the second one, with adjacent rest rooms, is on Ankeny Hill Road about a quarter mile southeast of the same junction.)

Baskett Slough NWR: Drive west of Salem approximately ten miles on Oregon 22 to the refuge's entrance and viewpoint where you will find an information kiosk with a detailed map of the refuge road system.

■ For More Information

Finley NWR, (503) 757-7236

Ankeny NWR, (503) 327-2444

Baskett Slough NWR, (503) 623-2749

INLAND

Down by the Ol' Mill Stream

29
Cedar Creek Bridge and Mill

> Since 1876, the Cedar Creek Grist Mill has been a romantic slice of Americana near Woodland, Washington.

The coho salmon migrate home to Northwest streams every fall, offering amazing visual testimony of the instinct that drives a species to survive and reproduce at all costs. Nature's law and salmon biology say but two out of three thousand survive beyond birth to continue their kind.

Two in three thousand! Just think of it! Despite the biological odds stacked against them and in spite of all that people have done to prevent the salmon from achieving their ultimate purpose, they endure. Along southwest Washington's Lewis River, a short cast from the Cedar Creek Salmon Hatchery, anglers cue up on the banks to catch a coho salmon before the run is done. Some successful fishermen will smile and laugh and proudly hoist their gleaming prize for a snapshot, while others sit patiently, waiting and watching their rod tips for the telltale signs of a salmon's bite on the bait. But if you sit too long, you'll miss the salmon's show along a nearby trail that puts you in touch with a distinctive chapter of Lewis River history.

The steep, winding road leading down to the Cedar Creek Covered Bridge isn't the only reason to put on the brakes at this open-frame, big-timbered covered bridge. The bridge's design is worth a moment or two to admire as well. The wooden structure was recently remodeled from the bottom up, thanks to funding secured by the local Friends of the Cedar Creek Grist Mill, a volunteer organization that spearheaded a campaign to restore the bridge. Although some parts of the restored structure are fairly modern (for example, all the necessary members for the decking could not be found, so a steel support frame was used), it is still made completely of cedar, fir, and stone and built in an otherwise traditional manner. The bridge's sides have been left open, which allows more air and light in to help keep the deck dry and to prevent rot, and thus to extend the life of the bridge. From atop the deck, glance twenty feet below and watch the show as the coho salmon parade past you in Cedar Creek. The small stream enjoys a sizable run of the silvery fish, which arrive in late September and continue on this migration route through October.

From the Cedar Creek Bridge, you'll be struck at how the past and present merge in a classic Americana sort of scene. It's really remarkable how the creek, the fish, and the bridge meld into a wistful, yet charming moment.

Across the creek there's even more to delight the visitor. Watch how the big-leaf maple leaves, yellow and burnished by the summer sun, flutter to the ground. Suddenly, your eyes lock on to the profile of an old-time flour mill and its huge churning waterwheel above a roaring stream. This is a Norman Rockwell moment: charming and alluring and guaranteed to put a lump in your throat when you stop to pay a visit.

George Woodham originally built the Cedar Creek Grist Mill in 1876, but it has taken on many faces and many lives in the years since. You can witness several of them when you step inside to take a gander at the historic photo display that shows how the mill looked when it greeted the twentieth century. One early photo shows water spilling over the wooden dam close to the mill building, while another includes a wooden fish ladder that later rotted away. In 1886, Gustav Utter leased the building, brought his own equipment, and installed the double turbine waterwheel that's still in use today. Utter ended up going out of business in 1891, and the mill was in near collapse when Goran Roslund bought it in 1905. He added a cedar shake mill on the side facing the creek and later added a blacksmith shop. The Roslund family held on to the mill and the surrounding eleven acres until 1955, when it was sold to the Washington Department of Fisheries. Today, the Friends of the Cedar Creek Grist Mill lease the site from the state.

The Friends of the Cedar Creek Grist Mill formed in the early 1980s and

FALL ~ Cedar Creek Bridge and Mill

coaxed new life out of the old, but enduring structure. After a decade of effort, grain was ground just as it had been more than a hundred years earlier. From the shore opposite the mill, you can see a 680-foot flume along the creek bank, where a short path leads to picnic tables. The flume channels the water into the mill to supply the power source for its entire operation.

You can visit the Cedar Creek Grist Mill year-round from 1:00 to 4:00 P.M. on Saturdays and from 2:00 to 4:00 P.M. on Sundays. That's when many Friends of the Cedar Creek Grist Mill volunteers and others will be on hand to explain how the mill operates. Friends of the Cedar Creek Grist Mill provide apples and press cider on the last Saturday in October. Visitors are encouraged to bring grains for grinding, too. (Note: There are no fees for the apples or the grain and grinding or for admission, but a donation is always welcome.) All in all, it's a fine way to while away a fall weekend, so put your world on hold and step back in time to enjoy a slower pace of life filled with a comforting nostalgia.

■ **Getting There**

From Portland, take Interstate 5 north to Woodland, exit 21. At the bottom of the exit ramp, turn right and immediately turn right again at the stoplight. Curve to the east to cross the North Fork of the Lewis River. At the fork, turn left toward Amboy onto Northwest Hayes Road, which becomes Cedar Creek Road. About eight miles east of Woodland, a sign points left to the mill.

■ **For More Information**

The Friends of the Cedar Creek Grist Mill, (360) 225-5832

COLUMBIA

Poem in Stone

31

Historic Columbia River Highway

Sam Hill had it right in the early years of the twentieth century when he noted the three things all tourists want most out of an adventure: "A good road to drive on, something worthwhile to see, and something worthwhile to eat."

Times haven't changed much, have they? But in the 1920s, Sam Hill's simple expectations were greatly surpassed by a vision-turned-reality with the completion of the Columbia River Scenic Highway. Hill was the chief backer for what's been called "a poem in stone," the first asphalt link between the Willamette Valley and the high desert. Hill and Sam Lancaster (his chief engineer) and other road builders designed this winding, narrow roadway to showcase the surrounding beauty and magnificence of the region and to replicate what Hill had seen on his many European travels: roadways with bridges, tunnels, and viaducts of stone and mortar with classic design and style. Gently carved from the contours of cliff and hillside, the completed highway was a work of beauty that took full advantage of nature's spectacular scenery in the Columbia River Gorge and was as much fun to experience as the scenery surrounding it. "On starting the surveys, our first business was to find the beauty spots, or those points where the most beautiful things along the line might be seen in the best advantage, and if possible to locate the road in such a way as to reach them," wrote Samuel C. Lancaster, historic Columbia River Highway engineer.

Thousands of laborers lifted picks and shovels and blasted rock and soil to carve the roadway out of sheer basalt walls from 1913 to 1922. They chose a line of least geographic resistance through the Columbia River Gorge in order to connect Portland on the west with The Dalles on the east. The road gave people a place to go with plenty of pretty scenery along the way. However, time and progress had a way of usurping Hill's lofty goals, and by the 1960s the new era of the interstate highway meant an end to Hill's scenic highway. Speed and commerce had become of greater importance than the experience of leisurely travel, and the old highway was forgotten, abandoned, even destroyed in parts. As a result, an entire generation of Northwesterners forgot the wonders of the old scenic highway.

Until recently, that is! Closed since Interstate 84 was completed in the 1960s, today sections of the old highway are being reconstructed in five sections totaling eleven miles of paved hiking and biking trail. The trail's width—eight to ten feet—is broad enough for a family to enjoy on bicycles, and the sections are close enough to Portland to make it a convenient day trip from there.

"I tell a lot of people it's really nice because this is one of the few trails that doesn't just go up into the Gorge. It's very family-friendly," Diane McClay, state park ranger for the Historic Columbia River Highway State Trail, recently told me. "It's a great opportunity for people to come out, recreate, take a leisurely walk, and see some beautiful areas of the Gorge. It's an outdoor recreational opportunity for everybody."

Most segments of the trail are more than ten years old. The most impressive and longest section, the Twin Tunnels, lies between Hood River and Mosier. According to Jeanette Kloos of the Oregon Department of Transportation, the tunnels originally opened in 1921, were seventeen feet wide, and could handle most of the traffic of the time. They were later widened to twenty feet to allow cars to pass, but vehicle sizes continued to grow and soon the tunnels needed stoplights to regulate one-way traffic. In the 1960s, the tunnels fell into disrepair and eventually were closed. Restoration of the two tunnels began in 1995 at a cost of $4.5 million and took five years to finish. The two tunnels span 463 feet, with new wooden beams, stone, and mortar window openings affording stunning views of the Gorge.

Pieces of the past remain. When you

FALL ~ Historic Columbia River Highway

Magnificent scenery is your constant traveling companion along the Historic Columbia River Highway near Mosier, Oregon.

■ Getting There

Section 1: Moffett Creek to Tanner Creek—1.4 miles. From Portland, take Interstate 84 east to exit 40, where you may park at the Toothrock trailhead. Hiking, biking, wheelchair accessible.

Section 2: Tanner Creek to Eagle Creek—1.4 miles. From Portland, take Interstate 84 east to exit 40, where you may park at the Toothrock trailhead. Note: There is a stairway at the Eagle Creek (east) end of the trail. Hiking, biking, wheelchair accessible.

Section 3: Eagle Creek to Cascade Locks—2.4 miles. From Portland, drive east on Interstate 84 to Eagle Creek, exit 41. Park at the Eagle Creek–Cascade Locks trailhead, which is adjacent to the Cascade Fish Hatchery. Hiking, biking, wheelchair accessible.

Section 4: Starvation Creek to Viento—1 mile. From Portland, drive east on Interstate 84 to exit 54, Starvation Creek State Park. Park in the area adjacent to the trailhead. Hiking and biking from Starvation Creek to Viento. Hiking, biking, wheelchair accessible from Starvation Creek trailhead for 0.5 mile east, including Starvation Creek Falls.

Section 5: Hood River to Mosier—4.6 miles. From Portland, drive east on Interstate 84 to exit 64 and follow the signs to the parking area and visitor station at the Senator Mark O. Hatfield West trailhead. Hiking, biking, wheelchair accessible.

■ For More Information
Columbia Gorge National Scenic Area, (541) 386-2333

are inside the western tunnel, look for the inscription that reads, "Snowbound, Nov 19 to 27—1921, Chas J. Sadilek, E.B. Marvin." The message demonstrates that the tunnels offered much more than passage through a mountain. Actually, a snowstorm once forced Charlie Sadilek to take refuge in the twin tunnels on his way home from a goose-hunting trip. He and another stranded motorist spent nine days admiring the sheets of snow from their perch high above the river, while cooking geese and baking apples on camping stoves. The only evidence that remains of their stay is the carving on an inner wall of the tunnel, but it provides a historic footnote for hikers and bikers who use the scenic trail.

Trail construction is expected to continue for many years as money allows, with the laudable long-term goal of opening even more closed sections of the old highway and completing an alternate route to Interstate 84 through the Gorge. Thanks to the new trail, perhaps you too will slow down to enjoy the Columbia River Gorge from a different point of view.

COLUMBIA

Cool Retreat
32
Ice Cave and Indian Heaven

Hey, where are my huckleberry hounds? Who wants to go pick some berries with me?"

That's my call to the family each September when the need to beat the heat drives us north of the Columbia River, not far from White Salmon, Washington, and into the Gifford Pinchot National Forest. It's a place where you will soon discover some truth to the well-known adage "Variety is the spice of life," for this region near massive Mount Adams will certainly satisfy your appetite for adventure and perhaps your hunger for a delicious treat too.

As you travel north from White Salmon on Washington 141 to Trout Lake, watch for the famous White Salmon River, born of glaciers high on the flanks of the nearby mountain. This river serves up a year-round whitewater rodeo of bumps, jumps, and thrills that rival any ride you'll find at a local county fair. For the adventurous, nothing quite compares to a whitewater rafting or kayaking trip on the popular White Salmon River.

Our plans called for a different sort of cool retreat deep down in the ground at the nearby Trout Lake Ice Cave. The cave is actually a lava tube that snaked through the ground during an explosive moment many thousands of years ago. When the lava cooled, a 650-foot tunnel was left behind, according to Linda Turner of the Gifford Pinchot National Forest. The Forest Service has constructed a wooden ladder beneath the main entrance, and Linda advised entering the cave prepared for a very different environment: "You need a flashlight or some source of light because it is absolutely pitch dark down there. Also, bring a hard hat because the ceiling drops as you progress and you don't want to be bumping your head all the time. Also, wear boots as the cave floor is rough, and of course dress warm, 'cause it's chilly down there."

With that, my family stepped down into the cave, lanterns and flashlights ablaze, and we immediately felt the cool air—perhaps thirty or fourty degrees cooler than the simmering surface temperature—surround us. As we made our way, adjusting to the dark, we inched slowly into the deeper recesses of the cave. I could hear water seeping down and across the basalt rock walls and noticed occasional pools of water on the floor. As Linda explained, the warmer surface air thaws some ice, which melts into the cave, where it freezes again. All of this—

➤ **Colorful and delicious huckleberries abound across the Gifford Pinchot National Forest.**

plus the darkness of the experience—contributes to an eeriness not lost on the visitor. Linda offered, "Yes, most people who walk in here feel a sense of exploration in a cave that you just don't get anywhere else. The dark contributes to that for sure, but it's also such a different environment." She paused in the silence for a moment and then offered with a chuckle, "And remember, with caves you can go exploring in them any time of the day or night. It doesn't matter!"

The geologic history and otherworldliness of the Trout Lake Ice Cave make for a compelling experience for sure, but the adventurous family needs to travel only a bit farther into the forest for a true taste of the season. In the nearby Sawtooth Berry Fields, be prepared to enjoy a seasonal treat of fresh-picked huckleberries. If you're lucky enough to meet Rick McClure of the U.S. Forest Service, you will also learn about the significance of huckleberries for countless generations of Native peoples. Rick is an archeologist with the Gifford Pinchot National Forest, and he has a keen interest and appreciation for the historic huckleberry fields of the region. He told me that the berries are as important a food staple and cultural icon to Native Americans as the salmon is.

"Berry picking," Rick recently noted, "brought together people from different tribes, different bands. It involved the entire family—men, women, children—everybody was needed to pick those berries. That's why they'd camp at places like the Sawtooth for five or six weeks. It's a lot of work to pick and prepare berries for winter, but it was critical to stockpile huckleberries because they were a very important food resource."

Traditionally used by Native Amricans, the Sawtooth Berry Fields, west of Mount Adams, are within the Indian Heaven Wilderness. The wilderness consists of 20,600 acres of broad, rolling countryside straddling the crest of the Cascade Range. Archeological evidence indicates the area provided a wealth of resources for Northwest tribes, and for almost ten

HUCKLEBERRY HOME COOKIN'

Rick McClure and Linda Turner of the Gifford Pinchot National Forest have provided the following fine huckleberry recipes. Both the pancakes and the crisp have become featured parts of the McOmie Family Recipe Book. Enjoy!

•

HUCKLEBERRY PANCAKES

¾ cup plus 1 tablespoon unbleached all-purpose flour
½ teaspoon baking soda
½ teaspoon salt
1 large egg
2 tablespoons sugar
1 cup buttermilk
1 teaspoon vanilla extract
4 tablespoons butter, melted and cooled
1½ cups huckleberries
Warm maple syrup

Sift together in a medium-size mixing bowl the flour, baking soda, and salt. In a smaller bowl, lightly beat the egg with the sugar, then stir in the buttermilk, vanilla, and 2 tablespoons of the melted butter. Add the liquid ingredients to the flour mixture and stir until just moistened. The batter should have the consistency of thick cream with some lumps.

Tart and tasty huckleberries are a unique treat in the Northwest.

Do not overmix. Heat a large griddle or two large nonstick skillets over medium-high heat, then brush each lightly with some of the remaining melted butter. Gently pour heaping tablespoonfuls of the batter about two inches apart on the heated skillets. Press a few huckleberries into each pancake and cook until the undersides are golden brown and bubbles are breaking on top, about 1½ minutes. Turn and cook 1½ minutes longer on the other side. Keep the pancakes warm in a low oven as you cook the rest of the batter. Divide the pancakes among warmed plates and serve with warm maple syrup.

•

HUCKLEBERRY CRISP

⅓ cup sugar
2 tablespoons cornstarch
¼ teaspoon cinnamon
¼ teaspoon nutmeg
¼ teaspoon salt
1 tablespoon lemon juice
1 cup huckleberry juice (drained from fruit)
4 cups huckleberries (slightly sweetened)
Topping (recipe follows)

Preheat oven to 400°F.

Combine sugar, cornstarch, cinnamon, nutmeg, and salt in a saucepan. Add lemon and huckleberry juices and stir until smooth. Cook over low heat until thickened and clear, stirring constantly. Stir in huckleberries and pour into a greased baking dish. Sprinkle topping over the huckleberry mixture.

Bake for thirty minutes or until topping is crisp and golden brown. Serve warm or cold.

•

TOPPING

⅓ cup butter
1 cup brown sugar
2 tablespoons flour
3 cups corn flakes

Melt butter in a saucepan. Combine sugar and flour and add to melted butter. Cook, stirring constantly over low heat for three minutes. Add cornflakes, mixing quickly until they are coated with syrup.

CASCADES

Updrafts and Thermals

33

Bonney Butte HawkWatch

thousand years Native people have been traveling to this area to pick berries. During the Great Depression, however, people picked so many huckleberries that an agreement was made between the Forest Service and Native Americans to reserve specific areas of the Sawtooth Berry Fields for harvest only by local tribal members. A handshake agreement in 1932 between William Yallup, chief of the Yakama Nation, and Gifford Pinchot National Forest supervisor K. P. Cecil, set aside about nine hundred acres for the Yakama Nation to gather its traditional food in the berry fields. As Rick McClure pointed out to me, that leaves thousands upon thousands of acres for exploring and gathering up to three gallons of huckleberries per person each year (free of charge, no permit required). Somewhat akin to the domestic blueberry, huckleberries vary in color from deep blue to near purple. Their taste is tart and tangy and absolutely delicious!

The annual huckleberry harvest is still an important part of Native American tradition. Please observe the signs reserving part of the berry fields for the local tribes.

■ Getting There
From White Salmon, Washington, travel north on Washington 141 to Trout Lake, then head west on Forest Service Road 24 for 5.5 miles.

■ For More Information
Gifford Pinchot National Forest, Mount Adams Ranger District, (509) 395-4300

As the summer slips by, birds migrating south are among the surest, earliest signs of the fall season. While shorebirds, ducks, geese, and other waterfowl are among the best-known migrating bird species, close on their tails are thousands of raptors. I have always tried to imagine what it must be like for the lonesome raptors to make their lengthy journeys—they're such an independent lot, not at all like the mass of feathers and wings of flocking species that find safety in numbers.

Imagine for a moment that you are one of the most powerful raptor species on the planet—say, a golden eagle—and you've only so much energy to use for a remarkable passage that stretches from Canada to Mexico. It is now September, time is passing, weather is changing, and your biological clock is ticking. As you learned many seasons ago, your mighty wings will allow you to soar on updrafts and warm thermals for hours at a time, so you make the flight largely by gliding. You rise above mountains and glide down valleys, ascend over ridges and skim down hillsides, using as little energy as possible—all the way—covering an awesome fourteen hundred miles.

The journey will lead you right into the heart of Oregon's Cascade Mountains and across spectacular Bonney Butte, where on a clear day the view onto the southern flanks of Mount Hood is brilliant and awesome. The butte is part of a lengthy north-south ridge lying south of Oregon's Mount Hood, a ridgeline that slices like a wing into the prevailing continental winds. There is high pressure on one side and low pressure on the other—precisely the conditions a raptor looks for and exactly where volunteers with the not-for-profit conservation group HawkWatch International and its Raptor Banding Project stake out each September to count—and to capture, then band—as many raptor species as possible.

The observation post is a lonely watch—from sunup to sundown—as

FALL ~ Bonney Butte HawkWatch

observers sit and count the passing raptors. Less than a quarter mile away, in the cover of a camouflaged blind, a team of scientists and volunteers has another awesome sight much closer at hand, one guaranteed to take your breath away, according to Perry Cabot, a HawkWatch International banding team member. Perry was my host during a recent visit to document the group's efforts for KATU.

◄ Sharp-shinned hawk, part of the tag and release program of HawkWatch International in Mount Hood National Forest.

◤ Bonney Butte is a first-rate and spectacular wildlife laboratory in the Mount Hood National Forest.

With binoculars in hand and sharp eyes peering into the wild blue yonder, Perry explained the group's mission: "We're looking for movement—for specks across the sky, for black dots flying—either against Mount Hood or just above the ridgelines or through the trees. It's often grueling work, just sitting and watching, 'cause the weather's not always clear and warm like today. But our time and efforts sure can pay off."

One small speck on the distant horizon soon becomes a large red-tailed hawk, but on this late-summer day its travel is briefly interrupted. The magnificent bird fixes on something in a clearing below and in front of our blind. But this "something" is actually a lure—or in this case, a pigeon or dove encased in a leather halter. It acts like bait, and the large bird dives into a small opening in the forest canopy, intending to capture its prey. Instead, it flies into a wall of fine-mesh net and is soon tangled. With catlike speed, Cabot bolts to the net and frees the bird.

"Speed is critical," Perry offered, as he quickly worked to release the young hawk's talons and wings from the soft net. "If we don't get them out fast, they could become a target for another raptor." The bird is then hooded and briefly encased in a small metal tube—a harmless confinement, as it immediately went quiet, somewhat like hooding a falcon. The container keeps the avians in the dark and the quiet, and they become very calm. A team of five quickly and quietly weighs, measures, and bands the captured bird to establish a record of it. The bird is then released back to the wild.

At Bonney Butte, the typical fall migration includes up to forty-five hundred migrant raptors made up of eighteen species. The most commonly seen species are the sharp-shinned hawk, red-tailed hawk, Cooper's hawk, turkey vulture, and golden eagle. The scientists with HawkWatch are trying to better understand how, when, and where raptors travel across Oregon, and Bonney Butte's geography has made it a first-rate laboratory. Unfortunately, according to Perry, too many of the massive birds are killed or injured by power lines, car accidents, or people shooting raptors for fun. Thus, while time is critical to every aspect of the operation, it may be most important for the future of raptor species. In addition, since raptors are top-level predators, occupy large home ranges, inhabit most ecosystems, and are sensitive to environmental contamination and other human disturbances, they serve as important biological indicators of ecosystem health.

"We really don't know a lot about the Pacific Northwest flyway," Perry told me and then added, "that's why Bonney Butte is so significant. We're the sole outpost here trying to create that data by getting the birds banded to provide more understanding about where and when so many of these birds are going." With vigilant eyes cast upward toward a backdrop of wonder and beauty, hope rises, too, that new knowledge will keep hawks and eagles soaring across Oregon.

■ **Getting There**
Travel east of Portland on U.S. 26 past Government Camp to Oregon 35 north. Drive four miles, crossing the White River, to the White River East Sno-Park. Turn south onto paved Forest Service Road 48. Drive seven miles and turn left on paved Forest Service Road 4890. Drive 3.7 miles and turn left onto rough and rocky Forest Service Road 4891 and follow signs for 4 miles to the Bonney Butte Campground. Continue past the campground entrance to the spur road on the left. Park here (do not block the road) and walk up to Bonney Butte.

■ **For More Information**
Cascade Chapter/HawkWatch International, (503) 972-6064

CASCADES

Back Road without Numbers
34
Aufderheide Scenic Drive

If the roadway flanking the North Fork of the Willamette River has a number, I care not to find it on a map. That's because I've such a love affair with this backdoor byway that it takes a bit longer to get place to place. I've heard it called "Box Canyon Road," but most travelers I know offer a nod of respect to the man for whom the Robert Aufderheide Memorial Drive was named in 1988. It honors a gentleman who devoted twenty-four years of his life to forestry. Robert Aufderheide was the supervisor of the Willamette National Forest from 1954 until his death in 1959.

The official byway breezes along for more than sixty miles in the Oregon Cascades, beginning near Westfir, just off Oregon 58, east of Eugene. This drive passes tree-framed pastoral farms crying "Photo opp!" and then heads into softly rounded hillsides with hidden campgrounds whose maple trees sport what calendars told us a month ago: the seasons are changing.

This drive parallels both the North Fork of the Willamette River and the South Fork of the McKenzie River, with views to cascading streams and large, old-growth Douglas fir. The paved, two-lane road ranges in elevation from 1,052 to 3,728 feet, with many turnouts for scenic viewing and access to backcountry recreation. The first major point of interest you come to is the Westfir Covered Bridge, which at 180 feet is the longest covered bridge in the state. You are now traveling upon the historic roadbed for a railroad line that was once used to haul fifty million board feet of timber per year from the North Fork drainage down to a mill at Westfir.

Countless feeder creeks trickle across spongy moss-covered rocks throughout the two river basins that are home to this drive. These creeks grow giant and stream-sized and are home waters to husky salmon that have muscled their way back from the salty sea to find their birth homes. Driven by biology, the fish are just in time to spawn and add yet another sign that summer has passed and now it is fall. But the colorful, wonderful show along this back road that I really cherish the most is to witness big-leaf maples, mottled with brown or gray, whose leaves sometime fall gently, gliding past my way. And oh, to be by an orange maple, the brightest of Oregon's autumnal colors: the searing hue of vine maple. At times, the fallen leaves collect in mountain-

▶ The changing seasons are meant to be savored along the wild and scenic South Fork of the McKenzie River.

ous piles along the roadway. Breezes easily kick up a leaf blizzard that makes me feel blissfully young at heart.

The drive can take two hours, an entire day, a never-lonesome week, or a lifetime, as there are many campsites along the way. About seventeen miles into the drive, you'll come to Kiahanie, a U.S. Forest Service campground with twenty-one campsites right on the North Fork. It is open from spring through fall and offers easy river access to the North Fork. Eight miles farther is Constitution Grove, dedicated in 1987 to commemorate the 200th anniversary of the signing of the United States Constitution. A self-guided trail leads you through stunning Constitution Grove, with scores of two-hundred-year-old Douglas firs. The Civilian Conservation Corps and the U.S. Forest Service built Box Canyon Guard Station, at thirty miles into this route, during the 1930s. A replica of the old log station stands near the summit of the drive.

Watch for a roadside monument in Robert Aufderheide's memory. You can spend some time here to enjoy a lunch break with history. Frissel Crossing, Twin Springs, and Homestead Campgrounds are clearly marked along the remainder of this route. You will find them virtually all yours to enjoy as there are usually few folks around. Not too far from Homestead Campground (seven miles on my odometer), you'll reach the French Pete Creek area. The nearby stream is a tributary of the South Fork McKenzie River and was named for French Pete, an early day sheepherder who ranged his band in this area. This South Fork of the McKenzie River is part of the National Wild and Scenic Rivers System and provides opportunities for catching rainbow and cutthroat trout. As the water handsprings over unseen rocks, leaves drop to placid pools where barely a ripple marks the moment. Anglers know these places and will likely be the only faces on a byway whose prime time is passing. So hurry soon, then slow down on a back road without a number—one of the very best around.

The Robert Aufderheide Memorial Drive is but a section of the much longer West Cascades Scenic Byway, a 220-mile scenic route filled with waterfalls, old-growth forests, countless campgrounds, and quiet Cascade lakes. An audiocassette or CD is available for travelers of the Robert Aufderheide Memorial Drive segment of the West Cascades National Scenic Byway. It can be picked up and returned, free of charge, at the Blue River Service Center, the Middle Fork Ranger District, and the McKenzie Ranger District offices.

■ Getting There
Take Interstate 5 to the junction with Oregon 58. Take Highway 58 east and drive thirty-two miles to the Westfir junction (the Oakridge Ranger Station is on the right). Turn left. Cross the bridge and turn left again. The official Memorial Drive begins in four miles.

■ For More Information
Willamette National Forest, (541) 465-6521

Oregon Parks and Recreation Department, (800) 551-6949

CENTRAL/EASTERN

Where the Antelope Play

35 ~ Hart Mountain

The waning days of fall can be lonely times on the high desert, when a cold, biting wind accompanies the dim morning light at Hart Mountain National Antelope Refuge in southcentral Oregon. The landscape surrounding the refuge is remote by any stretch of the imagination, and it is a place filled with contrasts: It is not the classic, snowcapped peak but more a massive volcanic ridge jutting above the desert. Its west side soars sharply from the Warner Valley floor to nearly a mile high via a series of rugged cliffs and steep ridges. The east side is rounded, more gentle, and easier to traverse. And it is distant—hundreds of miles from the nearest town of any size—yet, for all its loneliness, if you wait patiently and watch carefully, you may be taken aback by the number of foraging herds of pronghorn antelope, families of bighorn sheep and mule deer, plus flocks of sage grouse that make the refuge home.

At its western base, another gathering occurs each year when several dozen wildlife experts from state and federal agencies come together in a fascinating project called the California Bighorn Sheep Roundup. It's a capture-and-transplant project that's now moving into its fourth decade, and it's made the difference in restoring a species that was once near the brink of extinction. Original herds of the California bighorn sheep, a species native to the western U.S., disappeared from Oregon in the 1920s as a result of competition with livestock for food, too much hunting, and too many people building farms, ranches, and homesteads across the desert. But the bighorns scored some success in 1954 when a herd of twenty sheep was successfully reintroduced to the federally managed refuge. The herds were protected on the refuge and they have thrived.

The year I visited the project for a special KATU news report, I quickly discovered that the heart of the bighorn sheep roundup is teamwork and technology. The former comes through cooperative participation and the expertise of state and federal wildlife biologists, plus staff and volunteers from several sport and conservation organizations. The technology is in the form of a Jet Ranger 206 helicopter that makes capture of the elusive animals easier. During my visit, the plan was to capture up to fifty bighorns that were to be moved to four other Oregon sites.

State wildlife biologist Jim Torland told me that the helicopter makes the otherwise impossible job possible. "When you're going after the bighorns, you must go where they live," he explained. "This is such unforgiving, difficult country to cover on foot, and it's impossible with vehicles, so the chopper allows us access up narrow defiles, canyons, and steep slopes. If we can find the sheep on the flats at the top of the mountain, man, then it's all gravy at that point."

As news photographer Bob Jaundalderis and I climbed aboard the ship to document the capture, I could see every aspect of this annual Hart Mountain Bighorn Sheep Roundup (BSR) depended upon teamwork, especially between the helicopter pilot and his "gunner," the person who sits strapped into the ship near the open side door. The gunner and the pilot are in constant radio contact, as each scans the landscape for the bighorn herds. Once spotted, the twosome chooses an animal—either a male or female—and descends to just yards above it, then speeds with it across the ground. The gunner selects just the right animal and then fires his handheld "net gun." This high-tech tool, cradled and shoulder-mounted just as a hunter might handle a rifle, utilizes a .30-caliber blank cartridge. When fired, the blank propels four weighted ends of a heavyweight fifteen-square-foot mesh net. The weights are brass cylinders that shoot out and open the net in the air. It then descends around the animal like a huge bag.

It is a fascinating capture process and it happens in a heartbeat, but the effort takes precise timing and no small amount of courage for both the pilot and the gunner. After all, the sheep are fast—and elusive—as they dart across the ground at speeds reaching thirty miles an hour. Once an animal has been enveloped by the giant net, a critical third team member, called a "mugger," immediately jumps from the ship to the ground. He hobbles the animal's front and hind legs with leather straps and bindings to protect himself and the animal from harm. Then a critical period begins as the mugger monitors the sheep's temperature. The sheep's temperature is a reliable indication of its stress level. If it's above 107 degrees, the mugger must cool the animal with ice-cold water. I watched as a ewe, a young female, was cooled with canteen water and then carefully loaded into another, larger ventilated mesh bag for transport. Within minutes, the *whoosh-whoosh-whoosh* of the chopper's blades was heard, signaling its return. A cable was dropped from the ship, which the mugger attached to the bagged animal. Slowly and carefully, the animal was lifted into the cream-colored sky and then flown back to base camp.

Challenged by steep terrain, howling winds, and temperatures that can drop to thirty below zero, the BSR is certainly a test of teamwork, but it's teamwork that doesn't end with the capture, for it continues as the animal is gently dropped into the waiting arms of the biologists at base camp. Speaking little and only in hushed tones, each team of four scientists works quickly and efficiently on each captured sheep. Like a precise, well-oiled machine, the crews continue to monitor the bighorn's body temperature, collect blood samples, and then inject each animal with antibiotics to protect it against infections. An ear tag is also attached to each sheep to help with later identification. Biologist George Keister explained to me that every effort is made to ease the animal's stress. "We want the animals as calm as we can keep them through the entire process. Many, many studies over the years have shown that, given our level of care following capture, this procedure has the lowest immediate and long-term stress compared to other capture methods on these animals." It's also the most efficient method.

While the helicopter capture project is expensive, the costs are offset by the sale of hunting licenses, tags, and permits. Once hunted to near extinction, the California bighorn numbers now exceed five thousand in more than forty sites across eastern Oregon. It's a special program, blending human technology with a commitment to restore a species.

I hope your visit to Hart Mountain National Antelope Refuge is as exciting as mine have been over the years. I have learned that each season offers something new and special to see and experience. Binoculars or a spotting scope is a must for seeing bighorn sheep and other wildlife from either the base of Hart Mountain on the way into the refuge from the west or from Flook Knoll, eight miles east of refuge headquarters. All camping is located at the Hot Springs Campground, four miles south of refuge headquarters. Located within the campground is the Hot Springs Bathhouse, which consists of a hot spring enclosed in a cement building for year-round use. There are pit toilets; however, none are currently wheelchair accessible. No RV hookups, no drinking water, and no firewood are to be found. Free permits are required for all overnight stays. The permits are self-issued at refuge headquarters (open twenty-four hours a day), where there is also a rest room. No gas is available at Hart Mountain.

A bit of good news: There is abundant wildlife! The best way to see sheep, antelope, or deer is to take a daylong hike into one of the canyons from the base of the mountain. Keep in mind that there are no hiking trails, but some graded roads can be walked or driven. Warning: These roads are rough and rugged, so be prepared to be on your own in a wilderness setting for an extended time. Four-wheel-drive vehicles are highly recommended.

■ Getting There

From Lakeview, go north, then east, on Oregon 140 for twenty-two miles. Turn north at the Plush/Hart Mountain junction and go twenty miles to Plush. At the north end of Plush, turn east onto the Frenchglen/Hart Mountain Refuge Road for twenty-five miles to the refuge field station.

■ For More Information

Hart Mountain National Antelope Refuge, (541) 947-3315

◣ **Aspens and junipers hug Hart Mountain.**

CENTRAL/EASTERN

36 ~ Treasures from the Earth

Richardson's Rock Ranch

> The creamy center of a thunder egg reveals simple, exquisite beauty.

Call me "homesick," but I cannot help myself when the seasons transition and a longing builds to get back to the Oregon desert, toward a branch of the family's roots in central Oregon along the Deschutes River—especially during the in-between cycle from summer's blistering, white-hot heat to winter's bone-numbing cold. The fall months can be splendid times of climate moderation across the desert, and I love to point the family's travel compass east to Deschutes River State Park for the start of a relaxing, activity-filled weekend. It's a place you've likely seen along Interstate 84, but perhaps overlooked as an overnight destination. Too bad, for the rimrock-lined landscape just beyond the depths of the Columbia River Gorge and before you reach the flat-as-a-pancake sage and juniper country provides an intriguing, tree-shaded overnight oasis for campers.

Deschutes River State Park is a rambling state recreation area with camping that offers a front-row seat on a glorious and gorgeous waterway that swirls and ripples before the Deschutes and Columbia Rivers converge in a gigantic rocky canyon. There is no finer place for family outing activities like hiking, biking, camping, rafting, world-class steelhead and trout fishing, and equestrian trail riding. The Atiyeh Deschutes River Trail (named for former Oregon governor Victor Atiyeh, who was instrumental in protecting and securing public access to this stretch of river in the 1980s) reaches twenty-three miles upriver from the park. The river canyon is sheltered and warm and provides a great escape for enjoying both a national and state scenic waterway.

You'll find thirty-four campsites in the park with electricity and a day-use picnic area with shoreline picnic tables, as well as a large area for tent campers, with rest rooms (but no showers). There's even a covered wagon to entice and entertain the youngsters who can unroll their bags and make an adventurous overnight stay. It's a laid-back, relaxed campground where folks come pretty much for one reason. You see, beginning in late August and continuing through November, the lure of silver-bright oceangoing rainbow trout—steelhead—draws anglers from across the country. Park ranger Darryl Fitzwater told me that the park's reputation is well-known in angling circles, "Absolutely no question about it. People come here for the fishing. Some bring their boats and go upriver, and some raft down from up in the river canyon. Many have discovered that the Atiyeh Trail is perfect for mountain bikes, so they use them to go upriver and fish down."

The nearby Heritage Boat Landing is located across the river from the state park and is a popular launch point where river guides meet their clients or anglers cast lures into the river's seams between fast water and smooth in hopes of catching salmon, steelhead, or trout. Many anglers leave at first light and don't return until dusk, which means that during the day you have the campground all to yourself. Plus, as Darryl noted with a smile, "Fishermen are such early risers. They don't stay up late, so you can hear a pin drop in this campground after about nine o'clock."

If you're like me, you're bound to be curious when traveling the wide-open spaces of Oregon. I need to know everything I can. That's how it is when we leave Deschutes River State Park and head south on U.S. 97 searching for the sixty million years of geologic history found in the Oregon state rock: thunder eggs. I cherished these magical, mysterious golf ball–size rocks as a child for their drab exterior, but their oh-so-creamy and colorful agate interiors continue to be trophy prizes for young and old rock hounds alike. Technically a thunder egg is not a rock: It's a nodule or a geode that forms inside other rocks. Yet, if you were to judge by the throngs of visitors who stream through the Richardson's Rock Ranch, just off U.S. 97 near Madras, thunder eggs are without question the most popular rock in Oregon. The expansive fourteen-thousand-acre ranch allows rock hounds the opportunity to dig and discover countless secrets in the soil.

On a recent visit to the ranch, Jessie Richardson, the owner's granddaughter, helped guide the McOmie clan to a mother lode of thunder egg heaven. Armed with rock hammers, shovels, and insatiable appetites for the unexpected, the five of us were anxious to do some digging in the dirt—and it didn't take long to hit pay dirt. The technique isn't too difficult either. You simply kneel down and hammer, scrape, chisel, and mine the dirt away from the egg.

Thunder eggs were first discovered in this area during the 1920s by a rancher named Leslie Priday. For the last twenty-five years, the Richardson family has owned and operated its recreational rock ranch for eager tourists who can dig their own treasures or purchase them inside a small lapidary shop. As young Jessie, who's grown up exploring the nooks and crannies of the rock ranch, explained, "The really neat part is that when you dig up a thunder egg and bring it down to have us cut it open, well, you're the first person to have ever seen that rock. And to think it took sixty million years to make it, plus there's no two alike, they're all different—and the next one is going to be the very prettiest one you've ever cut."

Typically, an egg has a drab, gray-colored outer shell that can be knobby or smooth and may sport a ribbed pattern around its exterior. Eggs can range in size from less than an inch in diameter to more than a yard. When they are cut open, they reveal agates of various colors and exquisite designs that stand out when they're polished. Johnnie Richardson, the ranch owner and operator, teasingly declared that all you need to make a thunder egg "is a volcano that produces lava rich in silica, the stuff of which quartz is made. As the lava cools, steam and gases trapped within the lava form bubbles. The beauty is in the bubbles."

Inside the Richardson's Ranch lapidary shop, you'll discover that thunder eggs can be made into beautiful, varied jewelry, especially pendants, pen stands, and bookends. But I have discovered that the simple beauty and complexity of these geologic wonders are best appreciated when the egg is carefully cracked open and placed on display to reveal a moment from a distant past that's been frozen in time. Johnnie Richardson has a simpler explanation: "Everybody likes to get outdoors as a family and do something together and maybe you get a little dirty digging in the ground. But heck, you get to take your prizes home, and a five-gallon bucket of thunder eggs only costs about twenty-five dollars. That's not bad for a day together."

■ Getting There

Deschutes River State Park: Drive Interstate 5 east from Portland approximately ninety-five miles.

Richardson's Rock Ranch:

From Portland: Take U.S. 26 east over Mount Hood. Continue to Madras, and take U.S. 97 north about eleven miles to the Richardson's sign at milepost 81. Continue another three miles; signs point the way.

From The Dalles: From Interstate 84, take U.S. 197 south to U.S. 97, and go south (right) to the sign for the ranch about eleven miles north of Madras.

From east of The Dalles: Take Interstate 84 and exit at U.S. 97 south, and go south to the sign for the ranch about eleven miles north of Madras.

■ For More Information

Deschutes River State Park, (800) 551-6949; reservations, (800) 452-5687

Richardson's Rock Ranch, (541) 475-2680

Prineville Chamber of Commerce, (541) 447-6304

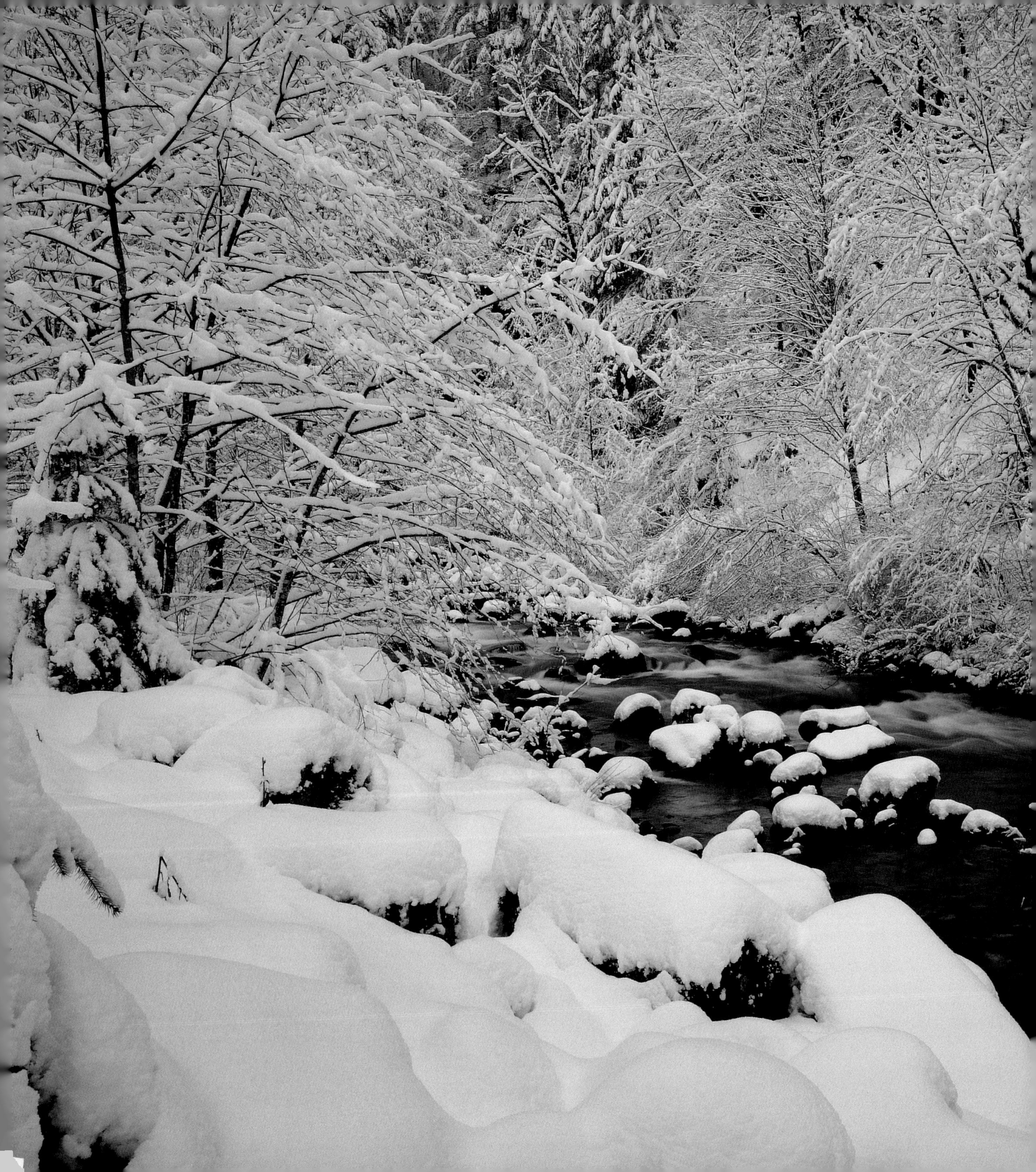

Winter

Adventure is not in the guidebook

and Beauty is not on the map.

Seek and ye shall find.

On the Loose, Terry Russell

◀ Nature's touch restores the soul along the Nestucca River Back Country Byway in Tillamook County.

COAST

37
Lewis and Clark Slept Here
Fort Clatsop National Memorial

According to Janice Elvidge, a spirited and always-enthusiastic park ranger who dons buckskins and fires flintlocks at Fort Clatsop National Memorial, park rangers will teach you—rain or shine—more about the day-to-day lives of the famous early explorers than any history book could. "We make the setting, create the feeling, serve up the moments that put you in the shoes of what it was like for Lewis and Clark and the Corps of Discovery to live in Oregon nearly four long winter months."

This memorial is the place where Lewis and Clark's Corps of Discovery camped near the Columbia River from December 7, 1805, until March 23, 1806. They comprised the first U.S. government–sponsored scientific expedition to the West Coast, within whose ranks were thirty-six inquisitive and determined men and one woman of commercial, military, scientific, and literary backgrounds. As Janice described, the corps filled the roles of biologist, botanist, cartographer, diplomat, ethnographer, geographer, geologist, physician, soldier, zoologist, and journalist.

"Their dedication to the task of finding a Northwest Passage across America was uncanny, their teamwork remarkable!" she said. "In spite of back-breaking labors, plaguing fleas, prickly pear cactus, hunger, and a myriad of other anxieties, they met their task and succeeded. We try to give visitors a sense of their accomplishments and their ordeals."

You could say "hands on" is the way of the world at Fort Clatsop, too. Park rangers like Janice will show you every aspect of the explorers' day-to-day life. From simple candle making to the more challenging job of carving a canoe, no detail is left unexplained. Curt Johnson, also known as "Mr. Fort Clatsop" to friends and staff, often has daily duty at this historic outpost. He worked here as a park ranger for twenty-one years, but no longer. Now retired, his love of U.S. history brings him back to Fort Clatsop as a volunteer. If you're lucky enough to spend a few moments with Curt, you'll learn much about this distant, yet distinctive, chapter of America's story.

"Think of it, Grant. For nearly nineteen months and four thousand miles, members of the Lewis and Clark Expedition risked their lives and limbs to reach the Pacific Ocean. The members hauled their boats against the Missouri River's currents. They suffered intolerably from the mosquitoes, walked hundreds of miles barefoot across prickly pear cactus, faced the formidable Sioux, ate animal-fat candles for lack of food. And then they arrived to live under endless cloudy, cold, and rainy conditions here along the Oregon coast. They were something special."

Covered head to toe in history as well as buckskin and fur, Curt has lost track of how many people he's taught about the hardships of the wilderness and how truly amazing an expedition it was.

"I have a gift for gab with people. It does get me in trouble once in awhile though!" he chuckled. "I get to talking with folks about the expedition and share information with them. For example, it

◂ A crackling, warming fire is an inviting touch inside the winter quarters of Lewis and Clark at Fort Clatsop near Astoria.

▸ Walk through these opened gates and you'll touch history at Fort Clatsop National Memorial.

was really the abundance of elk that led to the establishment of Fort Clatsop in this area. And boy did they kill elk! While half of the men built the fort, the other half formed hunting parties. Armed with flintlock rifles and muskets, the hunters didn't have to range far to find food. On December 13, they shot eighteen elk in one day. That was a Fort Clatsop record."

According to Curt, the elk provided the explorers with many things: food, hides for clothing and blankets, and fat for tallow candles. Antler was made into buttons. Brains were used for tanning hides into leather. Nothing was wasted. Extra meat was smoked and dried as jerky and stored in the fort's meat room for issue to the squads during the wet, gray winter.

A sunny day would have been rare at Fort Clatsop during the 114 days that Lewis and Clark stayed there: Only sixteen were without rain. The fort's thick log walls and pitched cedar roof were designed to keep the weather and invaders out. Speaking of the fort, keep in mind that what you see today is a replica, a 1955 community-built reproduction based upon the floor-plan dimensions drawn by Clark on the elk-hide cover of his field book. Two parallel rows of cabins, about fifty feet to a side, are connected by palisades and gates. The enlisted men's quarters occupied one side; interpreter Toussaint Charbonneau and his family's quarters, captain's quarters, an orderly room, and a storeroom occupied the other side. In 1958 the Oregon Historical Society donated the site of the fort to the federal government and it became part of the national parks system.

Curt is also quite adept at dispelling many myths about the Corps of Discovery, such as the one that Lewis and Clark were the only ones at the fort. They were not. "That's probably one of the biggest myths. Who was on the expedition and who did what? I try to stress that these many men were a team. I mean, think about it. They made five canoes in ten days. Pretty tough for two people to do alone, eh?"

Curt, like each member of the Fort Clatsop team, is eager to be your guide, especially if you have a hunger for history. They want to make certain you go home full of the truth. As Curt likes to say, "I want folks leaving and saying to each other 'By golly that was fun coming by Fort Clatsop today. I really learned something.' To hear that, just makes my day, makes my life worth living."

■ Getting There
Fort Clatsop is located approximately one mile south of Astoria on U.S. 101.

■ For More Information
Fort Clatsop National Memorial, (503) 861-2471

COAST

Keep the Beacon Burning

38

Heceta Head Lighthouse

Rushing to the coast to watch winter storms has long been one of my peculiar pastimes. That's because monster waves are such powerful events to watch, plus the coastline seems all mine to explore when winter is a bit ragged around the edges. Given that, the Heceta Head Lighthouse, perhaps Oregon's most famous lighthouse, seems a bright respite on a gloomy ocean, for its powerful beacon reaches far out to sea. Set atop a clearing amid otherwise forested cliffs that tower over the sea, Heceta (pronounced "ha-SEE-tah" by many, "HECK-ah-tah" by some, and "HEE-see-ta" by still others) displays a moody personality when the rainy season arrives each winter. That was perhaps even more true a couple of years ago when the light faded to black for several months. Not too long ago, I was invited to join a small gathering of experts charged with the awesome task of bringing Heceta Lighthouse back to life. Or should I say "back to light"?

First, the basics. As beacons of reassurance for mariners at sea, Oregon lighthouses (nine of them) have provided a tradition of service for more than a century. Heceta Head is the most powerful marine light on the Oregon coast and is named for Portuguese explorer Don Bruno Heceta who set sail from Mexico in 1775 to explore the Northwest coast and identified the headland in his writings.

Heceta Head Lighthouse first cast its light in March 1894 from its height of 205 feet above the ocean. The Chance Brothers of London made the glass prisms for what's known as a first-order Fresnel lens. It consisted of eight panels made up of 640 prisms, each one two inches thick. Back then, the lens revolved once every eight minutes, controlled by a system of weights called clockworks that were wound by hand every four hours, even during the night. The light source inside the lens consisted of a five-wick kerosene burner that generated eighty-thousand candlepower. In 1934, electric power was installed and the burner was replaced with a five-hundred-watt bulb that increased the candlepower to over a million. The manually operated clockworks were also converted to an electrical system and the lighthouse received a new flash system that enabled the light to flash every ten seconds. The light source was again updated in 1963, this time with a thousand-watt quartz iodide bulb, which produced a stunning 2,500,000 candlepower.

All of this history is important when you consider what occurred during the winter of 2001 when—after 107 years—the time had come for an overhaul. The U.S. Coast Guard, the U.S. Forest Service, and Oregon State Parks jointly undertook the first-ever cleaning and updating of the very old fixture. A process called "rust-jacking" had caused the base to deteriorate to such a point that its weight had shifted and it was out of plumb, hence the light beam was no longer accurate. In addition, the glue that held the prisms in place—known as "letharge"—was deteriorated. Jim Woodard, a serious-minded U.S. Coast Guard officer—and one of a handful of lighthouse experts in the world—was the manager on the scene for the eight-week project. He explained to me that Heceta's need for repair was critical and her light could shatter anytime.

"The glass is extremely fragile, and the material it's put together with is completely disintegrating. You have to be extremely careful, too, because this 107-year-old glass is very brittle. Unfortunately, the prisms are resting glass to glass. That is, the glue has failed, so there's nothing holding it together anymore."

A seven-person crew, whose motto was "Bodies heal, glass doesn't," painstakingly removed each glass prism—hundreds of them—as well as the massive iron base—2.5 tons worth—for repair. All of the pieces were slowly, gingerly roped down through the yardstick-wide spiral staircase with straps and winches. The $50,000 restoration was paid for by the U.S. government, but Woodard noted that Heceta is but one of scores of failing lighthouses across the country.

"It is worrisome to me in that all of these lenses are reaching their life expectancy and they all need to have some attention. Our nation's lighthouses really demand some love and care or we're going to lose them."

Heceta's repairs have given new life to a lighthouse that's not only a sentinel by the sea but also a link to another time. That's important—and a rare opportunity for you to touch a piece of history. The new light makes Heceta Head Lighthouse the brightest one on the West Coast—something to consider the next time you visit. Tours of the lighthouse are conducted mid-March through October and on weekends just prior to Christmas. There is no charge for tours, but donations for restoration projects are gladly accepted.

You may also wish to visit the nearby keeper's house, an interpretive center by day and a bed-and-breakfast by night. Placed on the National Register of Historic Places in 1978, the Queen Anne–style home has been restored to its original splendor. Perched on a cliff with a magnificent view of the Pacific Ocean and the beach below, the B&B welcomes guests year-round. A seven-course gourmet breakfast is served each morning in the dining room and is included in the price of the room.

Not far away and connected by a short hiking trail from Heceta Head Lighthouse and the keeper's cottage, is Heceta Head State Park, which includes nearby Devil's Elbow. You can choose just the right picnic site from a scattering of picnic tables offering dazzling views to the ocean. Bring your binoculars to enjoy the show on the nearby rock islands, where views of varied wildlife, including gulls and cormorants or sea lions, can be enjoyed.

■ Getting There
From Interstate 5, take Santa Clara–Florence exit 195B, Beltline Road. Stay on Beltline until it dead-ends at West 11th, which will be Oregon 126. Turn right and stay on Oregon 126 for approximately sixty miles until you reach Florence. Turn right (north) on U.S. 101 and drive twelve miles to the lighthouse.

■ For More Information
Washburne State Park, (541) 547-3416

Heceta Head Keeper's House B&B, (541) 547-3696

◣ Holiday lights on the Keeper's House Bed and Breakfast with Heceta Head Lighthouse at Devil's Elbow State Park.

INLAND

The Community That Flocks Together

Jackson Bottom Wetlands

39

"Whatizthat?"
"Whatizthis?"
"Wherezitfrom?"
"Wherewegoinnow?"
"Huh? Mr. McOmie, huh? Whatizit?"

Field trips are interesting affairs! I call them my "Whatizit?" trips—the times when I volunteer to lead groups of youngsters on an outdoor adventure to teach them more about the natural world, times when my energies are tested to the max, as a somewhat-uncomfortable knot develops in my neck from the quick swish panning this way or that to answer all of their questions.

"Mr. McOmie, Mr. McOmie, whatizthatbird, whatizthatplant, whatizthatfish?"

Yet I love to teach young people about the great outdoors! I started my professional life in a classroom, and I always considered my jump into television broadcasting but an expansion of the class size. But the truth be told, television audiences can never be reached in the same way. There's a special moment when you can see that light bulb of new knowledge click on in a youngster's eyes, followed by a nod and a knowing smile. That's my reward for time outdoors.

One of the friendliest places to see what's new in the outdoors is at one of the newest wildlife areas of the Portland metro region. Situated on the southern doorstep of one of the fastest-growing communities in Oregon, Jackson Bottom stretches across more than seven hundred acres near Hillsboro in Washington County. It offers varied wildlife habitat of marshes, meadows, ponds, and Douglas fir and ash tree stands that in turn attract all kinds of wild animals—especially birds: from waterfowl to blue herons to such raptors as hawks and eagles.

Pat Willis, who is the preserve's director, recently told me that attitudes about wetlands are changing. "Our wetlands and marshes have always been treated as forgotten corners of the local neighborhood or city. Most communities have looked the other way when they deal with these areas because marshes weren't considered very pretty. Truth is, these places are rich and diverse and hold many secrets about keeping our water clean—and our wildlife thriving. Wetlands really are critical to a healthy plant and animal community."

Jackson Bottom, notes Pat, was little more than "a dumping ground" for many decades. The open meadow areas were often grazed over by cattle, and even local businesses would dump all manner of waste and debris on the land. The attitude reflected a simple philosophy of "Out of sight, out of mind." That attitude began changing in the early 1970s when people saw that wetlands, marshes, and other so-called marginal lands might deserve a different perspective. That is, these places are important, and if wetlands could be restored, wildlife could be helped, too. According to Pat, an ambitious project and partnership began at Jackson Bottom using water supplemented in the drier summer by treated wastewater from the nearby Clean Water Services wastewater treatment plant. The landscape was sculpted with bulldozers into pondlike areas and filled with the treated wastewater, which helped restore the wildlife habitat. The water became even cleaner as it was filtered through native grasses and sedges, bushes, and trees, before it was returned to the nearby Tualatin River. Is it working? According to Pat Willis, absolutely!

A measure of that has been the dramatic increase in populations of wildlife, such as frogs, turtles, great blue herons, and waterfowl that nest in the cattails and sedges. In winter, the remarkable sight of several bald eagles is great testimony to the wetland's value. In fact, not only wintering bald eagles, but also a nesting pair, have made Jackson Bottom their home for the past four years. Pat noted that ten years ago, it was rare to see a bald eagle. Today, more often than not, you'll see one or two or more—perched like ornaments in tall trees from one of several viewing platforms that have been strategically placed across the preserve. With their bold white caps and tail feathers, the big raptors are easily identifiable. And the eagle nest is gigantic and hard to miss. Each year the pair of adult birds has added more sticks and branches to their nest, so that today the five-foot-tall nest is very distinct and prominent.

"The bald eagles really are more common," Pat offered, "and that's good because it shows that we've been doing something right in growing good habitat for many other smaller species. Without good habitat we wouldn't have an intact food chain to keep the eagles soaring. Those magnificent birds are a key indicator of healthy food, water, and shelter. Plus, the eagles have attracted more people to Jackson Bottom. It's the first time in Hillsboro's recorded history that bald eagles have nested in the city limits—and that's pretty amazing."

Aside from the designated view sites, you are encouraged to hike at Jackson Bottom, perhaps by strolling down the Kingfisher Marsh Trail to enjoy the sites and sounds of the thousands of Canada geese that winter on the preserve. Or step inside the new Jackson Bottom Wetlands Preserve Education Center to discover a six-thousand-square-foot education facility with classrooms, interpretive exhibit areas, and staff space. Another successful outreach program is the weekly "Lunch with the Birds," when you can visit with one of the preserve's staff members for an hour or two, learn more about the wildlife and the preserve, and almost always see some pretty amazing wildlife. Jackson Bottom Wetlands Preserve is a very special place that's exploding with amazing educational opportunities—and it's all there for your exploration and enjoyment.

◾ **Getting There**
From Hillsboro, drive south on Oregon 219 for approximately a half mile. Watch for signs to the viewing areas and the education center.

◾ **For More Information**
Jackson Bottom Wetlands Preserve, (503) 681-6424

◀ Don't forget your binoculars when you visit the birder's paradise called Jackson Bottom Wetlands Preserve near Hillsboro, Oregon.

▲ From wasteland to wetland, the Jackson Bottom Wetlands is a remarkable wildlife success story.

INLAND

In the Comfort of Your Car

40
Ridgefield National Wildlife Refuge

They come by the thousands to the crew-cut stubble fields, cornrows, and placid backwater ponds back-lit by dazzling winter sunshine. Tucked into the comfort of a camouflage blind, I relish a moment that's filled with the sound of flurry in flight. The sight of score upon score of Canada geese, packed in tight-knit waves, swooshing by just overhead on their fixed wings, takes my breath away. There is stillness at daybreak on this fine winter's day, and the calls of the excited geese echo across the scene. The big birds are jockeying for the best position on which to land on the widespread dining table of green grass, and they seem to bellow and blare this news: "We—Canada geese—some thirty thousand strong—have arrived at our new winter home at the Ridgefield National Wildlife Refuge along the Columbia River." The refuge was established in 1965 (along with three refuges in Oregon's Willamette Valley) in response to a need to protect vital habitat for the dusky Canada goose subspecies whose nesting areas in Alaska had been severely affected by the violent earthquake of 1964.

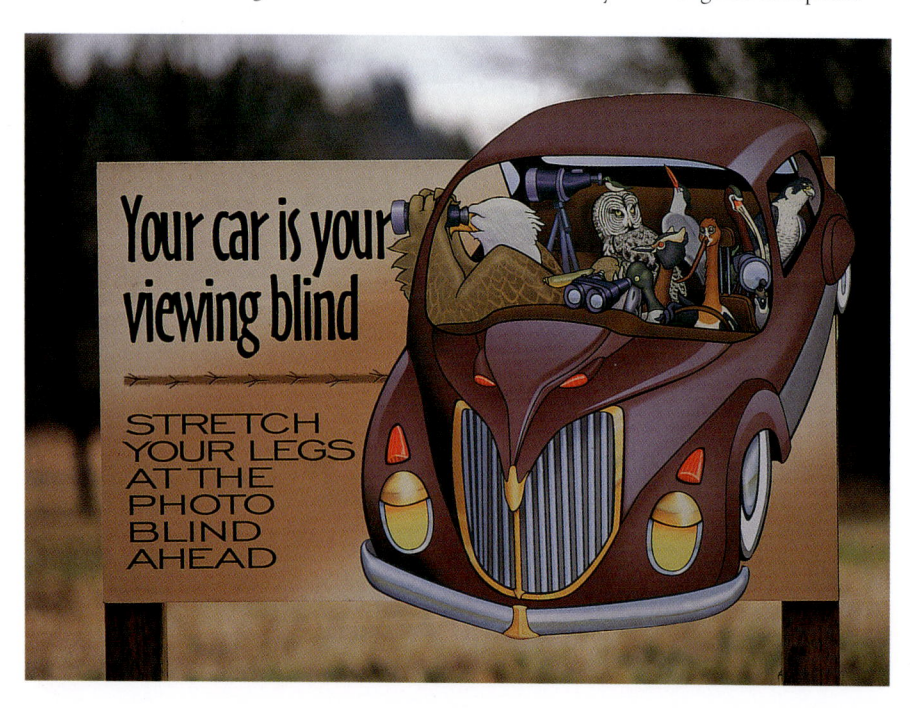

The sun plays peekaboo through the stark tree branches while the geese zoom past me. I am wrapped in the cover of the wooden blind at the end of the mile-long hiking trail along the new Ridgefield Auto Tour. The birds are so focused on their business that they pay me little heed as I move back to the warm comfort of my car. It's a pleasant meeting between travelers: one who's visiting but an afternoon, the others whose journeys cover thousands of miles and will reside here for the next four months.

I have always been a big believer that a community's wealth is really measured by its wildness: the wild places where the wildlife can be seen and enjoyed and appreciated. Ridgefield, Washington, has a dandy wild spot, and it's right off the Portland–Vancouver area's front steps. People who live far and near have discovered the many pleasures of the Ridgefield refuge, especially on the first-of-its-kind, 4.2-mile-long Ridgefield Auto Tour. The tour route crosses through the heart of the five-thousand-acre national treasure, and the best part is that the birds don't seem to mind your presence a bit.

◣ You'll see far more wildlife from inside your car on the unique **Ridgefield Refuge Auto Tour Route**.

◥ From forests to grasslands to wetlands, **Ridgefield Refuge** supports abundant wildlife including great blue herons.

106

Experience has shown that wintering birds become accustomed to motorized vehicles, and so these winged wonders allow people an up-close and personal viewing experience during the winter season. In fact, you could say the pace down the graveled lane is slow and easy. Between October 1 and April 30, you must remain in your vehicle to minimize disturbance (hiking and biking on the River S Unit are allowed May 1 through September 30), and the route has an information kiosk and separate observation blind for viewing more than 180 species of birds and other wildlife. The viewing blind offers escape from the sometimes-harsh winter weather and puts you out of the birds' sight.

Visitors seeking to hike on the refuge in winter may use the Oaks to Wetlands Trail on the Carty Unit. This trail follows the shoreline of floodplain wetlands and passes through oak and Douglas fir woodland. The hike provides opportunities to view many species of wildlife, some but a stone's throw away.

While transient species include many waterfowl species, year-round residents include mallards, red-tailed hawks, and great blue herons. The great blue heron presence at Ridgefield indicates abundant habitat. Standing four feet tall, with a wingspan reaching six feet, blue herons are often found in open areas adjacent to wetlands or ponds, so they are easier to see than many other animals. They often wade and watch, with great patience, for any small movement in the water of fish or other potential prey. Then they quickly reach out, spear, and grab (with their twelve-inch beaks) to make fast work of their catches.

Black-tailed deer are the largest mammal species on the refuge. Coyote, fox, raccoon, skunk, beaver, and otter are occasionally seen, too.

The best times to visit the refuge are early in the morning and late in the evening—when the animals are most active. Midday, the birds tend to idle around the wetlands. Time your visit accordingly, keeping in mind that some parts of this federal refuge are also open to hunting on certain days through mid-January and may be closed to nonhunters. You may also call the refuge office for more details.

■ Getting There

From Portland: Take Interstate 5 for about fourteen miles north of Vancouver to Ridgefield, exit 14. Drive three miles farther to the refuge's west entrances, just north and south of Ridgefield city limits. Follow signs from town, or phone for a map.

Auto Tour Route, River S Unit: The River S Auto Tour Route is accessed from Hillhurst Road, off Pioneer Street in Ridgefield. Although open year-round, visitors must stay in their vehicles November 1 through April 30 to prevent disturbance to the wintering waterfowl.

Oak to Wetlands Hiking Trail, Carty Unit: Open year-round, this 2.5-mile trail is located near downtown Ridgefield on the north end of Main Street. A sign designates the entrance to the parking lot, where a visitor's kiosk provides maps and trail brochures.

■ For More Information

Ridgefield National Wildlife Refuge, (360) 887-4106

INLAND

Oregon's Niagara Falls
41
Nestucca River Back Country Byway

Niagara Falls in Oregon? Oh yes, it's true! While Oregon's Niagara may not offer the same tremendous scale as its New York cousin, the adventure of finding Oregon's Niagara Falls in the Coast Range will leave you warm with satisfaction following a less-traveled route on a winter's day. Be prepared to spend some time and savor the trail that threads through the heart of these mountains, where milky white cloud wisps dance through the Douglas fir and western hemlock, and where the Nestucca River sings an ancient song as it makes its way to the sea. This is so significant a place that the Bureau of Land Management has designated much of the river canyon road a National Back Country Byway.

When you journey here, I suspect you'll call it lush and compelling, for the Nestucca River Back Country Byway travels through an Oregon old-growth forest where Douglas firs reach heights of two hundred feet and are more than four hundred years old. The eleven-mile byway parallels the ancient river run that carved through forty-million-year-old basalt and sandstone formations over tens of thousands of years.

On a day when sunshine takes over and beams through the forest, you're apt to find me as I head to Niagara in these mountains where the asphalt turns to gravel. It's a little-known fact that Oregon is home to its own Niagara, but unlike its larger, more distant relation, this falls must be tracked down through deep, dark canyon shadows where giant vine maples bend low and ferns and lichens and mosses are lit up by the prying sun. Nature's music gurgles up from adjacent spring-fed creeks, and taken together, these distinct sights and sounds lure you down the trail. It's all downhill, in fact, about a mile, which means that it's likely going to take you more time getting out than going in. Along the way, watch for four wooden bridges over the various creeks that feed into the Niagara canyon.

The lack of leaves on the big-leaf maples builds suspense as you get a peek of the falls from a distance, then round a final bend in the trail to find that the trailhead signs have fooled you because there are actually two waterfalls on this one hike. The first falls you encounter is Pheasant Creek, the second is Niagara. Both are born high in the heart of these mountains where the erosive stream water has shaped the old basalt rock into a spectacular amphitheater. There's even an inviting picnic table for drier, warmer times, but watch the winter sun closely for it will dip into the western horizon all too soon. And, unfortunately, you should, too!

Most, but not all of this byway is a paved two-lane road. In winter that may mean "caution" is the byword, for snow and ice conditions could make for hazardous travel.

There are four BLM-operated recreation areas and one Siuslaw National Forest campground along the byway. They are open to camping April through November. Dovre Campground offers ten campsites with fire rings, Fan Creek Campground has twelve sites, and Alder Glen has eleven; all have picnic tables. Elk Bend is primarily a day-use area, but it does offer four campsites. West of the

◀ **The Nestucca River sings on its way to the sea. Perhaps you've heard its song?**

▶ **Lacy waterfalls are a marvelous treat along the Nestucca River Back Country Byway.**

WINTER ~ Nestucca River Back Country Byway

Alder Glen recreation area, the byway enters the Siuslaw National Forest, where visitors will find the twelve-site Rocky Bend Campground, the only campground where drinking water is not available. All campgrounds are situated on the banks of the Nestucca River and provide excellent places for fishing or swimming.

■ Getting There

Nestucca River Back Country Byway (eastern access): Exit Interstate 5 at Wilsonville (exit 283) and proceed west on Wilsonville Road to Newberg. Follow Oregon 240 west to Oregon 47 at Yamhill, and continue south three miles to Carlton. From Carlton, drive Meadow Lake Road due west for about twelve miles, where it becomes the BLM's Nestucca River Back Country Byway.

Nestucca River Back Country Byway (western access): On U.S. 101 along the Oregon coast, drive twelve miles south of Tillamook to Beaver to Blaine Road. Continue east on Blaine Road to the town of Blaine. Keep to the right to get onto the BLM's Nestucca River Back Country Byway.

Niagara Falls: Travel south from Tillamook on coastal highway U.S. 101 to the town of Beaver. Turn east from town onto the Nestucca River Byway and head into the Siuslaw National Forest for approximately twelve miles. At the junction with Forest Service Road 8533, turn south and follow signs approximately four miles to Niagara Falls. Park your vehicle at the trailhead and walk about a mile to the falls.

■ For More Information
BLM, Salem District Office, (503) 375-5646

109

COLUMBIA

A Wildlife Parade
42
~
National Wildlife Refuges (Washington)

Mike Houck, the well-known urban naturalist and wildlife advocate for the Portland Audubon Society and urban greenspaces, loves to brag about the variety of winter wildlife adventures just off the Portland metro area's doorstep. "It is rather remarkable," he recently told me during an early morning outing on nearby Sauvie Island. "You can point a compass in any direction and find some place, reasonably close, that offers outstanding wildlife viewing opportunities. Plus, you'd swear you were a million miles away from a city of a million people." It is truly amazing what the Portland area offers the wildlife watcher. We were standing alongside Sauvie Island's Reeder Road, binoculars in hand, to chronicle the chilly dawn fly-out of bald eagles that travel from nearby nighttime roosting sites to hunt across the island's wetlands and marshes. It's quite the sight to see: eagle after eagle, sometimes by pairs, soaring across the dimly lit skyline. If you've not visited with Mike during an outing like this, you're missing quite an event. His enthusiasm for and knowledge of wildlife species are addictive. Houck not only leads Portland Audubon–sponsored field trips throughout the region, but he is also a coeditor and cowriter of the superb *Wild in the City*, a fantastic guidebook to the Portland area's natural spots.

Not long after our sojourn into the depths of winter, an unusual sun-kissed day broke through January's typical gray drizzle, and Mike directed me toward an unexplored trail in the Columbia River Gorge that I'd been itching to visit. The fact is, I really do relish the starkness of the winter season in wide-open expanses, especially on the Washington side of the gorge along Washington 14. You'll find a very different point of view there than what most visitors experience on Oregon's Interstate 84. I have been pleasantly surprised at the astonishing amount of bird life at three national wildlife refuges (NWR) within an easy-to-reach getaway east of Vancouver, Washington: Steigerwald Lake, Franz Lake, and Pierce Lake. While each refuge is currently closed to public access, you can peek into each at various overlooks and can hike around Steigerwald.

Steigerwald Lake is a wonderful example of how the best-laid plans of humans can go awry for wildlife and then go right again. Originally, the lake was a historic wetland and Columbia River floodplain

110

that in 1964 was diked and filled with dredging spoils to create an industrial park. Eventually, the 1,278 acres were purchased as mitigation for the expansion of nearby Bonneville Dam. The federal refuge landscape is framed by cottonwoods and white oaks, plus other riparian-associated plants that are established across largely open pasturelands, although Gibbons Creek, which holds populations of salmon and trout, courses across the refuge, too.

You may start your tour of the southern perimeter of this refuge at Steamboat Landing Park. This park on the Columbia River (with a floating dock) gives you access to the west end of a 3.5-mile paved dike road—perfect either on a bike or for a hike. From this trail you can marvel at the brilliant light and the deep shadows that play across the snowcapped basalt canyons on Oregon's side of the Columbia Gorge. The real show, however, is the abundant waterfowl that winter here—including Canada geese by the thousands. Mike explained the reason for so much winged activity: "In the years since 1986 when this became a refuge, there's been marked improvement in the management of the habitat, as well as the completion of many restoration projects. (Thanks to local volunteers!) There are many more projects on the way, too. Not only that, but this area is along a migration route for many birds that follow

◤ **Evening light on cottonwood and willow trees on Pierce Island, Columbia River Gorge National Scenic Area, Washington.**

the Cascade Mountains, so there's always plenty to see here."

Many bird species may be encountered on a hike around the southern perimeter of Steigerwald. (Mileage markers are posted along the route to give you a sense of how far you've hiked.) Note the fields on your left as you walk the dike. They attract thousands of Canada geese in the winter, and you may spot a few snow or greater white-fronted geese among them. Other waterfowl species include wood ducks, Eurasian wigeons, and both the common and Barrow's goldeneyes. Late in winter, great blue herons feed in these fields and other raptors can be seen here, too. As you walk east along the dike, the Columbia River will be on your right, and the large island that's just offshore is Reed Island, an undeveloped Washington state park. Plans to cut down the island's trees, put in a bridge to the mainland, build a marina, and even an airfield for private planes were blocked by the Vancouver Audubon Society to protect a great blue heron rookery and nesting bald eagles.

Not far from a large barn (milepost 1.5), watch for a shallow pond that attracts many ducks in the winter. At milepost 2 is the Gibbons Creek Fish Ladder, which was installed to help salmon, steelhead, and sea-run cutthroat trout return to the creek. Fish passage had been blocked for more than twenty years because of a pumping station in the nearby Washougal Industrial Park. The establishment of the refuge restored the creek, and hence the fish ladder was installed.

If you'd rather not hike the dike trail, you can drive Washington 14 and stop at a number of paved pullouts to view the refuge. The first one is about two hundred yards east of Washougal's sewage lagoons, at a field that attracts Canada geese. The next pullout is on the east side of Gibbons Creek, just past milepost 18. Someday, the "Gateway to the Gorge Visitors Center" will be located here and a hiking trail will extend to the dike. The U.S. Fish and Wildlife Service is planning to enlarge Steigerwald Lake and is attempting to remove nonnative grasses and to plant native trees and brush along the creek. Important: If you park near the dike road, please don't block the gates. Also, please do not cross any fences onto the Steigerwald Lake National Wildlife Refuge or adjacent private property.

Steigerwald Lake NWR is not the only mecca for varied winter wildlife in this part of the Columbia Gorge. Drive fifteen miles east of Washougal to Franz Lake NWR. It is closed to all public access, too, but watch for a scenic overlook at milepost 31. If you have a spotting scope or binoculars, look for a vast white carpet that seems to move—those are tundra swans, and they can be there by the hundreds to use the lake or the wetlands. There are nearly five hundred protected acres at this refuge, which is primarily a large shallow lake and adjacent wetlands. Group tours are available by arrangement.

Five miles farther east on Washington 14 is Pierce NWR. This refuge includes approximately 600 acres, of which 450 are Columbia River floodplain and 145 are inside the Indian Mary Creek watershed. The refuge includes wetlands and uplands along the north shore of the Columbia River and was donated to the U.S. Fish and Wildlife Service to give the geese sanctuary. Other wildlife includes waterfowl, raptors, songbirds, woodpeckers, upland game birds, fish, amphibians, and black-tailed deer. Pierce NWR is closed to all public use, but group tours can be arranged. The refuge can also be viewed from the summit of Beacon Rock and the Hamilton Mountain Trail (both located in Beacon Rock State Park).

■ Getting There

Steigerwald Lake NWR: From Portland, take Washington 14 east into the Columbia River Gorge and continue just east of milepost 16 to Steamboat Landing Park.

Franz Lake NWR: From Portland, take Washington 14 east into the Columbia River Gorge and continue fifteen miles east of Washougal.

Pierce NWR Refuge: From Portland, take Washington 14 east into the Columbia River Gorge and continue twenty miles east of Washougal.

Beacon Rock State Park/Hamilton Mountain Trail: From Portland, take Washington 14 east into the Columbia River Gorge and continue just past Pierce NWR. The trailhead is on the north side of Washington 14.

■ For More Information

U.S. Fish and Wildlife Service, Ridgefield National Wildlife Refuge Complex, (360) 887-4106

COLUMBIA 43

A Home for Eagles

Twilight Eagle Sanctuary

How can you miss on a day like this when the endless drizzle that blankets the land or the buckets of drenching wet that fall from above have oh-so-briefly disappeared? It's a day that's given way to indigo blue skies and fine, wide-angle views along a less traveled byway called U.S. 30. This route between Portland and Astoria may be among Oregon's oldest, albeit not the fastest, along the Columbia River. This green-bordered asphalt roadway skirts the southern shore of the mighty waterway and forces you to slow down to explore intersecting back roads where you may be surprised by what you see and hear.

For example, near Scappoose Bay, be on the lookout for flocks of sandhill cranes. They're hard to miss, for they are an imposing sight, standing nearly four feet tall and sporting striking red feather masks. Crane courtship is in full swing at this time of year, so if you spot a flock, watch as the males dance with their broad wings spread to reach sky high. They will jump and lunge and prance about all day long, putting on quite a comical show. And they will bend low and pick up sticks and small branches with their long, leathery beaks and then toss the woody debris into the air. All of this, biologists say, is how male cranes charm the nearby females—actions by which the lonesome boys hope to win a mate. Romance aside, it's an interesting way for you to spend a bit of time.

On these unusually warm winter days—when the thermometer peaks at fifty degrees—the surrounding hills along this drive seem to shake off their wetness for a time to form fog wisps that float above the hilly rims. Near Rainier, at the famous site of the Trojan Nuclear Plant, a former power station, pull off the highway to the inviting view of tundra swans—sometimes numbering as many as two hundred—lounging across adjacent wetlands and ponds. This power-generation site-turned-parkland is home to the swans from November through March. Sometimes called the "B-52s of the waterfowl world," the swans fill the air in swarms on six-foot wingspans, then glide to ground for a well-deserved break. Many of these huge birds will make a two-thousand-mile one-way journey from their Arctic breeding and nesting grounds to this site in Oregon. Although swans are not hunted in the Pacific Northwest, they remain a cautious bird, so don't expect to get too close. To ensure a close-up view, bring binoculars or a spotting scope and admire the snow-white plumage against the otherwise drab winter background.

Clatsop County draws you farther west along U.S. 30 to the Wolf Bay Wetlands, in the midst of the Twilight Eagle Sanctuary, where you can step up to a wooden deck and gaze out across the broad breadth of the Columbia River. Don't be surprised if some awesome sights are much closer at hand—for if you are lucky and gaze overhead at just the right moment, you may see our national symbol slowly cruise by. The sanctuary testifies to a community's efforts to protect wildlife habitat while providing an educational opportunity.

Nearly fifteen years ago, the Twilight Sanctuary was but a dream to a group of local Clatsop County folks who seized upon an opportunity to save a 15.3-acre parcel. The site was offered for sale by Cavenham Forest Industries, Inc., who had planned to log the last of the parcel's old-growth Sitka spruce and western hemlock trees. But the site also contained a nesting pair of bald eagles and served as a winter roosting site for many more. Cavenham agreed to sell the land to the Lower Columbia River Eagle Task Force, a local group. However, the first order of business for the citizen-based nonprofit organization was the challenging task of raising the money for the purchase—a princely $50,000.

Lest you doubt that "everyday people" can protect wildlife, you need to spend a few moments with Neal Maine, an energetic, innovative educator from nearby Seaside. I first met Neal when I was working on various news stories about the Twilight refuge purchase in the late 1980s. He was a member of the task force that spearheaded the fund-raising efforts to save the critical eagle habitat. He's also a big believer that folks of all ages can make a difference in helping wild critters. To that end, Neal told me that more than $68,000 was raised in little under two years in donations ranging from a few dollars to $5,000 from corporations, foundations, conservation groups, governments, local garden clubs, and individuals. He was especially proud of the role that local schoolchildren played in raising more than $3,000 for the purchase.

"Those kids—and there were hundreds from throughout Clatsop County, Grant," he smiled and softly noted, "did everything from bake sales to bottle drives to arm-twisting their parents, and these children really embodied our hope for the purchase. That is, each of us can make a difference saving wildlife habitat."

The Twilight Eagle Sanctuary is one of the few remaining sites adjacent to the Columbia River affording the roosting, feeding, and territorial requirements of bald eagles. A thick canopy provides shelter and moderates the otherwise cold winter temperatures. The eagles also prefer the area because of its riverine habitat since their winter feed consists mostly of ducks, geese, and swans. An estimated fifty bald eagles roost in or near the sanctuary during the winter, and that's nearly half of the remaining eagle population along both sides of the Columbia River.

The viewing platform is located about three-eighths of a mile from the sanctuary proper so visitors won't disturb the wildlife. The broad wooden deck overlooks a peaceful riverscape of wetlands, islands of grass, and sloughs. Interpretive signs at the platform explain facts about eagles and their habitat and also how people affect the birds' world. There are good chances to see bald eagles hunting or perching at or near the sanctuary at nearly any time of

◄ **Wolf Bay Wetlands is a sprawling wildlife mecca along the lower Columbia River near Astoria.**

year, but as Neal likes to say, there's an almost "money-back guarantee" that you will see eagles in the winter months.

■ Getting There

Scappoose Bay: There are two shore-based views into Scappoose Bay—one easy and one difficult. (1) From Portland, take U.S. 30 west to the Sauvie Island Bridge and turn right to take the bridge onto Sauvie Island. Follow N.W. Sauvie Island Road for approximately 2.5 miles to the junction with N.W. Reeder Road. Turn right and continue another 4.3 miles to the junction with Gillihan Road. Continue north on Reeder Road. At six miles, the pavement ends. Travel another 2.5 miles to a parking area. Take the six-mile round-trip trail to the northern end of Sauvie Island, where you find views to Scappoose Bay. (2) From Portland, take U.S. 30 west toward Astoria to milepost 25 and turn right onto Bennett Road, then left onto Old Portland Road. Scappoose Bay Marine Park and views to the bay are located to the right. You will also find canoe rentals, a boat launch, and store supplies at the marina park.

Trojan Park Wetlands and Pond: Follow U.S. 30 west from Portland for forty-two miles until you seen signs for "Trojan." The parking area is adjacent to the highway.

Twilight Eagle Sanctuary: Follow U.S. 30 west from Portland. Between mile markers 88 and 87, turn north on Burnside Road for a half mile.

■ For More Information

Oregon Department of Fish and Wildlife, (503) 872-5268

Audubon Society of Portland, (503) 292-6855

COLUMBIA

44
Eulachons or Hooligans?
Cowlitz River Smelt Run

They call it a run, but that's not really true. Packed fin to fin, the small fish called "smelt" glide and swim in the clear, shallow river water. You can easily see them by three, four, and scores galore! But wait! The fact is—as measured by the commercial fishing nets stuffed with thousands and thousands more—it's not a run at all. Each February, in southwest Washington's Cowlitz River, you could say there's a stampede of the tiny fish. It's an annual event for dedicated anglers who could care less about cold, bone-chilling winter water. Some fishing folk, clad in neoprene rubber waders, will stand waist deep or even higher just to find the right spot. Then, armed with telescopic-handled dip nets, the anglers reach far out, then drop their nets into the icy river and, with a downstream sweep, attempt to snare as many of the prized, silvery, wriggly, squirmy masses of smelt as possible.

Steve King, Senior Fishery Biologist of the Oregon Department of Fish and Wildlife, recently told me that "smelt" or "hooligans" are eulachons (pronounced "YU-la-kons"), the Native American name for the Columbia River smelt, known in scientific circles as *Thaleichthys pacificus*. Smelts are small, not reaching more than a foot in length, and like Pacific salmon, the smelt are anadromous, spawning in freshwater but migrating to the ocean to feed and grow. The tiny fish swim in large schools and begin a spawning migration at age three or four. They typically enter the Columbia River in early to mid-January,

---

"LITTLE CHIEF" SMOKED SMELT

Courtesy of Luhr Jensen

Smelt
1 cup noniodized salt
1 cup brown sugar
1 tablespoon paprika
1 tablespoon chili powder
1 tablespoon garlic salt
1 tablespoon onion salt
1/2 teaspoon black pepper
1 cup soy sauce
1/2 cup cider vinegar
1 tablespoon Worcestershire sauce
3 cups warm water

Some prefer whole smelt, others remove smelt heads and entrails with a pair of scissors. Either way, wash smelt in clear water. Combine dry ingredients with soy sauce, cider vinegar, and warm water. Let the brine cool and add the smelt. Brine the smelt four or more hours. Rinse thoroughly and let air dry. Smoke until fish surfaces have a dark golden-brown sheen (five to seven hours).

114

finding tributaries in mid- to late January. Most tributary spawning is in the Cowlitz River, but the fish usually run up Washington's nearby Kalama and Lewis Rivers and occasionally Oregon's Sandy River. The females deposit their eggs over a sandy river bottom, and the eggs attach to the sand and silt. After hatching, the tiny fry move out to the ocean to feed and grow.

In Kelso, Washington, the self-proclaimed "Smelt Capital of the World," recreational smelt fishing brings out thousands of people a day. They perch on shoreline rocks, or wade in the river to dip and catch up to ten pounds of the fish, each person's daily limit. Smelt are a high-protein fish that, in addition to being pan-fried or smoked for human consumption, are widely used as fish food at aquariums and marine parks. Smelt dipping is a Pacific Northwest pastime, and you'll often see young kids, their parents, and their grandparents making an afternoon adventure of the event. It is great outdoor fun, and some say, hints of warmer spring days to come. Smelt dipping nets can be purchased in area sporting-goods stores. They may also be rented at many signed locations in this area of the Cowlitz River, and it's common to see roadside rental stands and even local grocery stores renting the nets for a modest hourly fee.

When the run is on, it doesn't take long to build an appetite either! So, what do you do with a bucketful of fresh, squirmy smelt? Check out the selected recipes—tried and true—that may get you hooked on something new (see sidebar).

■ **Getting There**
From Portland, drive north on Interstate 5 to Kelso, exit 47. Proceed west across the Cowlitz River on Allen Street. Immediately turn right on Washington 411 (West Side Highway) and proceed north. Washington 411 parallels the Cowlitz River. You will encounter fishermen all along this route for the next fifteen miles.

BEER-BATTERED SMELT

Beer Batter
The flavor is improved by use of milk in their preparation before cooking.

Smelt
Milk
1 tablespoon dried oregano
1 tablespoon seasoned salt
1 teaspoon seasoned pepper
1 teaspoon garlic salt
1 teaspoon paprika
1 cup flour, plus flour for dusting fish
½ cup lemon juice
Beer

Soak fish in milk for half an hour before frying.

Mix together oregano, salt, pepper, garlic salt, paprika, flour, and lemon juice. Thin batter with beer to consistency of pancake batter. Dust fish with flour, then dip in batter. As batter is used, add more beer to maintain consistency.

Note: This batter may also be used for other fish, onion rings, or chicken. Also, this recipe is prepared for use in a manufactured electric home soaker. These units are widely available for purchase at sporting-goods stores.

■ **For More Information**
Washington Department of Fish and Wildlife, (360) 902-2200

◂ There's always room for another dip net when the smelt run is on along the Cowlitz River near Longview, Washington.

CASCADES

Away from the Crowds
~46~
Wind River

trails for skiers. We especially enjoyed the moonlight ski tour, which offers an ethereal, unworldly nighttime skiing experience. For those who need them, cross-country ski instruction and skiing equipment are available for rent at Diamond Lake Resort.

"Steep & Deep" is the motto of the oldest Snowcat skiing operation in the country. Snowcat skiing at nearby Mount Bailey offers the kind of epic days one expects from helicopter skiing, but the turbo-diesel Snowcat operates in all weather conditions and at a fraction of the cost. Run by and for hard-core skiers and riders, Mount Bailey Snowcat Skiing offers up to twenty-five skiers and snowboarders access to a sixty-thousand-acre area that reaches the 8,368-foot summit and includes three primary cirques (bowls), an extensive array of steep chutes and broad faces, and long and undulating ridges. It is a steep and deep powder adventure like you've not experienced in Oregon before.

■ Getting There
From Portland: Take Interstate 5 to exit 124 in Roseburg. Drive east on Oregon 138 to the Diamond Lake Recreation Area in the eastern portion of the Umpqua National Forest. Follow signs to the resort.

From Bend: Drive south on U.S. Highway 97 to the Diamond Lake junction at Oregon 138. Continue west on Oregon 138 to Diamond Lake.

■ For More Information
Diamond Lake Resort, (800) 733-7593

Across the Columbia River, little more than an hour from Portland, is a well-kept secret in Pacific Northwest snow country. Although a bit off the beaten path, it is hard to miss soaring Mount Adams (elevation 12,776 feet), Washington's only major mountain named for a U.S. president. Here's another surprise: Southwest of the mountain is the little-traveled Wind River basin that, like the mountain, is so seldom visited that it maintains a quiet charm. You might say part of the area's character is to hide miles of groomed cross-country skiing trails suitable for beginners through advanced. In the Wind River area, you really have a chance to ski away from the crowds. U.S. Forest Service Ranger Tom Linde told me that despite development and publicity of more popular nearby ski areas like Mount Hood Meadows, the Wind River basin still hasn't been "discovered" by crowds of people.

"On a busy weekend when the conditions are ideal, we may have two hundred people skiing across our many sno-parks. During the week, there may be twenty or thirty people. So, if you do the math and consider how much territory is out here, you know you'll have it all to yourself."

Tom smiled as he explained that a recent U.S. Forest Service program called "Snofoot Trails" has made the cross-country ski experience even better. More than thirty miles of trails are groomed exclusively for skiers each week. The trails are closed to snowmobiles and other motorized vehicles and are identified with trailhead signs bearing trail name, number, and distance to destinations. Some routes are trails and others follow snow-covered roads. Many have been designed to allow loop trips back to your starting point. Trail difficulty ratings are shown on the map and trail signs. Ratings are based on trail length, steepness, and skiing skills required. A free map, available at the Wind River District office, shows you how the loops fit together.

Recently, I arranged to meet local resident Phil Zoller, who offered his Snowcat and sleigh as unique transport for a family outing into the Wind River Sno-Park. We met Phil for a day of fun in the sun and snow near the Oldman Pass Sno-Park (approximate elevation 2,600 to 3,400 feet, depending upon where one skis).

Phil is a bear of a man with the heart of a pup, and he's lived and loved the life of an outdoorsman for more than fifty years. His life's work has been as a river guide, but during winter months, he mans the controls of his Snowcat and contracts with the U.S. Forest Service to groom trails for cross-country skiers. He

WINTER ~ Wind River

▶ **You'll be smiling too when you discover solitude and beauty along the many Wind River Sno-Parks of Skamania County.**

explained that each year the Wind River District received funding from the Washington State Parks Winter Sports Commission's sale of Washington sno-park permits to provide grooming and setting of cross-country ski tracks on approximately thirty miles of trails and roads. Trail grooming usually starts when approximately two feet or more of snow are on the ground, and normally that occurs around Christmas. The trails are usually groomed approximately every week on Thursday, or Friday if needed.

As always, our conversations ran the gamut of local and regional history, and Phil offered some interesting insight to the entire Mount Adams region when he told me, "You know, Grant, Lewis and Clark had Adams mixed up with Mount St. Helens, so I suppose you could say it's always been tucked away and kind of hidden. In many ways, we're at the end of the road. You don't go through here to get anywhere else. That's a plus, though, because there hasn't been any significant development on or near the mountain, and people around here kind of like that."

Mount Adams was the last major Cascades mountain to be "discovered" by white explorers, and unlike neighboring Mount Hood, Mount St. Helens, and Mount Rainier, the twelve-thousand-foot wonder was named for U.S. president John Adams. Remarkably, the region still offers a wilderness experience, both for skiers and snowshoers. The Wind River drainage includes four sno-parks exclusive to cross-country skiers: Oldman Pass, Hardtime, Koshko, and McClellen Meadows. Each is accessed from the Wind River Highway and U.S. Forest Service Road 30.

The skiing experience is rewarding, and we really enjoyed the Oldman Loop, a little

119

SNOW SAFETY

While Phil's reference to "losing yourself" is a fine romantic notion, outdoor experts caution that the dangers in Northwest snow country are very real. Even on a nice day, the winter sun may provide a "false sense of security" when you and your family are out and about in the snow, according to search-and-rescue veteran Mark Kelsey. Mark is a mountain guide who lives in Government Camp, on the doorstep of famous Mount Hood. He's seen far too many people get into trouble in recent years for their lack of winter knowledge. He advises people not to be deceived by fun in the sun and to be ready to meet winter at its worst.

When you head to the mountains, prepare yourself for 'what if?' by asking yourself a few simple questions: How am I getting back? Am I going to walk through six feet of new snow? How much energy will I expend? Will I be wet?

These are solid questions that deserve preparation and planning. Mark told me that the key to planning is knowledge about shelter building. "When time is of the essence and the weather's getting worse, an easy-to-build emergency pit shelter may save your life." Using a snow shovel (a must-have on Mark's essential items list), dig a pit about four feet deep and no more than five feet across, stacking snow blocks along the rim. Cover the pit with your tarp and secure your tarp with snow blocks, leaving an entrance/exit inside. Once inside, secure the entrance/exit portion of the tarp with snow, and prop the shovel up, raising the tarp so that it forms a pitched roof.

It's equally important to figure out where to get water and, hopefully, to have some food with you. According to Mark, aluminum foil can be used to shape a cup or bowl to drink or eat out of. Just punch a hole in the ground and you've got a form for shaping foil into a cup or bowl. Coupled with the foil, candles provide a way to melt snow. "Set the candle in the snow, get your aluminum cup, and start melting snow for water," said Mark. These are little things that can become critical in keeping you alive in a worst-case scenario.

Essential Items
Lightweight snow shovel (small, with a telescopic handle)
Tarp
6 food bars
Flashlight
Compass (preferably with a reflective mirror)
Emergency candles (for light and warmth; a single candle can raise inside air temperature by 10 degrees)
Aluminum foil

---

over a mile long and perfect for beginners. It runs through the forest with rolling hills and flats and open areas where the timber had been clear-cut. In fact, one of the clear-cuts allowed a spectacular view to Mount Adams. I complimented Phil on his fine work, for the groomed ski tracks make the travel relatively easy. But it was the lack of distractions I favored the most—no typical ski-area hubbub here. Instead I found a real freedom to explore the forest in silence. Phil put it most aptly when he said, "The Wind River [and greater Mount Adams region] is a place where you can still lose yourself but find the soul of an outdoor adventure."

■ Getting There

Note: Access to the Upper Wind River Winter Recreation Area is via the Wind River Highway (which becomes Forest Service Road 30), a two-lane, paved highway. The road is plowed by Skamania County when necessary, but it is not a main route. Snow tires are recommended, and all vehicles should be equipped with chains and a shovel.

From Portland, travel Interstate 84 east to Cascade Locks and cross the Columbia River on the Bridge of the Gods. Continue east on Washington 14 to Carson, and turn north onto the Wind River Highway, which becomes Forest Service Road 30, for approximately 24.4 miles to Oldman Pass Sno-Park.

■ For More Information

Gifford Pinchot National Forest, Wind River Information Center, (509) 427-3200

CENTRAL/EASTERN

A Bull Elk Romance
47
Elk Horn Wildlife Area

Here's a lesson that twenty years of covering wildlife stories has taught me: Always expect the unexpected!

For one thing, critters never keep appointments. They can be the most daunting story subjects to capture on tape, and I've plenty of photography partners in the TV news business who will testify to that frustration. We have spent countless hours—no, make that days—traveling across hundreds of miles, often in the worst of weather, hoping to capture just the right moment when a wild animal will display some unique behavior. Be it salmon jumping a waterfall, sage grouse strutting across their springtime desert leks or breeding grounds, or hiking into distant, craggy mountains searching for cougar or bear dens, I have learned that when it comes to encountering wildlife, it pays to be a lucky rather than an accomplished journalist. Not long ago, one of the luckiest wildlife encounters occurred right in a small eastern Oregon town and left a lasting impression that will be the talk of that town for years. In the "Valley of Peace" at La Grande, Oregon, in the shadow of the Blue Mountains, a very lonely Rocky Mountain bull elk went looking for love and found himself stranded in a sea of human hubbub. The story started in a suburb of this small Union County burg, on a crisp, cool, and brilliant September morning. Local resident Jim Brown was going about his weekly chore of cleaning the leaves from his yard. He had yard work, not wildlife, on his mind, until his neighbor urgently called him aside and whispered that he'd better take a gander into the side yard, where Jim had a number of guests.

"I put the ladder down and went over," he explained to me. "And there—in the middle of my yard—is the biggest bull elk I have ever seen, just lying down back there. Talk about amazed. Good lord! It was something."

It was something alright! Nine hundred pounds of something that sported a towering set of sharp antlers, six points to a side. The elk was huge and awesome and resting on Jim's green grass. But how, you may wonder, did a backwoods critter end up smack in the middle of La Grande? Jim Cadwell, a local wildlife biologist, told me that the bull's behavior had a simple explanation: The elk had love on his mind.

"La Grande sits on the doorstep of the magnificent Blue Mountains, and we have cow [female] elk coming into the outskirts of town all the time. Since September is the peak of the rut or breeding season, there's a good possibility that this male was looking for a mate."

◄ **Bring a camera, film, and patience when you visit the Elk Horn Wildlife Area in eastern Oregon.**

Yes, it seems the bull elk was looking for love—and he ran past the local Safeway grocery store, cruised through downtown along Main Street, zipped by the Elks Lodge without hesitation, and then made a sharp turn onto 2nd Avenue to find it. His route to romance picked up quite a gawking crowd, too. Three miles and twenty minutes later, the poor boy was nearly exhausted and practically collapsed in Jim Brown's side yard. Word spread among the locals like wildfire, and soon nearly a hundred people were watching from a short distance. The police had their hands full controlling the swelling crowd, who sported cameras and binoculars amid a carnival-like atmosphere.

According to Stan Terry of the Oregon State Police, love had put this bull and the police in a pickle. He explained, "I was really afraid that somebody might get gored, because the elk was really agitated. He'd snap his teeth, scratch the ground with his hooves, and he was definitely aggressive. We didn't have a lot of answers about what to do next either."

For nearly two hours, folks wrestled with ideas and ways to move him out of town. Some said they could rope the bull, others thought to drug him with a tranquilizing dart, and a handful suggested they could solve the dilemma with their hunting rifles. All these ideas were ruled out due to safety concerns, but the police were nervous because time was running out. The poor beast might collapse from the trauma of it all.

That's when Brian Chamberlain stepped forward with a better plan: He'd call the big bull out of town! Brian, an accomplished hunter, had a simple idea to give the big boy what he wanted. Brian was adept at using a special cow call that—with practice—emits the not-so-sultry sounds of a female elk looking for a mate. The cry is somewhat akin to a high-pitched squeal from an out-of-kilter, floppy fan belt. But if it's presented correctly, the sound is an offer that bull elk cannot refuse. Brian moved up the street a block or two and gave two short whistles. Stan Terry described what happened next:

"It was the darndest thing. That bull perked up his tall ears and swiveled them around like radar dishes. He listened, then his head snapped to the left and his eyes got big as saucers. I swear he smacked his lips before he shot off like cannon fire in Brian's direction. That bull elk was on a dead run, and he had lust on his mind!"

Brian suddenly realized he'd better move or he'd soon have a lap full of elk. "Stan yelled at me, 'Start running now, Brian!' I looked around the corner and thought, 'Oh my gosh! He's headed right at me.' His nose was up in the air and he was looking all around."

I quickly asked, "Looking for love?"

Brian laughed nervously and said, "Oh yeah, probably—but not from me. That's why I wanted to keep ahead of him—so I started running, too. Only faster! He was just picking his up his feet and putting them down."

For block after block, that's how it went down, as Brian, the elk "Pied Piper," called, then ran, then led a romantic elk up and down streets for miles. Finally, they reached the forested foothills, and thankfully, the elk was home free.

"It must have been pretty funny for folks to gape up the street and see this bull chasing after me." Brain chuckled and hinted at a certain pride at having saved the day and saved a majestic elk from certain death.

Stan Terry was very thankful no one was hurt and said the tale of "La Grande's Romantic Elk" is destined to become legend. "Yeah, it's one for the memory banks for sure—the day a lonely bull elk went looking for love and became the biggest show in our town."

You won't need to chase elk or be chased by them to enjoy one of the finest winter elk tours in eastern Oregon at the Elk Horn Wildlife Area near Baker City. From mid-November through February, you can go aboard the hay wagon and let Pat and Mike, two gigantic Percheron draft horses, pull you safely along and get real close to as many as a hundred and fifty Rocky Mountain elk. A deer and elk feeding program has been in place for many years at the ten-thousand-acre refuge so that the animals will not venture into the Baker Valley and damage farmers' haystacks. According to the area's manager, Eddie Miguez, it's a program that's worked very well. "Preventing crop damage was the reason the state created the wildlife area in the early 1970s, and it's why we've added acreage and feed sites several times since."

The state's solution has been a success, too, as the problem of elk and deer marauding haystacks is only a memory for most landowners in the Baker, Bowen, and

North Powder valleys. You are encouraged to bring your camera and lend a hand on the elk chow line, which pauses often and gets you close to the massive and beautiful animals.

Our feeding trip was largely filled in with students from nearby North Powder School—bundled up against the chilly fifteen degrees, with a light dusting of snow falling across our trail. We witnessed interesting behaviors of young male elk sparring with one another—testing each other's strength with their antlers. We learned that elk and deer are not the only wildlife here, for predators are often seen flanking the herd. In fact, we quickly spotted a coyote in the nearby tree line—intently watching the herd. It's not unusual to see several coyote—even an occasional cougar—checking out the herd. You can learn a lot about predator-prey relationships as nature's often dramatic struggle between life and death is played out here all winter.

■ Getting There
From Portland, drive east on Interstate 84 to midway between La Grande and Baker City, exit 285. Follow the "Wildlife Viewing" signs to the Elk Horn Wildlife Area.

■ For More Information
Oregon Department of Fish and Wildlife, (541) 898-2826

Baker County Visitors Bureau, (800) 523-1235

La Grande/Union County Visitors Bureau, (800) 848-9969

T and T Wildlife Tours, (541) 856-3356

CENTRAL/EASTERN

48 ~ Into the Deep
Wallula Gap near Pasco

On our way from this place to that with no particular schedule to hold us back, my family loves to travel and explore all the corners of our region, and at any time of year—especially along the Columbia River, where a pause from the rush of traffic on Interstate 84 can lead to new knowledge and understanding about Northwest cultural and geological history.

So it was a few years back, when the McOmies were bound for Spokane, Washington, to visit with friends on a late winter weekend adventure. As we motored across the desert on the straight-as-an-arrow interstate, I realized we were in a much bigger hurry than was really necessary. So, not far beyond McNary Dam, just off Washington 730, I put on the brakes to take advantage of an opportunity to explore and teach my youngsters about this seldom-visited stretch of waterway.

As we passed vast Lake Wallula, created in 1957 by the construction of gigantic McNary Dam, I pointed out to the boys how different the landscape was from the lush, steep canyon walls of the Columbia Gorge we'd passed only hours earlier. Here was a terrain of stark contrast to that place measured by wide-open vistas, very few trees, and an arid climate. The lake behind McNary Dam (one of seven major dams on the mighty mainstem Columbia River) offers a range of recreation facilities, from full-service campgrounds and picnic areas to undeveloped remote beaches. Upriver from the lake, near the junction of Washington 12 and 730 at the confluence of the Columbia and Walla Walla Rivers and just across the border into Washington, is an area known as the Wallula Gap. Here, the Columbia River canyon narrows. It is the site of colorful Indian lore and a place where interesting natural phenomena occurred during an ancient catastrophic event known as the Great Missoula Floods.

As we pulled off of the highway to gaze at the surrounding, nearly vertical rimrock cliffs of Wallula Gap, I explained to the boys that long ago, perhaps fifteen thousand years, there had been a gargantuan, whirling river that lapped at the tops of the soaring rock walls hundreds of feet above us. The story goes that in distant northern Idaho a lobe of ice that had acted as a dam, and stood perhaps three thousand feet high, burst apart. The dam had shut off the drainage of the Clark Fork River and had formed a large lake in western Montana. But as the Ice Age ended, and this monstrous dam suddenly failed, it released five hundred cubic miles of glacial meltwater. A two-thousand-foot

123

WINTER ~ Wallula Gap near Pasco

wall of water roared out across the region and drained the entire lake in a matter of days. This tremendous flood was diverted west by southwest across the entire Columbia Plateau and toward the narrows of Wallula Gap, where we stood. We could easily see how the gap was a choke point of sorts along the otherwise wide Columbia River. Here, it narrowed like the neck of a funnel to less than a mile from shore to shore. Geologists say that during this event only one-sixth of the water arriving at the gap could pass through it, so the building floodwater backed up and formed a twelve-hundred-foot-deep lake stretching thirty-five hundred square miles across southeastern Washington. For several weeks, as much as two hundred cubic miles of water per day were delivered to a gap that could only discharge less than forty miles per day. Water filled the nearby Pasco basin and the Yakima and Touchet valleys to form temporary Lake Lewis and, for several days, it stopped and reversed the tributaries of the Columbia River.

Today, all of this is worth a pause to consider as you fix your eyes on Wallula Gap and realize how immense this event must have been—ten times more water poured through Wallula Gap than is carried by all of Earth's rivers combined. And it happened over and over and over again. Geologists speculate that this type of freeze and flood exchange occurred over a hundred times during the last Ice Age (between one hundred thousand and thirteen thousand years ago). It was a process that left countless lasting marks upon the entire region as slurries of ice, water, rock, mud, and other debris flushed across the Columbia River Basin. Many geologists suggest that future ice ages may well wash over this area again—perhaps sooner (geologically speaking) rather than later.

There is another chapter of Northwest history—cultural history—that distinguishes this area and dates to the more recent events of the Lewis and Clark Expedition. On October 18, 1805, William Clark noted in his journal the spying of Mount Hood on the distant western horizon:

> *I discovered a high mountain of emence hight covered with Snow, this must be one of the mountains laid down by Vancouver.*
> —from the journal of William Clark

According to historians Gary Lentz (park ranger at Lewis and Clark Trail State Park) and Dave Nicandri (director of the Washington State Historical Society), Clark witnessed the great snowy icon of the state of Oregon from the plains above Wallula Gap. Mount Hood was especially important because it served as a course marker for the expedition's ultimate destination: the Pacific Ocean. For the first time since they had left present-day North Dakota the previous April, the expedition could place itself on a map and could paddle or hike the river boundary between today's Oregon and Washington.

I seriously doubt Lewis and Clark, nor any member of their Corps of Discovery, would have objected to the fine comforts you'll experience at either of two state parks that my family has enjoyed near Walulla Gap. Each of these parks (one in Oregon, the other in Washington) sports unique features that provide all the comforts of home and offer a welcome break following a long highway journey.

When I visit this region for extended vacation time, I usually tow my boat as well, in order to see the area from a different point of view and to enjoy fishing and water skiing. Camping and boating are the draws to Hat Rock State Park, which lies on the south shore of Lake Wallula behind McNary Dam on the Columbia River. Except for the west boat ramp, this park is closed from October 31 and reopens in early spring (the exact date will be determined by the weather). There is no fee to use this park, unless you want to reserve the picnic area. In addition, there is historic significance to be explored here, for Hat Rock (so named for the nearby basalt monolith) was the first distinctive landmark passed by the Lewis and Clark Expedition on its journey down the Columbia. It's also one of the few remaining geological sites not submerged by Columbia dams.

If I am simply passing through this region and am in need of a short respite and lunch, Sacajawea State Park is the place for me, a 284-acre day-use-only marine park at the confluence of the Snake and Columbia Rivers. It features ninety-one-hundred feet of freshwater shoreline at the confluence of the Snake and Columbia Rivers about five miles southeast of Pasco. Just a stone's throw from Wallula Gap, the park is marked by a landscape spread under a magnificent sky with excellent views of the Snake and Columbia as they flow together, as well as the dramatic, towering canyon walls on the Washington side of the Columbia.

■ Getting There

Hat Rock State Park: From Portland, drive east on Interstate 84 to Umatilla, exit 166, and the junction with U.S. 730. Proceed east nine miles on U.S. 730 to the park entrance.

Sacajawea State Park: From Pasco, drive east on Washington 12 toward Walla Walla. Take a right on Tank Farm Road. Continue across railroad tracks. The park is at the end of the road.

■ For More Information

Hat Rock State Park, information, (800) 551-6949; reservations, (800) 452-5687

Sacajawea State Park, information and reservations, (509) 545-2361

◄ Ancient, compelling history is yours to explore at Wallula Gap near Wallula, Washington.

Source Notes

P. 33—In gathering material about Clear Lake and the McKenzie River Scenic Highway, I found Shirley Lewis's background information especially helpful.

P. 36—In gathering facts about Silver Falls State Park, I found Craig Tutor's (Oregon State Parks) background information especially helpful.

P. 55—In gathering geologic history about Erratic Rocks, I found Jim O'Conner's (USGS) background information especially helpful.

P. 62—In gathering information about the history of the Cloud Cap Inn, I found Bill Shepherd's background information and the Crag Rats historic journals especially helpful.

P. 82—In gathering historic facts about the Cedar Creek Grist Mill, I found Jeff Claire's background information especially helpful.

P. 86—In gathering material about the Historic Columbia River Highway, I found Mike Ferris's (U.S. Forest Service) background information especially helpful.

P. 102—In gathering historic facts about Heceta Head Lighthouse, I found Debra Bender's (Oregon State Parks) background information especially helpful.

P. 110—In gathering details about Washington's Columbia River National Wildlife Refuges, I found Wilson Cady's (Audubon Society) and Yvette Donovan's (U.S. Fish and Wildlife Service) background information especially helpful.

Recommended Reading

Bannan, Jan. *Oregon State Parks*. Seattle, Wash.: The Mountaineers, 1993.

Beckham, Stephen Dow, and Robert M. Reynolds. *Lewis and Clark from the Rockies to the Pacific*. Portland, Ore.: Graphic Arts Center Publishing, 2002.

Davis, James. *Seasonal Guide to the Natural Year: A Month-by-Month Guide to Natural Events*. Golden, Colo.: Fulcrum Publishing, 1996.

Ewing, Susan. *Going Wild in Washington and Oregon*. Portland, Ore.: Alaska Northwest Books, 1993.

Heinl, Russ, and Sallie Tisdale. *Portland from the Air*. Portland, Ore.: Graphic Arts Center Publishing, 2000.

Houck, Michael C., and M. J. Cody, editors. *Wild in the City*. Portland, Ore.: Oregon Historical Society Press, 2000.

Jarvela, Andrea. *The Oregon Almanac: Facts about Oregon*. Portland, Ore.: WestWinds Press, 2000.

Jones, Phillip M. *Canoe and Kayak Routes of Northwest Oregon*, 2nd ed. Seattle, Wash.: The Mountaineers, 1997.

Lichatowich, Jim. *Salmon Without Rivers: A History of the Salmon Crisis*. Washington, D.C.: Island Press, 1999.

McOmie, Grant, and Steve Terrill. *Grant's Getaways: Outdoor Adventures with Oregon's Grant McOmie*. Portland, Ore.: WestWinds Press, 2001.

Ostertag, Rhonda. *Best Short Hikes in Northwest Oregon*. Seattle, Wash.: The Mountaineers Books, 2003.

Ritter, Harry. *Washington's History: The People, Land, and Events of the Far Northwest*. Portland, Ore.: WestWinds Press, 2003.

Schafer, Rick, and Craig Lesley. *Oregon IV*. Portland, Ore.: Graphic Arts Center Publishing, 2002.

Sheehan, Madelynne Diness, and Dan Casali. *Fishing in Oregon*, 8th ed., revised and updated. Portland, Ore.: Flying Pencil Publications, 1995.

Thoele, Mike. *Footprints Across Oregon: A Roving Chronicler's Favorite People and Places*. Portland, Ore.: Graphic Arts Center Publishing, 1989.

Whitehill, Karen, and Terry Whitehill. *Nature Walks In and Around Portland: All-Season Exploring in Parks, Forests, and Wetlands*, 2nd ed. Seattle, Wash.: The Mountaineers, 1998.

Willamette Kayak and Canoe Club. *Soggy Sneakers: A Guide to Oregon Rivers*, 3rd ed. Seattle, Wash.: The Mountaineers, 1994.

Yuskavitch, James A. *Oregon Wildlife Viewing Guide*. Helena, Mont.: Falcon Publishing Company, 1994.

Index

Italic page numbers indicate photographs

aircraft, 76, 76–77
Alfred A. Loeb State Park, 16, 17
Alsea Falls Recreation Area, 22–23
Ankeny NWR, 80, 81, *81*
Ape Cave, 65–66
Atiyeh Deschutes River Trail, 96
Aufderheide Scenic Drive, 93

Bald Peak State Park, 84, *84*
Baskett Slough NWR, 80, 81
Bastendorff Beach County Park, 46
biking, 58, 86–87, *87*, 96–97, 107, 111
birds and birding. *See also* wildlife refuges and viewing
    Ankeny NWR, 80, 81, *81*
    Baskett Slough NWR, 80, *81*
    Bonney Butte HawkWatch, 90–92, *91*
    Fern Ridge Reservoir, 56–58, *57*
    Finley NWR, 80, 81
    Franz Lake NWR, 111
    Free Flight Bird and Marine Mammal Rehabilitation Center, *18*, 18–19
    Jackson Bottom Wetlands, 104–5, *105*
    Malheur NWR, *42*, 43
    Pierce NWR, *110*, 111–12
    Ridgefield NWR, *106*, 106–7
    Sauvie Island, 110
    Scappoose Bay, 113
    South Beach, 20–21
    Steigerwald Lake NWR, 110–11
    Trojan Park Wetlands and Pond, 113
    Twilight Eagle Sanctuary, 113–14
    Wolf Bay Wetlands, *112*, 113–14
boating
    Atiyeh Deschutes River Trail, 96
    Clear Lake, 34–35
    Deschutes River State Park, 96–97
    Fern Ridge Reservoir, 56–58, *57*
    Hat Rock State Park, 125
    Kingfisher, 48–50, *49*
    Malheur NWR, 41–43, *42*
    Metolius River, 60–62, *61*
    Owyhee River, 38–41, *39*
    South Slough Estuary, 47
    Timothy Lake, 30–32, *31*
    Willamette Mission State Park, 85
Bonneville Fish Hatchery, 26–28, *27*
Bonney Butte HawkWatch, 90–92, *91*
Bridge of the Gods, 58–59

camping
    Alsea Falls Recreation Area, 22–23
    Atiyeh Deschutes River Trail, 96
    Aufderheide Scenic Drive, 93

Bastendorff Beach County Park, 46
Camp Sherman, 61–62
Cloud Cap Road, 62–64
Deschutes River State Park, 96–97
Eagle Cap Wilderness, *69*, 69–71
Fern Ridge Reservoir, 56–58, *57*
Hart Mountain Natl. Antelope Refuge, 95
Hat Rock State Park, 125
Lake Owyhee State Park, 40
Metolius River, *60*, 60–62
Nestucca River Back Country Byway, *108*, 108–9
Paradise Campground, 33–34
Silver Falls State Park, 38
South Fork of the McKenzie River, 93, *93*
South Slough Estuary, 46–48, *47*
Timothy Lake, 30–32, *31*
Trask County Park, 51–53
Wallowa Mountains, *69*, 69–71
Cape Arago Highway, 46, 47
Cape Meares Beach, 21
Cascade Locks, 58–60
Cascades getaways
    Ape Cave, 65–66
    Aufderheide Scenic Drive, 92–93
    Bonney Butte HawkWatch, 90–92, *91*
    Camp Sherman, 61–62
    Cloud Cap Inn, 62–64
    Crater Lake, 116–118, *117*
    Diamond Lake, 116, 117–18
    McKenzie River Highway, 33, 33–35, *34*
    Metolius River, *60*, 60–62
    Mount St. Helens, 64–66
    Silver Falls State Park, *36*, 36–38
    Timothy Lake, 30–32
    Wind River Sno-Park, 118–120, *119*
    Windy Ridge, 64, 66
caves, 65–66, 88
Cedar Creek Bridge and Mill, 82–83, *83*
central/eastern getaways
    Deschutes River State Park, 96–97
    Eagle Cap Wilderness, *69*, 69–71
    Elk Horn Wildlife Area, *121*, 122–123
    Hart Mountain Natl. Antelope Refuge, 94–95, *95*
    Malheur NWR, 41–43, *42*
    Owyhee River, 38–41, *39*
    Richardson's Rock Ranch, 96–97, *97*
    Wallowa Mountains, *69*, 69–71
    Wallula Gap, 123–25, *124*
Clear Lake, 34–35
Cloud Cap Inn, 62–64

coastal getaways
    Alfred A. Loeb State Park, 16, 17
    Bastendorff Beach County Park, 46
    Cape Arago Highway, 46, 47
    Cape Meares Beach, 21
    Fort Clatsop Natl. Monument, *100*, 100–101
    Free Flight Bird and Marine Mammal Rehabilitation Center, *18*, 18–19
    Heceta Head Lighthouse, *102*, 102–3
    Kingfisher, 48–50, *49*
    Lincoln City, 78–79
    Redwood Trail, 16–17, *17*
    South Beach, 20–21
    South Slough Estuary, 46–48, *47*
    Tillamook Air Museum, 76–77, *77*
    Tillamook Bay, 50–51
    Trask County Park, 51–53
    Trestle Bay Wetlands, 21
    Yaquina Head Lighthouse, 74–75, *75*
    Yaquina Head Outstanding Natural Area, 74–75
Columbia River getaways
    Bonneville Fish Hatchery, 26–28, *27*
    Cascade Locks, 58–60
    Cowlitz River smelt run, 114–115, *115*
    Eagle Creek, 58, *59*, 60
    Franz Lake NWR, 111
    Historic Columbia River Highway, *73*, 86–87, *87*
    Horsethief Lake State Park, 28–30, *29*
    Indian Heaven Wilderness, 89–90
    Pierce NWR, *110*, 111–12
    Sauvie Island, 110
    Sawtooth Berry Fields, 88–89
    Scappoose Bay, 113
    Steigerwald Lake NWR, 110–11
    Trojan Park Wetlands and Pond, 113
    Trout Lake Ice Cave, 88
    Twilight Eagle Sanctuary, 113–14
    Wolf Bay Wetlands, *112*, 113–14
covered bridges, 33, 82–83, *83*, 92
Cowlitz River smelt run, 114–15, *115*

Dee Wright Observatory, 35
Deschutes River State Park, 96–97
Diamond Lake, 116, 117–18
drives
    Alsea Falls Recreation Area, 22–23
    Aufderheide Scenic Drive, 92–93
    Bald Peak State Park, 84, *84*
    Cape Arago Highway, 46, 47
    Cloud Cap Road, 62–64
    Heritage Tree Program, 24–25

Historic Columbia River Highway, *73*, 86–87, *87*
Malheur NWR, *42*, 43
Marys Peak, 22–23, *23*
Maude Williamson State Park, 84–85
McKenzie Pass, 35
McKenzie River Highway, 33, 33–35, *34*
Mount St. Helens Natl. Volcanic Monument, 64
Nestucca River Back Country Byway, *108*, 108–9
Steigerwald Lake NWR, 111
Wheatland Ferry, 84–85
Wildlife Safari, 53–55, *54*
Willamette Mission State Park, 85
Windy Ridge, 64, 66

Eagle Cap Wilderness, *69*, 69–71
Eagle Creek, 58, *59*, 60
Elk Cove Creek, 45
Elk Horn Wildlife Area, *121*, 122–23
Erratic Rocks State Park, *55*, 55–56

Fern Ridge Reservoir, 56–58, *57*
ferries, 84–85
Finley NWR, 80, 81
fire danger, 35
fish hatcheries, 26–28, *27*
Fisher Butte Trail, 57, *57*
fishing
    Atiyeh Deschutes River Trail, 96
    Aufderheide Scenic Drive, 93
    Camp Sherman, 61–62
    Cascade Locks, 59
    Cedar Creek Bridge and Mill, 82–83, *83*
    Cowlitz River smelt run, 114–15, *115*
    Deschutes River State Park, 96–97
    Glacier Lake, 70–71
    Kingfisher, 48–50, *49*
    Metolius River, *60*, 60–62
    South Fork of the McKenzie River, 93, *93*
    Tillamook Bay, 50–51
    Timothy Lake, 30–32, *31*
    Trask County Park, 51–53
Fort Clatsop Natl. Monument, *100*, 100–101
Franz Lake NWR, 111
Free Flight Bird and Marine Mammal Rehabilitation Center, *18*, 18–19
geology, 55–56, 64, 65–66, 88, 96–97, 123–25
Ghost Ridge, 63
Gifford Pinchot Natl. Forest, 88
glassblowing and glass floats, 78–79, *79*

127

Index

Hart Mountain Natl. Antelope Refuge, 94–95, *95*
Hat Rock State Park, 125
Heceta Head Lighthouse, *102*, 102–3
Heritage Tree Program, 24–25
Hidden Creek Trail, 46–47
hiking
    Alfred A. Loeb State Park, *16*, 17
    Ankeny NWR, 80, 81, *81*
    Ape Cave, 65–66
    Atiyeh Deschutes River Trail, 96
    Aufderheide Scenic Drive, 93
    Baskett Slough NWR, 80, 81
    Deschutes River State Park, 96–97
    Eagle Creek-Cascade Locks Trail, 58, *59*
    Erratic Rocks State Park, *55*, 55–56
    Fern Ridge Reservoir, 56–58, *57*
    Finley NWR, 80, 81
    Fisher Butte Trail, 57, *57*
    Hart Mountain Natl. Antelope Refuge, 95
    Heceta Head Lighthouse, 103
    Hidden Creek Trail, 46–47
    Historic Columbia River Highway, *73*, 86–87, *87*
    Jackson Bottom Wetlands, 105
    Leslie Gulch Succor Creek Byway, 40
    Malheur NWR, *42*, 43
    Marys Peak, 22–23, *23*
    McKenzie River Natl. Recreation Trail, 34
    Nestucca River Back Country Byway, *108*, 108–9
    Quarry Cove Tidepools, 75, *75*
    Redwood Trail, *16*, 16–17
    Ridgefield NWR, 107
    Sawtooth Berry Fields, 88–90
    South Slough Estuary, 46–48, *47*
    Steigerwald Lake NWR, 111
    Trail of Ten Falls, *36*, 36–38
    Valley of the Giants, *24*, 25–26
    Wallowa Lake State Park, 71
    Willamette Mission State Park, 85
    Yaquina Head Outstanding Natural Area, 74, 75
Historic Columbia River Highway, *73*, 86–87, *87*
horses, 69, 69–71, 96–97
Horsethief Lake State Park, 28–30, *29*

Indian Heaven Wilderness, 89–90
inland getaways
    Alsea Falls Recreation Area, 22–23
    Ankeny NWR, 80, 81, *81*
    Bald Peak State Park, 84, *84*
    Baskett Slough NWR, 80, 81
    Cedar Creek Bridge and Mill, 82–83, *83*
    Erratic Rocks State Park, *55*, 55–56
    Fern Ridge Reservoir, 56–58, *57*
    Finley NWR, 80, 81
    Heritage Tree Program, 24–26
    Jackson Bottom Wetlands, 104–5, *105*
    Marys Peak, 22–23, *23*
    Maude Williamson State Park, 84–85
    Nestucca River Back Country Byway, *108*, 108–9
    Ridgefield NWR, *106*, 106–7
    Valley of the Giants, *24*, 25–26
    Wheatland Ferry, 84–85
    Wildlife Safari, 53–55, *54*
    Willamette Mission State Park, 85

Jackson Bottom Wetlands, 104–5, *105*

Kingfisher, 48–50, *49*

Lake Owyhee State Park, 40
Lake Wallula, 123
lakes
    Clear Lake, 34–35
    Crater Lake, 116–18, *117*
    Diamond Lake, 116, 117–18
    Fern Ridge Reservoir, 56–58, *57*
    Glacier Lake, 70–71
    Lake Owyhee State Park, 40
    Lake Wallula, 123
    Moccasin Lake, *70*
    Timothy Lake, 30–32, *31*
    Wallowa Lake State Park, 71
Leslie Gulch Succor Creek Byway, 40
Lewis and Clark expedition, *100*, 100–101, 125
lighthouses, 74–75, *75*, *102*, 102–3

Malheur NWR, 41–43, *42*
Marys Peak, 22–23, *23*
Maude Williamson State Park, 84–85
McKenzie Pass, 35
McKenzie River, *33*, 33–35, 34, 92, 93
Metolius River, *60*, 60–62
Moccasin Lake, *70*
Mount Bailey, 118
Mount Hood, 62–64, 71
Mount St. Helens Natl. Volcanic Monument, 64–66, *65*
museums and visitor centers
    Ape Cave Headquarters, 65–66
    Bonneville Fish Hatchery, 26–28
    Cascade Locks Museum, 59
    Cedar Creek Bridge and Mill, 83
    Fort Clatsop Natl. Monument, *100*, 100–101
    Free Flight Bird and Marine Mammal Rehabilitation Center, *18*, 18–19
    Heceta Head Lighthouse, 103
    Jackson Bottom Wetlands, 105
    Lincoln County Historical Society, 50
    Malheur NWR, 43
    Mount St. Helens Natl. Volcanic Monument, 64
    Safari Village, 54
    South Slough Estuary, 46–48, *47*
    Tillamook Air Museum, 76–77, *77*
    Yaquina Head Outstanding Natural Area, 75

Nestucca River Back Country Byway, 99, *108*, 108–9
Niagara Falls, 108
North Falls, *36*, 37

Oldman Pass Sno-Park, 119
Owyhee River, 38–41, *39*

Paradise Campground, 33–34
petroglyphs, *29*
Pheasant Creek Falls, 108
Pierce NWR, *110*, 111–12

Quarry Cove Tidepools, 75, *75*

recipes
    Beer-Battered Smelt, 115
    Crawfish Boil, 51
    Grilled Fish Fillets, 50
    Huckleberry Crisp, 89
    Huckleberry Pancakes, 89
    "Little Chief" Smoked Smelt, 114
    Mango Salsa, 50
    Rockfish Tempura, 50
Redwood Trail, *16*, 16–17
Richardson's Rock Ranch, 96–97, *97*
Ridgefield NWR, *106*, 106–7
rock climbing, 28–30

Sacajawea State Park, 125
Sauvie Island, 110
Sawtooth Berry Fields, *88*, 88–89
Scappoose Bay, 113
Siletz Bay, *20*
Silver Falls State Park, *36*, 36–38
skiing, 117–18, 118–20, *119*
snowmobiling, 116–17
South Beach, 20–21
South Fork of the McKenzie River, 93, *93*
South Slough Estuary, 46–48, *47*
Steigerwald Lake NWR, 111
Sumpter Valley Dredge State Park and Railway, *67*, 67–68

thunder eggs, 96–97
Tillamook Air Museum, 76–77, *77*
Tillamook Bay, 50–51

Timothy Lake, 30–32, *31*
Trail of Ten Falls, *36*, 36–38
Trask County Park, 51–53
trees
    Alfred A. Loeb State Park, *16*, 17
    Heritage Tree Program, 24–25
    Redwood Trail, *16*, 16–17
    Valley of the Giants, *24*, 25–26
    Willamette Mission State Park, 85
Trestle Bay Wetlands, 21
Trojan Park Wetlands and Pond, 113
Trout Lake Ice Cave, 88
Twilight Eagle Sanctuary, 113–14
Twin Tunnels, 86

Valley of the Giants, *24*, 25–26
volcanoes, 62, 64–66, *65*

Wallowa Lake State Park, 71
Wallowa Mountains, *69*, 69–71
Wallula Gap, 123–25, *124*
waterfalls, *36*, 36–38, *108*, 108–9
West Cascades Scenic Byways, 93
wetlands, 104–5, *105*, 111, *112*, 113–14
Wheatland Ferry, 84–85
wilderness, *69*, 69–71, 89–90
wildlife refuges and viewing. *See also* birds and birding
    Ankeny NWR, 80, 81, *81*
    Baskett Slough NWR, 80, 81
    Bonney Butte HawkWatch, 90–92, *91*
    Elk Horn Wildlife Area, *121*, 122–23
    endangered species, 53
    Finley NWR, 80, 81
    Franz Lake NWR, 111
    Free Flight Bird and Marine Mammal Rehabilitation Center, *18*, 18–19
    Hart Mountain Natl. Antelope Refuge, 94–95, *95*
    Jackson Bottom Wetlands, 104–5, *105*
    Lake Owyhee State Park, 40
    Pierce NWR, *110*, 111–12
    Ridgefield NWR, *106*, 106–7
    Sauvie Island, 110
    South Slough Estuary, 46–48, *47*
    Steigerwald Lake NWR, 110–11
    Twilight Eagle Sanctuary, 113–14
    Wildlife Safari, 53–55, *54*
    Willamette Mission State Park, 85
Wind River Sno-Park, 118–20, *119*
Windy Ridge, 64, 66

Yaquina Head Lighthouse, 74–75, *75*
Yaquina Head Outstanding Natural Area, 74, 75

NWR = National Wildlife Refuge